nplications of the Antiballistic Missile Program

Scope, Magnitude, and Implications
of the
Antiballisitic Missile Program

Hearings
before the
Subcommittee on Military Applications
of the
Joint Committee
on Atomic Energy Congress
of the
United States
Ninetieth Congress
First Session
on
Scope, Magnitude, and Implications
of the
United States Antiballisitic Missile Program

NOVEMBER 6 AND 7, 1967

GOVERNMENT REPRINTS PRESS.
Washington, D.C.

© Ross & Perry, Inc. 2001 All rights reserved.

No claim to U.S. government work contained throughout this book.

Protected under the Berne Convention. Published 2001

Printed in The United States of America
Ross & Perry, Inc. Publishers
717 Second St., N.E., Suite 200
Washington, D.C. 20002
Telephone (202) 675-8300
Facsimile (202) 675-8400
info@RossPerry.com

SAN 253-8555

Government Reprints Press Edition 2001

Government Reprints Press is an Imprint of Ross & Perry, Inc.

Library of Congress Control Number: 2001094516

Formerly pulished as "Scope, Magnitude, and Implications Of the United States Antiballis
Missile Program" printed by the U.S. Government Printing Office.

http://www.GPOreprints.com

ISBN 1-931641-91-9

CONTENTS

HEARING DATES

STATEMENTS OF WITNESSES

STATEMENTS INSERTED IN THE RECORD

CHARTS INSERTED IN THE RECORD

APPENDIXES

SCOPE, MAGNITUDE, AND IMPLICATIONS OF THE UNITED STATES ANTIBALLISTIC MISSILE PROGRAM

MONDAY, NOVEMBER 6, 1967

Congress of the United States,
Subcommittee on Military Applications,
Joint Committee on Atomic Energy,
Washington, D.C.

The subcommittee met at 2 p.m., pursuant to call, in room 1202, New Senate Office Building, Senator Henry M. Jackson (chairman of the subcommittee) presiding.

Present: Senators Pastore, Gore, Jackson, and Aiken; Representatives Hosmer, Bates, and Anderson.

Present also: Senator Smith.

Staff members present: John T. Conway, executive director; Edward J. Bauser, assistant director; George F. Murphy, Jr., national security affairs; William England, professional staff member; and Francesco Costagliola, staff consultant.

Senator JACKSON. The committee will come to order.

The Subcommittee on Military Applications of the Joint Committee on Atomic Energy opens its hearings today on the problems of antiballistic missile defense—a field in which the Joint Committee has had a long and continuing interest. Senator John O. Pastore, Chairman of the Joint Atomic Energy Committee, in a major policy address in connection with the launching of the nuclear submarine *Narwhal* at Groton, Conn., on September 9, 1967, announced that the Military Applications Subcommittee would undertake a thorough study and review of this subject. (See app. 3, p. 103.)

These hearings will review the plans and programs relating to our ABM program in the context of three recent developments of utmost seriousness, which relate to the credibility of the Western nuclear deterrent.

First, is the fact of the Soviet offensive buildup. Moscow has been working hard to narrow the missile gap that limited its range of options in the Cuban missile crisis of 1962. It has recently doubled the number of its operational ICBM's. Also, the larger missile payload the Soviets can mount on their bigger missiles gives them the capability to deploy higher yield nuclear warheads per missile than we can. A second development is the Soviet defense buildup. The Soviet leaders have deployed an ABM system around Moscow, and our best intelligence is that they will expand and improve that system over the years.

A third important development is the emergence of Red China as a thermonuclear power, with the advantages this will give China to exploit the weakness of its neighbors—unless it has reason to fear the consequences.

(1)

The main purpose of these hearings is twofold:

We want to bring to the Congress and the public the latest information on plans by the executive department concerning the U.S. antiballistic missile program. The decision, announced on September 18, 1967, that our Government would undertake the development of a so-called thin ABM defense, has significant implications for our national security. We expect the responsible officials, within the bounds of security, to discuss in public and in detail this recently announced program. I believe it is important that as much information as possible should be made available to the American people so that they can better understand the issues involved. (See app. 4, p. 105.)

It is also our sincere hope that these hearings will help to make clear some of the longer term problems of ballistic missile defense as they relate to maintaining the credibility of the Western deterrent, which is the first essential of our national security and individual liberty, and of the survival of our allies in freedom.

Let me say a word about the meaning of deterrence.

What I mean by deterrence is a combination of forces in being and state of mind about the credibility of those forces.

The Western deterrent must be credible to the adversary. If the Soviet rulers came to believe that their ballistic missile defense, coupled with a nuclear attack on the United States, would limit damage to the Soviet Union to a level acceptable to them, whatever the level is, our forces would no longer be a reliable deterrent. The Western deterrent must be reassuring to our allies. If our allies came to believe that the Russians had an effective ABM system, and knew that we did not, their confidence in the American deterrent and their will to resist Soviet blackmail would be undermined. The Western deterrent must be reassuring to this country and to the American President. If a President came to believe that the Soviets had a relatively effective ABM system, and knew that the United States did not, this could inhibit our Government from standing firm in a period of crisis.

Under conditions where the credibility of the Western deterrent was in question, the Soviet Union would be emboldened to take greater risks in expanding the frontiers of its influence—for example, by moving on Berlin, or by acting adventurously in the Middle East or elsewhere. The circumstances would thus be created for the most dangerous confrontation—a showdown between nuclear powers in which Moscow did not feel deterred by our forces.

During these hearings, which are expected to extend into next year, we will also review the implementation of the nuclear test ban treaty safeguards jointly with members of the Nuclear Safeguards Subcommittee of the Senate Armed Services Committee. This is an annual review in connection with the annual report to the Senate on the implementation of the safeguards program.

I might also note that the Preparedness Subcommittee of the Senate Armed Services Committee and its staff have been following closely the main developments affecting the overall East-West balance of strategic forces. They are continuing their work in that area under the able leadership of the chairman of the Preparedness Subcommittee, Senator John Stennis.

Before welcoming the two witnesses who will be testifying this afternoon, I want to ask if any member of the committee has any statement he wishes to make at this time?

Representative HOSMER. Mr. Chairman, I have a statement I would like to put in the record, as though read. It seeks the range of estimates on the additions to Soviet ICBM weapons and establishes a period between 1969 and 1972 in which they might be expected to obtain parity with the United States in numbers.

It goes on from there to calculate what possible damage we might impose in retaliation and opens the question of what is that amount of assured destruction as defined by the Secretary.

Chairman PASTORE. Have these figures been checked for clearance and classification?

Representative HOSMER. These are unclassified figures. I expect to question Mr. Nitze possibly from this information. Is that satisfactory, Mr. Chairman?

Chairman PASTORE. Yes.

Senator JACKSON. We can leave the statement in the record. I think what we should do rather than reading the whole statement, the Secretary——

Representative HOSMER. I would just like to have it in as though read.

Senator JACKSON. The two Secretaries should have an opportunity, of course, to go through the statement, and they may wish to comment on that tomorrow or at a point later in the day.

Representative HOSMER. In 1966 the Pentagon estimated the U.S.S.R. then had 340 ICBM's. Estimated additions to this arsenal range from 200 to 400 per year. The United States has 1,000 silo-based Minuteman missiles and 54 Titan II's—1,054 landbased missiles. Roughly 400 of its 656 Polaris missiles can be assumed to be on station at any one time. Thus the total of available U.S. strategic missiles is 1,454, and this figure remains steady. Depending on Soviet rate of additions, the table below indicates when the Soviets will achieve numerical parity and thereafter superiority:

	1967	1968	1969	1970	1971	1972	1973
Yearly added rate:							
200	540	740	940	1,140	1,340	1,540	1,740
300	640	940	1,240	1,540	1,840		
400	740	1,140	1,540	1,940			

It makes little difference whether these additions are in ICBM configuration or take the form of orbiting weapons. In either event they will carry large hydrogen warheads and their purpose is the same.

The precise reason the Soviets maintain, improve, and expand their strategic nuclear system is to be able to make a surprise attack which so severely damages us that our retaliatory forces are rendered incapable of hitting back with unacceptable destruction. The fact they continue to spend billions of rubles on this system makes it obvious they intend to use it when it can be employed successfully on its offensive mission.

The precise reason we maintain our strategic nuclear system is to deter such an attack. Deterrence is a defensive maneuver and its success depends on obviously being able to suffer such an attack and still have sufficient undamaged surviving weapons to impose unacceptable retaliatory destruction on the attacker's homeland.

Secretary of Defense Robert McNamara properly points out that the keystone of deterrence is a capability to "absorb any surprise nuclear attack and to retaliate with sufficient strength to destroy the attacking nation as a viable society." He believes this involves not so much the atomic punch of our warheads as it does laying them down with precision on their targets. He feels it depends not so much on the number of our missiles as it does their survivability. He contends survivability does not necessarily require ABM's to intercept enemy warheads, but that what is important is hardened ICBM sites capable of withstanding the explosions and functioning afterward.

He promises—and has convinced President Johnson—that enough of our strikeback strength will survive any conceivable attack to impose "assured destruction." As the Soviets come closer and closer to us in numerical parity, more and more of the validity of his promise turns on whether they are using warheads sufficiently powerful to penetrate our hardened silos and destroy our ICBM's.

In announcing the Soviet orbital system last Friday Mr. McNamara again contended that Soviet yields are in the 1- to 3-megaton range—insufficient to penetrate our silos. He refuses to recognize the Soviet penchant for large yields in the 10- to 30-megaton range, or the superior thrust of their rockets which enables them to carry the more powerful warheads—presumably capable of penetrating and destroying our ICBM's in their silos. Nor, have I ever heard him admit that even if he is right about Soviet yields at this moment, there is any guarantee that tomorrow their strategic nuclear system cannot or will not be retrofitted with the larger warheads.

Secretary McNamara surely cannot speak about today's Soviet warheads with any more verity than his Joint Chiefs of Staff who apparently disagree with him on the issue. Nor can he speak with any more assurance about future Soviet warheads than even members of this Joint Committee and others privy to the same intelligence estimates that he is.

As the trend toward parity continues it becomes increasingly important to determine—as best we can—whether or not, utilizing the proper yield warheads, a Soviet surprise attack at numerical parity actually will leave us undamaged an "assured destruction" capability. For the purpose we must assume continued improvements in their guidance will bring accuracy to within around 2,000 feet and it is reasonable to assume their force has been programed against our 1,054 landbased ICBM's, locations of which are known.

Under these circumstances the Rand Corp.'s "Bomb Damage Effect Computer" calculates a 92 percent destruction probability—destruction of 970 of our 1,054 landbased ICBM's, leaving 84 undamaged to retaliate.

It can be assumed our 25 Polaris submarines actually at sea with about 400 Polaris missiles will be subject to some attrition from a fairly large number of Soviet submarines and other attackers. To round out calculations generously we can assume 79 percent—316 Polaris missiles—will actually get away on retaliatory missions.

Our total retaliatory force will thus be 400 missiles with what generally are assumed to be 1 megaton warheads. If the Soviet ABM defense system is only 50 percent effective, 200 will get through to their targets.

Will that 200 impose "assured destruction?"

The answer does not require revelation of national secrets. It can be done with substantial confidence using the laws of probability. We can assume that all 1,454 of our missiles are targeted for destruction of the Soviet Union, because any lesser assumption simply decreases the retaliatory damage calculation about to be made. It also is logical to assume the 100 percent destruction mission will be divided proportionately between landbased and Polaris missiles according to their respective ratios in the stockpile, 72 percent and 28 percent, and that they will be destructive in the same relationship as the number reaching target is to the total available the moment before surprise attack—7.9 for landbased missiles and 39.5 percent for Polaris. Thus—

[In percent]

	Planned damage	Missiles on target	Actual damage
Land based	72	7.9	5.7
Polaris	28	39.5	11.1
Total	100		16.8

Prior to World War II, the U.S.S.R. lost 10 percent to 15 percent of its population during the purges. During World War II it lost over 13 percent of its population. From the Soviet viewpoint it is questionable whether a 16.8 percent population loss from retaliation would be unacceptable and therefore constitute "assured destruction." In World War II the U.S.S.R. suffered a total loss of 40 percent of its industrial capacity. By comparison it might regard a 16.8 percent loss to be a bargain-basement price for world domination.

I anticipate a quarrel with my figures by claims that our arsenal has a large "over-kill" capability and several missiles may be assigned to the same target, thus "assuring" destruction. It will be said there are about 150 city-industrial complexes in the U.S.S.R. worth hitting, so that starts us with about 10 bombs in stockpile for each—and if 200 get through, that still allows 1⅓ per complex to assure destruction.

My answer is straightforward. In assuming that 200 missiles penetrated Soviet defenses, I assumed that all were assigned to the city-industrial complexes. Actually not less than 25 percent would likely be assigned to purely military targets. That leaves 150—one per complex. Further, it is unreasonable to assume that ICBM's are perfect and there would be no malfunctioning. It is more realistic to assume 5 percent loss for rocket power failures, another 5 percent for guidance system troubles, another 5 percent for warhead defects, then allow 5 percent more for post-attack human judgment degradation at our retaliatory command and control centers and another 5 percent loss to account for Soviet civil defense. This totals another 25 percent and leaves only 100 missiles, two-third of a missile per complex.

Since complexes actually should need about four warheads to accomplish the 100-percent destruction we assumed, that means the remaining warheads will account for but 25 complexes—whether by 25-percent destruction of 100 complexes, 100-percent destruction of 25 complexes, or some combination in between. Thus, since 25 complexes is 16.6 percent of the 150 complexes started with—destruction amounts only to 0.2 percent difference from the 16.8 figure arrived at by another route and the refutation of my calculations does not stand up.

I also anticipate an effort to attack my calculations by asserting they neglect MIRV. This is a multiple individual reentry vehicle package attaching more than one warhead to a missile. But since the Russians are as smart technically as we are, there is no validity to a contention that they are not also going to MIRV and thereby canceling out whatever advantage we might otherwise anticipate. And, since they are blessed with rockets capable of carrying larger payloads than ours, there is no assurance they just might pack more warheads per delivery vehicle than us and gain an advantage.

My conclusion is that we should (1) be adding to our numbers of ICBM's; (2) we should be putting in an ABM system against the Soviets, not just the Chinese; (3) we should not phase out the B-52's and B-58's, which I did not include in this discussion and which may well be the balance of power on our side at this moment making deterrence work; and (4) we should be analyzing whether a second mission for the orbiting weapon is to knock out any antiballistic missile system we put in and thereby clear the way for a rain of Soviet ICBM's to follow.

It is interesting to note that decisions affecting nuclear deterrence which a President makes on the advice of his Defense Secretary and others probably will not affect the strategic power of the Nation during his term of office. But they may largely determine the degree of strategic superiority—or inferiority—available to his successor.

This is an ironic fact of life in the nuclear age. The decisions made by President Eisenhower gave President Kennedy the opportunity to build superior weapons systems. The decisions President Kennedy and President Johnson have made may determine whether their successors have the opportunity to build superior strategic systems to defend the Nation. If they have made mistakes, their administrations will not suffer for it, but in the future the Nation may be hard pressed to cope with nuclear blackmail or even a disastrous surprise attack.

(See p. 47 for Deputy Secretary of Defense Nitze's reply to this statement by Congressman Hosmer.)

Senator JACKSON. Are there any other comments?

If not, let me say the committee is very pleased to welcome as our first witnesses in these hearings the Honorable Paul H. Nitze, Deputy Secretary of Defense, and Dr. John S. Foster, Director, Defense Research and Engineering, of the Department of Defense.

The Chair would like to suggest that Mr. Nitze complete his statement in full, that we then proceed to the statement by Dr. Foster, and then turn to questions. I think this procedure would be more orderly and we will have ample opportunity to ask the questions of the two witnesses that are appearing here for the Department of Defense.

If there is no objection then we will proceed in that order.

Mr. Nitze, we are delighted to have you with us this afternoon. You have a prepared statement, I believe, and you may proceed in your own way.

STATEMENT OF PAUL H. NITZE, DEPUTY SECRETARY OF DEFENSE

Mr. NITZE. Mr. Chairman, I am pleased to appear before your committee today to testify on antiballistic missile defense.

For more than a decade we have been carrying on an antiballistic missile development program at a very high priority and at a total cost of over $3 billion. This research and development effort, known since 1963 as the Nike X program, has covered a wide range of possible tasks; the most demanding being that of assuring protection of our population against massive attacks by sophisticated reentry systems. During the course of this work it has been demonstrated that it is possible to shoot down incoming warheads. Against the most demanding task, that of assuring protection of our people against a massive threat, two problems became evident. First, Nike X was originally conceived as a terminal defense system operating at moderate range, each unit of the system able to defend only a relatively small area. Such a system, even if widely deployed, would leave unprotected large areas of the country which could be targeted at will by the enemy. Second, even with respect to the area defended it would not be an impenetrable umbrella; it would be one in which missiles are expended to shoot down missiles; thus it would always be possible for the Soviet Union with its massive and sophisticated capabilities to program sufficient offensive missiles to exhaust any reasonable level of defense at points of its choosing. For this reason, an ABM deployment aimed at providing assurance of security for our population as a whole against the Soviet threat is infeasible with today's technology and has not been authorized.

The Nike-X system, fortunately, was designed as a family of components consisting of a number of different types of radars and missiles which can be tailored to various purposes, including those lower than the most demanding task. In 1965, a concept of an area defense operating outside the earth's atmosphere was introduced into the Nike-X development program. The consequent introduction of the long-range Spartan missile made it possible to plan defense systems which would blanket the entire country while requiring only about 15 to 20 Spartan batteries to do so. Such an area defense could be effective provided the threat was not massive. Such a threat began to come into being a few years ago when the Chinese Peoples Republic (CPR) demonstrated progress in their nuclear and missile programs.

The CPR threat to this country cannot become actual before the early 1970's, and, initially at least, will certainly be small in number and of relatively primitive technology. We can now deploy what is, in effect, a third-generation defense, having passed through the old Nike-Zeus system, then to the Nike-X, and having now added area defense. We are confident that this sophisticated defense can provide us with high assurance of denying damage to the United States from the type of attack the CPR will be able to launch in the mid-seventies. With further foreseeable improvements we believe we can maintain such protection at least until the 1980's.

This winter, Mr. McNamara testified before the Armed Services Committees that it was not then necessary to make a decision on a Communist Chinese oriented ABM because the estimated timing of the CPR threat was such as to allow us to delay a decision. Since that time, the Chinese threat has progressed not more rapidly, but as rapidly, as was then estimated as possible and this September, 9 months having passed, it became timely to make a decision on deployment if we wished to match the emerging threat with an adequate defense.

The question naturally arises as to why we do not rely on our capability for assured second strike destruction to deter the CPR as we do rely upon it to deter the Soviet Union. The primary difference between the Soviet and the CPR case is that it is feasible to provide a damage denial ABM against the CPR but it is not feasible to do so against the Soviet Union. If we could assure effective defense of our population against an attack such as is within Soviet capabilities we would recommend that we do so. But at the present state of technology, we cannot. Against the CPR, we can.

There is, however, an additional consideration. The Chinese first generation ICBM capability will undoubtedly be small in numbers and thereby vulnerable to attack. A small and vulnerable nuclear delivery system presents a problem to its possessor. In time of crisis, it must be launched first in a surprise attack or it runs the risk of total elimination. This characteristic of a small, vulnerable system could create pressures toward reckless behavior, even in a people not by nature reckless. An area ABM defense for the United States would eliminate such pressures because even a surprise attack would then be ineffective.

This area ABM, by denying a threat by Communist China of destruction of U.S. cities should provide an additional indication to Asians that we intend to deter China from nuclear blackmail against them. This should contribute toward our goal of discouraging nuclear weapon proliferation among the present nonnuclear countries.

Finally, our decision to go ahead with a limited ABM deployment in no way indicates that we feel an agreement with the Soviet Union on the limitation of strategic nuclear offensive and defensive forces is any the less urgent or desirable.

Thank you, Mr. Chairman.

Mr. Foster will proceed in more detailed fashion.

Senator JACKSON. Thank you, Secretary Nitze.

Dr. Foster, we are very pleased to have you with us this afternoon. You have a prepared statement and charts, I believe.

You may now proceed in your own way.

STATEMENT OF JOHN S. FOSTER, JR., DIRECTOR OF DEFENSE RESEARCH AND ENGINEERING

Dr. FOSTER. Thank you, Mr. Chairman. It is a pleasure to appear before you today. Before describing some technical features of the deployment I would like to amplify Secretary Nitze's remarks on the history of our experience with ballistic missile defense.

The original need to provide a defense against ballistic missiles came in the 1940's with the introduction of the German V-2 short-range ballistic rocket, and the experience subsequent to World War II with this class of weapon. By the middle fifties the potential threat to the United States had become serious because of the extension of missile ranges to intercontinental distances. The ICBM presented a unique threat because of its speed and thermonuclear warhead. Traveling at 4 miles a second, it would reach this country in 30 minutes compared to the hours previously required by enemy bombers.

For almost a decade, the ICBM was considered by many to be the ultimate weapon against which no defense was possible. However, by the midfifties a concept had evolved that we hoped would be an effective defense.

In 1956, the Nike-Zeus development program was started. Its design resembled in many respects that of its predecessors, Nike-Ajax and Nike-Hercules, which were antiaircraft systems. Radars were used to detect and track incoming targets, and a rocket interceptor equipped with a nuclear warhead was launched and guided to the target. A system was installed and tested at Kwajalein in the mid-Pacific Ocean. Successful intercepts were made against actual ICBM targets launched from California in the early 1960's.

The Nike-Zeus system used a family of mechanically slewed radars and consequently its traffic handling capability was severely limited. The only way to provide the capability of handling simultaneous targets was to increase the number of radars; consequently, the larger cities would have required as many as 30–40 radars total of four different types. Even with this large number, the system could still be easily overwhelmed by the enemy's use of multiple objects such as chaff and decoys and balloons, since each of them would have to be taken under direct fire.

These defects were corrected in 1963 by the introduction of the Nike X concept. Phased array radars were introduced which steer their beams electronically in a few millionths of a second. The traffic-handling capability was thus vastly improved. Also, the SPRINT missile, a very high acceleration interceptor, allowed launches to be delayed until after the cloud of objects had reentered the atmosphere. The atmosphere slowed down the pieces of chaff and balloons, and the radar could discriminate them from the warheads which did not slow down until much lower altitudes.

In spite of these improvements, the system, when measured against the Soviet threat, had grave weaknesses. As Secretary Nitze stated, Nike X was originally conceived as a terminal defense system operating at moderate range. A battery at the most could defend one city; in the larger cities, more than one battery was required. The deployments were consequently very expensive even if one were to attempt to defend a few of our cities. The cost to defend only 25 cities was about $10 billion investment; to defend 50, about $20 billion, and any reasonable deployment would still leave hundreds of cities unprotected. (There are more than 200 cities above 100,000 population.)

But system cost has not been a major factor. The major factor is that the Soviets could, if they chose, concentrate on one or more cities and by the simple process of exhausting the interceptor force, penetrate the defense. This could be done either by using many individual ICBM's or by using missiles carrying many multiple warheads. It was possible, therefore, for the Soviet economy and technology to defeat the defense by buying more or improved offensive weapons.

Finally, in 1965 we introduced area defense. The basic additions were the PAR (Perimeter Acquisition Radar) and the long-range Spartan missile. Because of its long range, a relatively few batteries can protect the entire country, against a light and relatively unsophisticated attack.

Area defense removed one of the defects of Nike X by providing coverage to all U.S. cities instead of certain selected ones. However, by its very nature, it would still be penetrated by heavy or sophisticated attacks such as the Soviets could mount.

In 1966, a new threat appeared—the probability that the Chinese People's Republic (CPR) were developing an ICBM. This is obviously vastly different from the Soviet threat. It will not materialize until the early 1970's, and when it does it will be small in numbers and relatively unsophisticated. As Secretary Nitze has just said, against this threat we have high assurance of providing damage denial for the whole country. Furthermore, we think we can maintain this capability against a growing Chinese threat at least until the 1980's, through modifications to the original deployment.

The Chinese-oriented deployment is called Sentinel. Let me describe it in some detail. (See app. 9, p. 134, for additional information on Sentinel system.)

Shown here on this chart (fig. 1) are the four major components of the Sentinel system. They are two radars types and two missile types. The first radar type is the PAR. It is a long-range radar designed to acquire targets as soon as they come over the horizon. The PAR——

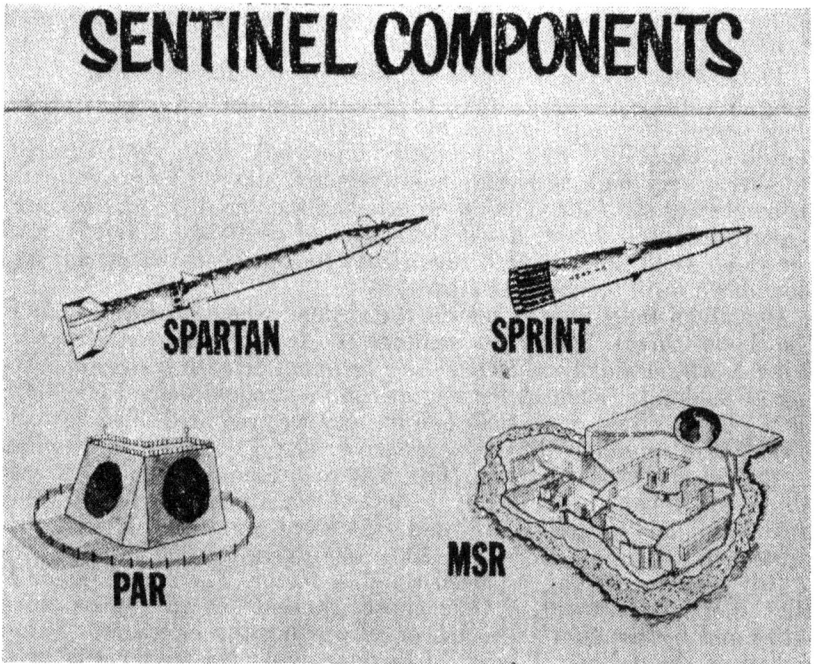

SENTINEL COMPONENTS

SPARTAN   SPRINT

PAR   MSR

FIGURE 1

Senator JACKSON. That stands for what?

Dr. FOSTER. Perimeter acquisition radar.

The upper left-hand missile, the Spartan, is used to make the long-range intercept and the Sprint is used to defend terminal locations such as radars or Minuteman missiles.

This picture (fig. 2) is a long-range early warning radar. It is actually a radar that is situated at Eglin Air Force Base in Florida. I show it here because it is very similar to the perimeter acquisition radars that we intend to deploy with the Sentinel system. It is a low-frequency radar capable of acquiring and tracking incoming objects as soon as they come over the horizon.

As you can see here, the front face of this large building appears to be concrete and indeed it is. But actually imbedded in the concrete are thousands of different elements. There are individual elements on the right-hand side that form part of the receiving system and on the left-hand side elements that form part of the transmitting system. Then in the back of this wall, of course, are the actual components of the radar, the transmitters and receiving units, as well as the associated electronics and computers.

The next picture (fig. 3) shows the other radar, the missile site radar. It is this radar that launches our interceptors, the Spartans or the Sprints, and guides them to the intended impact point. This is a higher frequency radar and is used to provide the precise guidance commands necessary to assure an intercept of the interceptor missile with the incoming objects.

This particular radar is designed to handle a very heavy traffic.

Shown here (fig. 4) are two missiles. The one on the right is actually the old Nike-Zeus missile. I show it, however, because it is very similar to the Spartan missile that is under development. Spartan is a little bit larger than the Zeus missile. The Spartan missile will have the capability of going out to several hundred miles to make an intercept. It will be three stage, solid propellant, and will have a thermonuclear warhead in the megaton range. It will be guided with sufficient accuracy so that the yield of the warhead is adequate to assure destruction of the incoming object.

On the left is the Sprint missile, a very high performance missile that can jump up tens of thousands of feet in a few seconds. It is a two-stage missile, again solid propellant and carries a smaller warhead, in the kilotons range, because this warhead is intended to make intercepts

FIGURE 3

FIGURE 4

in the atmosphere. And, of course, is then a shorter range missile.

Now, let me put these pieces together and try to describe to you how area defense works.

Shown here (fig. 5) is an object launched from China on its way to land over the continental United States. As soon as this object comes over the horizon a PAR deployed in the northern edge of our country picks up the incoming object and tracks it for a short time. After tracking, the PAR radar can predict the subsequent trajectory with sufficient accuracy so that the local MSR radar can launch a Spartan to the intended intercept point and destroy the incoming object.

Chairman PASTORE. Would the explosion take place over our own country?

Dr. FOSTER. Yes, sir; it would.

Senator GORE. Mr. Chairman, could I ask a question at this point?

Senator JACKSON. Yes.

Senator GORE. I had understood, perhaps in error, that the Sprint missile could be used to protect a given city with a defense installation the same as it could be used to give specific protection to a radar or other defense site. Is that correct?

Dr. FOSTER. Yes, Senator Gore, it certainly could. It is not the intention of the Sentinel deployment to provide that type of coverage for cities.

Senator GORE. So your answer to me a few minutes ago was with respect to intention rather than capability.

Dr. FOSTER. It was with respect to the deployment I am describing.

Senator GORE. Thank you.

Senator JACKSON. Can you at this point make a distinction between a point defense and area defense? The Sprint is a point defense system

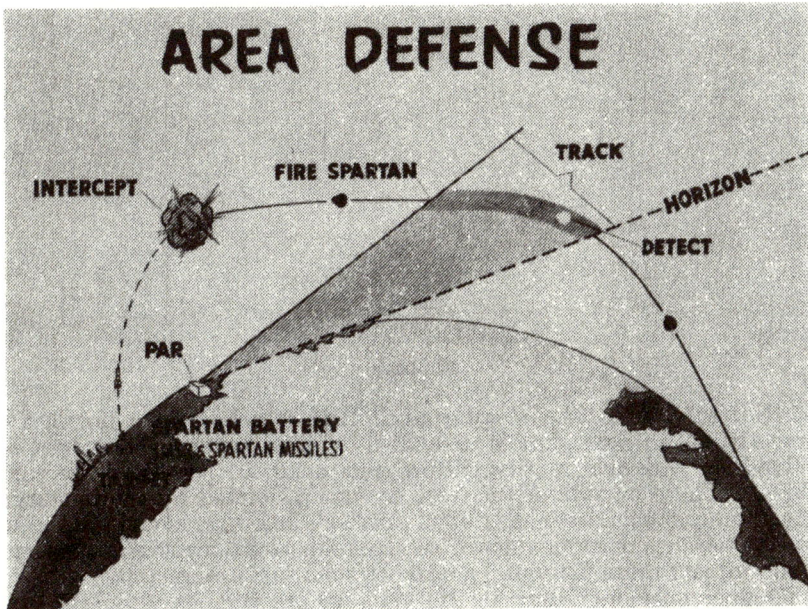

FIGURE 5

and the Spartan system is an area defense system. Can you elaborate on that?

Dr. FOSTER. Yes, Mr. Chairman. The defense capabilities of the the United States permit us to consider attempting to defend whole areas with long-range missiles and the associated radar. This is adequate against relatively light and unsophisticated attacks. However, against heavier attacks it is necessary to have more defense. defense in depth, and so to defend against concentrated attacks which come on specific targets we would propose to put in additional missiles of the Sprint type, quickly acting missiles. Now, in this particular deployment, the deployment we are pursuing at the moment, we deploy against the Chinese an area defense. There can be terminal defense in this system and that terminal defense is associated with protection of the eyes of the system, the perimeter acquisition radar. And further, if we wished, additional protection of the Minuteman silos.

Let me move now to the type of defense, the coverage that is provided by an individual battery. Shown here (fig. 6) is a rough map of

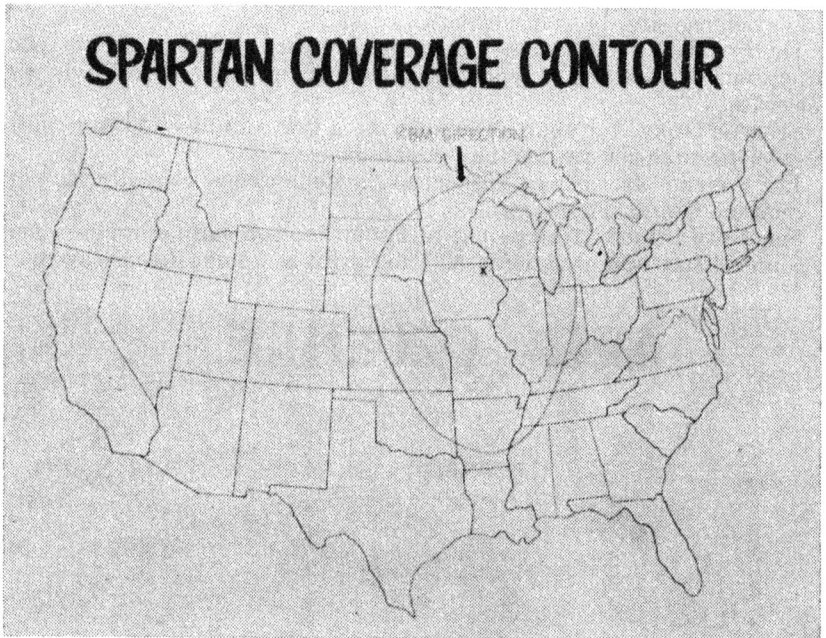

SPARTAN COVERAGE CONTOUR

FIGURE 6

the United States. We imagine an ICBM attack from a northerly direction on an area that is defended by this battery. That area is defined by this oval. Cities within that oval are protected by this battery. Those outside of the oval are not protected by the battery. The area of defense extends a little further south than north, and east or west because it is possible for the battery to intercept missiles that would impact quite far south simply by shooting straight up.

To give you some feeling for the coverage provided by the perimeter acquisition radar, this chart (fig. 7) attempts to indicate the coverage

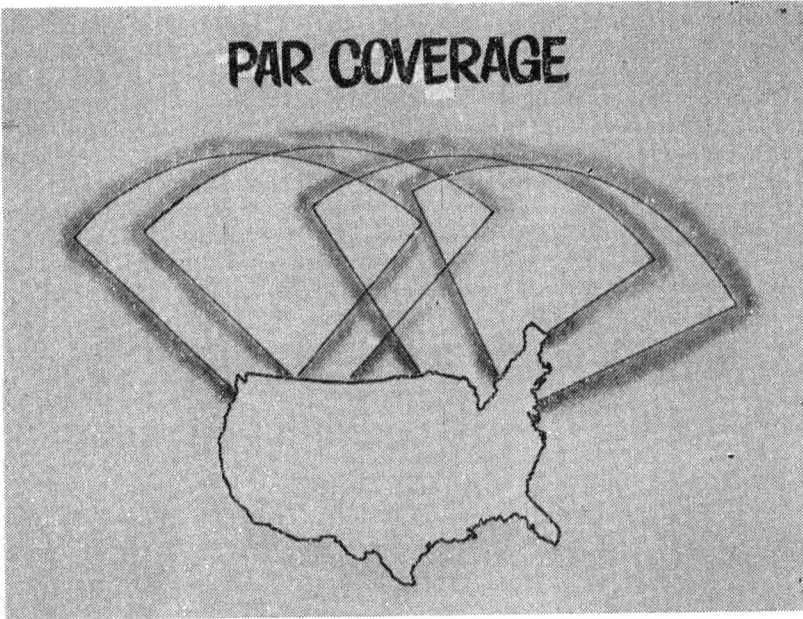

FIGURE 7

when one has several perimeter acquisition radars situated in the northern regions of the United States. This coverage extends out to the horizon which, as I indicated for ICBM's, is about 1,500 miles.

When one puts many batteries in the United States one gets a coverage as indicated here (fig. 8). You see virtually the whole of the

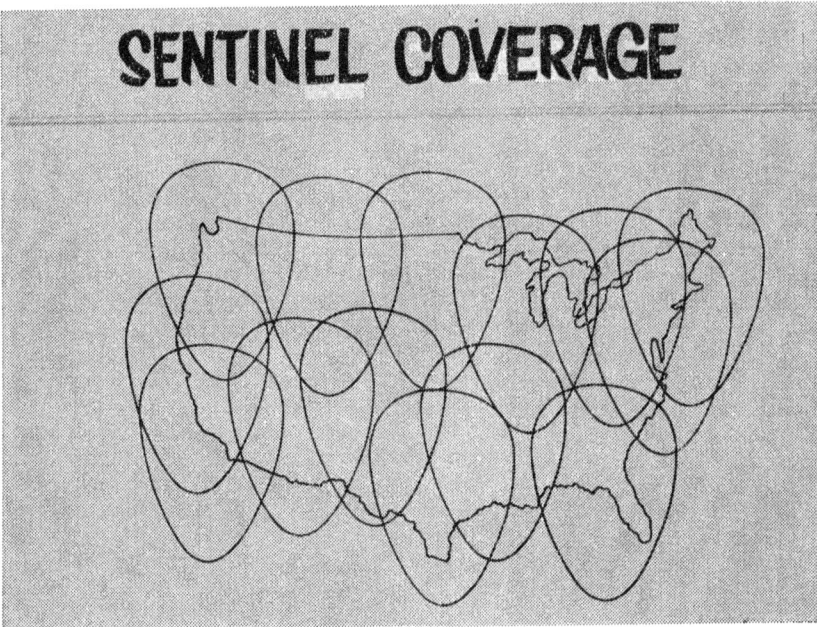

FIGURE 8

United States is covered by this area defense. Again, however, let me stress that while we have covered the United States with a few batteries and we have provided protection for Alaska and Hawaii, this defense system as proposed can be defeated by a very heavy or sophisticated attack on either the interceptors or the radars and with that attack one can knock out the radars and hence defeat the defense or, by exhaustion, remove all of the interceptors and there is no defense.

One often asks what effect, then, there will be on the country if one were to use this area defense against a Chinese ICBM attack. First of all, one has to be concerned with three main effects, the flash, the blast, and the fallout. (Fig. 9 illustrates.)

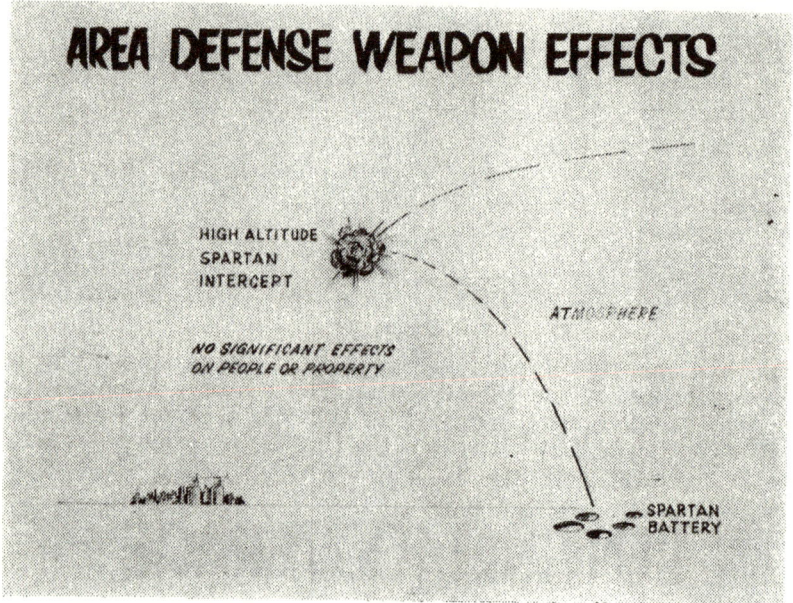

FIGURE 9

With regard to the flash, when the Spartan is launched and goes out beyond the atmosphere and detonates, the detonation of a few megatons will give rise to a blinding flash. Most people working in the regions underneath will not notice it. Those who are outside, especially those who are looking up and on a very clear day, will experience a blinding flash. There is no permanent damage but somewhat the same as if someone is exposed to a photographer's flash.

As far as the blast is concerned, because the detonation occurs above the main atmosphere, there will be a very light response or, at most, a kind of sonic boom. From the point of view of fallout, the moment of detonation of course produces some nuclear effects but these will not be felt on the ground. Nevertheless, radioactivity is produced and the detonation of dozens of these Spartan warheads would release a large amount of radioactivity as would the Sprint detonations of a few kilotons in the atmosphere. In the ensuing weeks and years this radioactivity would settle down onto the country worldwide. The effects of this fallout would be very similar to the effects that we have been experiencing from our last atmospheric test series in 1962.

Chairman PASTORE. Yes, but wouldn't that be less harmful than the actual offensive missile coming from the enemy actually striking?

Dr. FOSTER. Yes, Senator Pastore, it would be negligible compared to the fallout from a single burst on our country.

Chairman PASTORE. That is by comparison, not a big problem.

Dr. FOSTER. I should end up by saying there would be a negligible effect on the property and people of the country in the event this system has to be used.

The question is how effective might this defense be against Chinese attack? I have plotted here (figure 10) on the abscissa, various numbers

FATALITIES VS CPR MISSILES

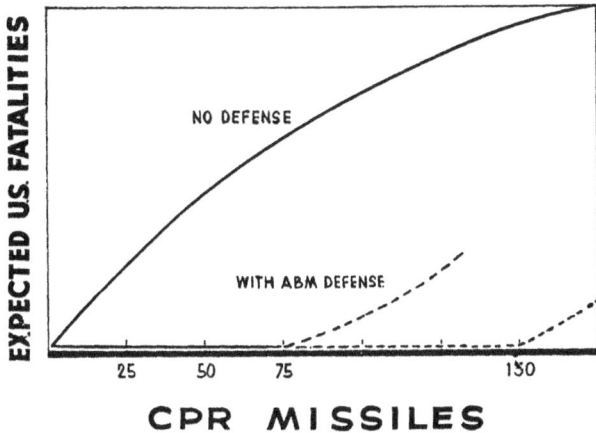

FIGURE 10

of Chinese missiles that could be in their hands in the next decade. I have plotted vertically with no particular scale the deaths that one might have to expect. Without defense you can see we would suffer considerable fatalities. The intention, however, of the Sentinel deployment is to provide a high assurance that there will be no fatalities in the event of a Chinese attack for at least a decade after the initial capability.

So, you see here that we have no fatalities shown until, say, they have 75 missiles. At that time there is an indication that fatalities could occur. It is for that reason that we intend to maintain a very aggressive research and development program in the next decade as we have in the past in order to assure to the best of our ability that we will be able to maintain a high probability of no fatalities for as far into the future as we know how.

Senator GORE. What are the indications on your chart as to fatalities? You list the number of missiles but there is no index on possible fatalities.

Dr. FOSTER. Yes, Senator Gore. That depends a great deal, of course if we had no defense, on exactly the targets that the Chinese might pick. When one goes through calculations associated with 20 or 30 missiles one frequently comes up with deaths amounting to 10 to 20 million.

Senator GORE. Mr. Chairman, what I was asking, if I may—on his chart there is no index on the perpendicular.

Dr. FOSTER. That is correct, Senator Gore. I mention that simply because we realize, if there were to be 10 or 20 or 30 thermonuclear warheads detonating over our country we would have enormous losses. I did not want to quibble over their level. Rather to point out that as a consequence of the decision which has been made and announced by Secretary McNamara we intend to deploy a system that regardless of what it might otherwise have been there will be a high probability of no fatalities for a decade after the initial operation of such a system.

Mr. Chairman, that completes the brief review of the system.

Senator JACKSON. Thank you, Dr. Foster, for your statement and explanation.

Mr. NITZE. Mr. Chairman, I have had a chance to glance through Mr. Hosmer's statement. I would like to have the opportunity to introduce into the record after his statement a more considered reply to his statement. (See p. 47 for Secretary Nitze's reply.) If you will permit, I would like to make a few remarks on the statement at this time.

The first point I would like to make is that as to the estimates of Soviet upcoming numbers, this you will have an opportunity to go into classified testimony in great detail, with the intelligence community as well as with ourselves. But there does seem to be in the statement an emphasis upon megatonnage. The question is raised as to whether Mr. McNamara was right on Friday when he said that the FOBS missile would have three megatons or less. That estimate is wholly in accord with the best estimates of the intelligence community.

Furthermore, the suggestion is made that all of their missiles will have 10 to 30 megatons, which is not correct. Their SS11 missile is more comparable to our Minuteman missile than to the type of missile which would have such a capability.

It further suggests an emphasis upon megatonnage as a criterion of management. I think one ought to look at that criterion as to whether it is the right criterion.

In the 1950's we built a large number of very high yield weapons for our bombers. During the Eisenhower administration it became clear that those weapons would not be deliverable against defenses anticipated in the sixties, and the Eisenhower administration recommended that those high yield weapons be phased out of the inventory or at least phased down. This has been done, was done during the Kennedy administration.

If we are really interested in megatons, it would have been possible to keep those in the inventory and added some 10,000 megatons over and above what was kept in the inventory.

Instead, we put into the inventory weapons which were deliverable, which were much improved weapons and which had a much higher target kill capability.

Another point in connection with this, it would seem to me that if one takes that line of argument, one could cast doubt about the decision to build the Polaris system. The Polaris system has, after all, 41 boats. Two years ago the decision was made to augment it with the Poseidon system. The Poseidon system will cost some $7 billion on top of the $11 billion that has gone into the Polaris system. It is a wholly right decision to have so done because it will greatly increase the throw-weight, and the accuracy; one can use that throw-weight either for more megatonnage, but preferably we would use it for more reentry vehicles so that we could accurately destroy more targets.

Clearly I think it has been wholly right to either invest or commit $18 billion in this system. The aggregate megatonnage that it will deliver is a fraction of the 10,000 megatons which will have been retired when we retire these big weapons.

I would like to also say that we have every intention to maintain our assured destruction through the full period of estimates that Mr. Hosmer suggests. I do not see in this statement reference to the capabilities of our bombers during this period.

We do not intend to phase out our bombers; we will maintain a strong bomber force. We believe that our bomber force alone will be able to have a 20 percent destructive capability at the high estimate of the upcoming threat; we believe that at a medium estimate it would have a 30 percent destructive capability; at the low estimate, 35 percent capability.

The same is true of our ICBM's and of our submarine-launched missiles. We propose to continue to have a thoroughly credible deterrent and frankly I do not think it helps the position of the United States to make denigrating remarks about our nuclear posture when it is not true. We can go into this in the executive session in much greater detail.

Thank you, Mr. Chairman.

Representative HOSMER. May I make three corrections perhaps because you had a hasty chance to read it.

The hypothecation, the workout is based on the Soviet Union achieving numerical parity with the United States in numbers of delivery vehicles. It does not discuss a present situation or denigrate the present retaliatory capacity of the United States in terms of assured destruction.

Secondly, the paper does not talk in terms of cumulative megatonnage but only megatonnage of an individual warhead in relation to its capability to destroy one of our retaliatory missiles in a hardened site.

Third, there is a reference to the bomber fleet toward the end of the statement. It was one of my conclusions, the third one, that we should not phase out the B–52's and B–58's which I did not include in this discussion and which may well be the balance of power on our side at this moment making our deterrent work.

Thank you, Mr. Chairman.

Senator JACKSON. It is my understanding that it is not proposed to phase out the B–52, the G's and H's, until well into the 1970's.

Mr. NITZE. That is correct, Mr. Chairman.

Senator JACKSON. The B–52, E's and F's, are being phased out.

Mr. NITZE. As the FB–111's come in.

Chairman PASTORE. Do I understand in summation that you have no doubt that the striking power, nuclear and thermonuclear, of the United States exceeds that of the Soviet Union?

Mr. NITZE. In terms of target-kill capability under any circumstances throughout the full period that Mr. Hosmer's paper relates to we will maintain it.

Chairman PASTORE. Thank you.

Senator JACKSON. I don't think there is any dispute about our capability at the present time and for some years to come to maintain a strategic nuclear deterrent. But in discussing this subject, of course, we deal with the problem of leadtime.

Chairman PASTORE. I thought that was exactly what this paper raised. It raises that question. It says there may be a doubt about that.

Senator JACKSON. It assumes certain conclusions based on an assumption that if you don't do anything about the present situation, this could happen. I believe this is the point you are endeavoring to make.

Representative HOSMER. If you permit them to obtain parity, numerical parity, and if you do not know for sure that they are not using large enough warheads to kill off ours before they get off the ground, then the result in that paper will occur, calculated both by use of the Rand bomb damage computer and other mathematical probability formulas.

Mr. NITZE. I would prefer to go into the rebuttal in executive session if you would like.

Senator JACKSON. May the Chair suggest, too, that consideration be given to the submission, say by tomorrow morning, of a response in writing to be submitted in the open session to the extent that it can be made in the open session, so that the press will have that information—(see p. 47) to the extent that it can be done within the bounds of security.

Representative HOSMER. May I state I will not be here tomorrow but I will be at the Conrad Hilton Hotel in Chicago at the American Nuclear Society meeting and will be available for any questioning by reporters at that time.

Chairman PASTORE. Yes, but don't make the same speech.

Senator JACKSON. The Chair would like to make a few remarks here before asking questions, and then I will turn to my colleagues.

Let me make a short comment on Secretary McNamara's Friday announcement that the Soviet Union may be testing an orbital bomb. (See p. 128, app. 8, for the text of Secretary McNamara's press conference.) This Soviet "first," of course, has major implications for the U.S. antirocket defense program, which is the subject of these hearings.

As an immediate counter our Government will surely have to speed the development of antisatellite weapons and also build a lot more advanced detection radar.

As I see it, the Soviet development of an orbital bomb should finally put to rest two oversimplified notions. One, the notion that military technology has reached a kind of "plateau" and that the "scientific military revolution" has been stabilized; and two, the notion that if the United States does not act to develop a weapons system, the Soviet Union will not act—the theoretical tit-for-tat, action-reaction model of the Soviet arms buildup.

Secretary McNamara said that this new Soviet weapon "is not a violation" of the outer space treaty which the American Government ratified this year and which forbids signatory nations from placing "in orbit around the Earth any objects carrying nuclear weapons or any other kinds of weapons of mass destruction". (See app. 2, p. 99, for text of "Outer Space" treaty.) The argument seems to be that the Soviet weapon is just a near-orbit or fractional-orbit bomb, and so is not covered by the terms of the space treaty. Yet Secretary McNamara conceded that when launched, the Soviet weapon could circle the earth for several orbits before firing its payload of bombs.

At a minimum, then, there is a "good faith" violation of the space treaty. The whole point of that treaty was to avoid just this sort of object carrying nuclear weapons in space. Obviously, if the Soviet Union develops, tests, and stockpiles this kind of weapon—all ready to go without warning—then the prohibitions of the space treaty won't be worth the paper they are written on.

I would like in the light of this, Secretary Nitze, to ask you, Why did the Defense Department give away for nothing a major bargaining point against Soviet space weapons?

Mr. NITZE. I think, Mr. Chairman, that you raised a number of questions. Could I take them up in order?

Senator JACKSON. Yes, certainly.

Mr. NITZE. The first one is the question as to whether or not anybody in the Defense Department considers we reached a technological plateau and it is not worth while continuing to work on this. This is quite contrary to fact. We have increased the R. & D. program with respect to such weapons. We propose as an example to continue at a high level R. & D. in the ABM field. I think Mr. Foster might expand on this point and then I will come back to other points which you raised, Mr. Chairman.

Senator JACKSON. This point has been debated and discussed. I am not saying the notion is held by scientists in the Defense Department, but by prominent scientists who have maintained there is this technological plateau and they have raised the question whether there is anything more of importance to discover in the weapons field.

Dr. Foster.

Dr. FOSTER. Mr. Chairman, I am absolutely delighted with your attitude on the absence of any technological plateau. I completely agree with you. That is why we come here once a year and ask you for funds to make sure that it is not so in the future.

You indicated that the Soviets were first with this program that may be a fractional orbital bombardment capability. As a matter of fact, I suspect that at the time the Soviets were making their decision about this, it was just at the time we were making it. It is not surprising to me now to look back and see that we decided not to go ahead—nor that the Soviet decided to go ahead.

The matter is simply this: When we saw that it was possible, not so much a fractional orbital bombardment system, but a system that could evade the then in-being ICBM detection system, the BMEWS, we investigated alternative methods of detection. That was back in 1963. At that time Secretary McNamara initiated what is now called the over-the-horizon radar program. It went through several years of research and development and experimental test in the field and this fall is now for the first time in limited operation.

This system has picked up Soviet FOBS. Those Soviet FOBS provide no less warning to us today than the ICBM's do with BMEW. In other words, we are warned when the Soviets launch missiles and we have time to launch our forces, put them on the alert, if we wish to.

Senator JACKSON. But if they are in orbit and you don't know what they are going to do, and they have a lot of them in orbit——

Dr. FOSTER. Then our forces are already up.

Senator JACKSON. But the time in which you would have to respond with an ABM system is how much as compared to a conventional intercontinental ballistic missile?

Dr. FOSTER. Mr. Chairman, you actually have more time under those conditions to respond. However, we are not planning to deploy any extensive antiorbital bomb satellite capability. Those bombs don't represent any more of a threat to us, in fact they are less of a threat to us, than the ones that remain sitting in silos in the Soviet Union. The reason is simply this.

Once an orbital system is put up, it takes many hours before it can be in a position to hit the target that they want. So, if you have many of them up there and you want to launch a simultaneous attack, it is not possible. It is possible with ICBM's in silos. That is why we have chosen that approach.

For all I know the Soviets, too, have chosen this approach. This particular system is not a FOBS at all. Nor have they used the multiple orbital capability nor to my knowledge have they ever put a nuclear weapon in orbit.

Senator JACKSON. Of course, we have no way of knowing.

Dr. FOSTER. That is correct.

Chairman PASTORE. Then what good is your warning system?

Dr. FOSTER. I beg your pardon, sir?

Chairman PASTORE. You say we don't know whether it is a weapon. Therefore what good is your warning system until they are all set to drop it?

Dr. FOSTER. To be a serious threat by the Soviet Union to the United States they would not launch one or two fractional orbital systems to evade our detection system. I made it clear that our detection system cannot be avoided by a fractional orbital bombardment system. Therefore, they would have to consider launching many, 50, a hundred. Before they had launched more than a few, our bombers would be alerted and off the runways.

The whole purpose, it is assumed, of a fractional orbital bombardment system is to catch the soft forces by surprise, our B-52's and our air defense forces. I want to assure you that if we make such detections, and we will if they launch fractional orbital systems, our forces will be off the ground.

Chairman PASTORE. Yes; but how many would they have to put up in order to knock out your warning system? Would it have to be massive?

Dr. FOSTER. Yes; it would have to be rather massive.

Chairman PASTORE. In other words, they would not have to send up only one or two?

Dr. FOSTER. No; the warning system depends on many installations. That is a very good point, sir.

Mr. NITZE. Mr. Chairman, another question was raised and that was as to whether or not it is a violation of the space treaty. Article 4 of the treaty requires that the states party to the treaty undertake not to place in orbit around the earth any objects carrying nuclear weapons or any other kind of weapons of massive destruction or storing such weapons in celestial bodies or station such weapons in outer space in any other manner.

The FOBS is a land-based system which acts essentially as an ICBM. An orbital bombardment system on the other hand would involve weapons based or deployed in space for longer periods of time. This is what is banned by the treaty.

The language and intent of the treaty have the purpose of preventing the stationing of mass destruction weapons in space. The deployment of a space system such as FOBS at ground installations is not a violation nor is the development of space weapons, provided the mass destruction weapons are not placed into orbit during the course of test launching.

We have therefore concluded that this is not a violation of the treaty.

Chairman PASTORE. In order to violate article 4, a weapon must be placed in orbit?

Mr. NITZE. That is correct.

Senator JACKSON. Mr. Secretary, this is a very tortured construction of the treaty provisions.

Mr. NITZE. I think this was all gone through prior to the time that the treaty was negotiated.

Senator JACKSON. Mr. Secretary, isn't it true that this weapon system on command can be made into a full orbital device?

Mr. NITZE. I think it would have to be substantially changed from what we believe that the present system is in order to do that.

Senator JACKSON. Can we be completely sure? I understood Secretary McNamara at the press conference to say that it could go into a full orbit.

Dr. FOSTER. Mr. Chairman, we have no evidence as to whether or not it could operate past one orbit or not. I think Mr. McNamara was expressing an opinion that if they did not construct a satellite to come down after completing most of one orbit, it could go on and do another one. I suspect that he is right.

Senator JACKSON. The point I am trying to make is that with all the talk about trying to get an arms limitation agreement with Moscow, a good faith agreement—because treaties don't mean anything unless the signatories will act in good faith—it seems to me that we are off to a very bad start here with the Soviets having in being a number of weapon systems that can be placed in orbit, albeit at the present time it may not be for a full orbit. But the clear intent of that space treaty was to do away with terror weapons in space. If this is not a terror weapon, I don't know what it is.

Mr. NITZE. Frankly, it is not a terror weapon. It is not any more terrible than the ICBM. The same launcher could launch a heavier missile which should be more destructive. The point of it is that this weapon is one which we believe has the intention of trying to go after our soft targets if we don't have warning. We have taken steps to get warning.

Senator JACKSON. At least they are not flying ballistic missiles over the United States. This weapon system can be flown over the United States, and according to the Department of Defense interpretation of the treaty, there is no violation.

Mr. NITZE. It would be a violation if it had a weapon in it.

Senator JACKSON. Wait a minute. I don't understand that. I thought in order to be a violation of the treaty that it would have to be in full orbit with a weapon in it. Does the Department take the view that if there is a weapon in it, even if it is a fractional orbit, it is a violation of the treaty?

Mr. NITZE. I believe you are correct, it would have to be a full orbit.

Senator JACKSON. The point I am making is that it is not like an ICBM. They could fly this system over the United States with a weapon in it, and return. Whether this can be done technically is another matter. But they certainly have been flying some, presumably without warheads in them. We don't know whether they have had warheads in them. We have no way of detecting it. Isn't that right? We have no way of detecting whether there is a weapon system, a nuclear weapon system, within the orbital bomb?

Mr. NITZE. We could not tell.

Chairman PASTORE. May I ask a question at this point? Are you actually saying, Mr. Nitze, that unless you have a full orbit, any fractional orbit is no more terrible than a landbased missile? Is that what you are actually saying?

Mr. NITZE. That is what I am saying. That is right, because in order to do damage they would have to have lots of them and under those circumstances we would have warning, we would flush our bombers and fighters.

Senator JACKSON. Senator Gore?

Senator GORE. In order that this might be put into perspective— whether or not it is a terror weapon—is either an orbital weapon or an ICBM weapon more terrifying than the possibility of weapons from submarines?

Mr. NITZE. I believe not.

Senator JACKSON. I say, Senator Gore, that again I emphasize that the treaty does not ban, according to the Department of Defense's interpretation, an orbital bomb flying over the United States and the Soviet Union with a nuclear warhead.

Mr. NITZE. A fractional orbital bomb.

Senator GORE. Mr. Chairman, in that connection we have a treaty with the Soviet Union banning nuclear weapons tests in the atmosphere, but one condition on which the Senate ratified that treaty was a commitment by the President that we would maintain a readiness to conduct atmospheric tests on very short notice.

So, if maintaining readiness to conduct tests in the atmosphere is a violation of that treaty, then the Senate ratified it under an erroneous impression.

I do not see that the Soviet Union's readiness to place a weapon in orbit is any more a violation of the outer space treaty than our readiness to conduct atmospheric tests is a violation of that. I don't think either is.

Mr. NITZE. This is quite correct. We consider it would be perfectly within the treaty for us to build a fractional orbital bomb system, and if we thought that was to our advantage, we would have done so.

Chairman PASTORE. But Mr. Gore is saying this fractional orbit— can that not be used as a full orbit? Or do you have to have new technology, new research?

In other words, what they have and can use for fractional orbit, can they use the same device for a full orbit?

Mr. NITZE. I believe if it were even an orbital weapon, the development of such is not banned by the treaty. What is banned by the treaty is the deployment of such a system with nuclear warheads in space.

Chairman PASTORE. What you are bringing out here is the fact that if for some reason this treaty became abrogated, they are already prepared for full orbit, and we don't even have fractional orbit.

That is the point he is making.

Dr. FOSTER. Senator Pastore, I think it is extremely important that each member of this committee understand very clearly what such a system might mean to the United States.

Let us assume for the moment that these flights are associated with the fractional orbital system. Then the only reason we can understand for such a development and such experiments is an attempt by the Soviet Union to be able to cope with the readiness state of the B-52's in our strategic forces that they have seen for the last 25 years.

The U.S. strategic forces are ready on a few moments notice to be airborne and off the airfield, ready to go to war, if they have to. The Soviets have looked at that now for more than two decades.

What they perhaps thought back in 1963 was that with their large payload they could go around the southern route, go around the 60-minute trip, and avoid or evade the BMEW.

There is another possibility, and that is that there is a tunnel—we don't know it very well, and neither do they—that they might scoot through between the BMEW radars and come in undetected, if they were low enough. Hence the trajectory is at about a hundred mile altitude.

Now, the question is, then, What good is it today?

Well, today we have deployed and have operational an early warning radar, so we have as much warning today against the fractional orbital attack by the Soviet Union as we would if they used that same booster to deliver a warhead the conventional ICBM route.

At the present time we have two major difficulties: No. 1, the payload is one-half to one-third when it is a fractional orbital system, so the yield is a half to one-third. No. 2, it is less accurate, and so less of the target is destroyed.

I don't see any advantage to this system, if indeed it is a fractional orbital bombardment system.

Now, it may not be. If they put it in multiple orbit, I think it is even less useful, because they cannot call it down on targets of their choice at any moment. They may have to wait 3, 5, 9, 10 hours before a particular one passes over the target they want to bombard. It seems to me that then makes it worse than bombers.

Senator JACKSON. How much, Dr. Foster, will we have to spend in improving our detection system because of this development to provide for an antisatellite capability? Do you have any idea?

Dr. FOSTER. Mr. Chairman, independent of this development, we intended to finish our full deployment of the over-the-horizon radar program, and that amounts to just a few tens of millions of dollars.

Senator JACKSON. How much?

Dr. FOSTER. A few tens of millions, in the next few years.

Senator JACKSON. That will be adequate?

Dr. FOSTER. That will be perfectly adequate; yes, sir.

Senator JACKSON. How about an antisatellite rocket system to knock down satellites?

Dr. FOSTER. We have an antisatellite capability now. It cannot catch any orbit on the first orbit. The Sentinel system that I have just described would be more than adequate to take care of any array of such orbital systems within a few orbits.

Senator JACKSON. Now I want to ask either one of you gentlemen this question: Have we taken this matter up with the Soviet Union since the signing of the space treaty? Mr. Brezhnev boasted as early as July 3, 1965 about "intercontinental orbital rockets," to the military academy graduates in Moscow. Have we taken this matter up with Moscow, the question of a violation or good faith breach of the treaty?

Mr. NITZE. I think the question of the orbital bomb was taken up. The question of the FOBS I do not believe has been, because we do not consider——

Senator JACKSON. It seems to me this is something that the administration should certainly be bargaining with the Soviets on, in light of the fact that we are still trying to reach some kind of an agreement with them in connection with the ABM deployment. But if we are off to this kind of start, in which we know that they are putting at least into fractional orbit a——

Mr. NITZE. Mr. Chairman, I think this is an important point.

When we negotiate a treaty, we ought to be precise as to what the language means, and what is permitted, and what is not. Otherwise, it leads to great confusion.

We were clear and precise as to what this language meant, prior to the negotiation of the treaty. Therefore I do not think your inference is correct, that it would have undermined the treaty had we decided we wanted to develop a fractional orbital bomb.

We felt that the treaty condition was such that we could develop such, if we wanted to. Similarly, the Russians, if they have decided they want to do this, this is within the language of the treaty.

But you want to be clear what the treaty provides, and what it does not provide.

Senator JACKSON. I am talking about the "good faith" aspects of the treaty. When one of these devices is launched into orbit, you have prima facie evidence that it is a weapon system, do you not?

Mr. NITZE. So far one of these has not been launched into a full orbit. They have only been launched in less than a full orbit.

Senator JACKSON. I understand that we have sufficient information which made it possible for the Secretary of Defense last week to announce that they had launched a number of these devices.

Mr. NITZE. That is correct.

Senator JACKSON. What I am saying is that I think it is important that we not try to leave the impression that this is no different than an ICBM situation.

First, they can have it over the United States, they can have a nuclear warhead in it—I am not trying to scare anyone, I am just trying to clarify what our interpretation of the treaty is—they could have it over the United States, and if they could return it, there would be no violation, according to our unilateral interpretation of the treaty.

I am submitting that there is certainly here a good faith breach of the whole purpose of the space treaty. I think that the average American would say, and most people would, that this is a good faith breach of this treaty having a nuclear or a whole series of nuclear warheads over the United States, and then returning them.

They are not firing ICBM missiles over the United States, and it is an entirely different situation. I think that point ought to be made clear.

Mr. NITZE. They have not put weapons—incidentally, none of these has flown over the United States.

Senator JACKSON. I understand, but they can fly them over the United States.

Mr. NITZE. You are saying that they might do something which you think might be a violation.

Senator JACKSON. They could fly them over this country and we don't know what they have in them. The treaty makes no provision for inspection so as to determine whether orbiting bodies are armed.

Dr. FOSTER. Mr. Chairman, the treaty does permit nations to develop orbital weapon systems. That is a specific provision in the treaty. They can develop them. They cannot deploy them.

Senator JACKSON. Is this a deployment?

Dr. FOSTER. No, sir. We have some evidence that they may be developing one, not an orbital system, perhaps a fractional orbital system, that as far as we know provides no additional military capability. Rather, it has less military capability, as we see it, than had they used the missile in its conventional form.

Senator JACKSON. How would you define "deployment"?

Dr. FOSTER. I would suppose that deployment would consist of putting this concept into a production line, and building missiles, and installing them with this particular capability.

Senator JACKSON. They now claim, as I understand, Mr. Breshnev claims, they now have the system.

Mr. NITZE. I do not believe he has claimed that they are doing what is prohibited by the treaty, which is stationing weapons in orbit. That is prohibited by the treaty.

Senator JACKSON. I think it is quite clear, at least to my way of thinking, that any time they have on launcher a weapon system that can either be put in partial or full orbit—and I think we have to assume this capability for a full orbit. The Secretary of Defense did in his remarks at the press conference last week, in response to a question——

Mr. NITZE. He did say that this type of system could probably do more than the fractional orbit.

Senator JACKSON. That is right, but the fact that Moscow has such a system in being, ready to launch, and that it can be put into that kind of orbit, I am submitting, is certainly a violation of the "good faith" provisions of the treaty.

I make that comment only in that light, because I think as we look ahead, we certainly have to consider the way in which the Soviets are acting insofar as existing treaties are concerned and certainly insofar as the most recent one is concerned.

Senator GORE. Mr. Chairman, will you yield there?

Senator JACKSON. Yes, sir.

Senator GORE. I do not wish to be an apologist for either the administration or the Soviet Union on this issue, but since it is a matter of such delicate and crucial importance, and since ultimate agreement for nuclear limitation and disarmament is so important to our people and the people of the world, I think that I should say that as a U.S. delegate to the United Nations, I was assigned on behalf of my Government the responsibility of debating and ultimately negotiating an outer space agreement with the Soviet Union which ultimately became a United Nations agreement, and which, as you know, was the precursor of the treaty, the treaty being but a formalization of the United Nations resolution.

At no time during these conferences and debates did I ever understand my Government to insist, or that there was any understanding that an agreement against orbited missiles of mass destruction in any way precluded research and development.

I understood it was the actual deployment of terror weapons in outer space which was precluded.

Senator JACKSON. I don't think there is any dispute about that.

Mr. NITZE. That is my understanding, too.

Senator JACKSON. I don't think there is any question about what the Senator from Tennessee said.

The point is that the Soviets have a system in being that is beyond research and development. It has actually been launched.

Mr. NITZE. I really don't understand that, Mr. Chairman. If it is permitted to have research and development, then obviously it is permitted to have the conclusion of research and development, is it not?

Senator JACKSON. Mr. Secretary, I have never said that they have technically violated the treaty; I have addressed myself completely to the "good faith" point, the good faith point being that they have "in being," apparently, a series of these devices which can be used either as a fractional orbital system or as a full orbital system.

We have no way of knowing, under the treaty, no way of finding out, whether or not they have technically violated or will violate the treaty until the nuclear bombs hit.

Now, there is no provision in the treaty authorizing physical inspection so as to determine whether orbiting bodies are armed. That is one of the weaknesses of the treaty. Am I correct that there is no provision for inspection?

Mr. NITZE. I believe not.

Senator JACKSON. I understand that under article X there is a provision for a request by other states to the treaty to be afforded an opportunity to observe the flight of space objects launched by those states. That is under article X of the treaty.

Do we have any plans to make a request along that line?

Mr. NITZE. There are not any objects up there to request inspection.

Senator JACKSON. No, but they are acquiring such a system and they have actually fired a number of them. Would it not be appropriate to find out from them whether they are putting weapons in such devices, and whether they have plans for a full orbital bombardment system, as a part of it?

Mr. NITZE. If we believed they were putting weapons in orbit, we certainly would take action under the treaty.

Senator JACKSON. Mrs. Smith.

Senator SMITH. Thank you, Mr. Chairman.

Mr. Nitze, I quite agree with you that treaties and international agreements should be specific, but I would ask by whose interpretation?

Unless there is good faith, such as the chairman has already discussed, is it possible to have a treaty so precise and so specific that loopholes cannot be found?

Mr. NITZE. As Senator Gore said, this was discussed with the delegation while the treaty was under negotiation, as to what the treaty meant, and what was prohibited, what was not prohibited.

The R. & D. along these lines was not prohibited by the treaty.

Senator SMITH. This is not an R. & D., is it? It is in being.

Dr. FOSTER. As far as we understand, this is research and development. It is not deployed, that we know of.

Senator SMITH. Mr. Secretary, back on March 31 of this year I made a speech in the Senate, in which I expressed my doubts about the proposed antiballistic missile defense system, and said that I thought Secretary McNamara was right in his disapproval of it, but for the wrong reason.

I said that I was not convinced that the state of the art on an antiballistic missile defense system has reached a relatively static status. I expressed the fear that the proposed ABM defense system was the very system that may be obsolete or become obsolete in the near future.

When Secretary McNamara recently called a few of us over in his office, you may remember, to give us advance notice of his then forthcoming announcement of his decision to go ahead with a thin ABM defense system, I reiterated my reservations about such a system either being obsolete or becoming obsolete before it could be established.

Secretary McNamara's announcement over the weekend on Russia's fractional orbital bombing system seems to me to have confirmed the already obsolescence of the proposed ABM defense system.

Mr. Chairman, I have no questions, unless the Secretary has some observations he wishes to make.

The CHAIRMAN. Mr. Nitze, would you like to comment on Mrs. Smith's observation?

Mr. NITZE. Dr. Foster, would you make a comment?

Dr. FOSTER. Senator Smith, I appreciate your concern for the tendency for systems, once deployed, to become obsolescent. That is a concern that is also shared by Secretary McNamara, and Secretary Nitze, and myself.

The reason why we think we have a chance to have this Sentinel system survive for a decade is specifically because we have been through three generations of ballistic missile defense, in a sense, on paper and in some hardware in the field, tested it against the ICBM developments of the United States, and looked at the Soviet systems, and tried to see what system to deploy that could be capable of stopping them.

We see no reason to believe that the Chinese system would be radically different.

Nevertheless, let us suppose that the Chinese, as their system begins to evolve, choose the route of a fractional orbital system, coming in low, giving one less time for the perimeter acquisition radar to make the detection and force then a faster response by the defense.

I can assure you that if this is the approach that the Chinese make, we will have in development and ready for deployment equipment, at the time that the Chinese have their system, that will be able to cope with them.

Senator JACKSON. Senator Pastore.

Chairman PASTORE. I have followed you gentlemen very, very closely on the thesis you have developed here today, which leads me to this question: If our concern is establishing an antiballistic missile system merely because of the Chinese threat, then how do we resolve in our own mind the motivations of the Russians in bringing Moscow under the protection of their own antiballistic missile system?

Would you say that the Soviets are fearful of the Chinese threat, or the American threat?

Mr. NITZE. I would think that they were fearful of the American threat.

Chairman PASTORE. Therefore, if it is good for them, why is it not good for us?

Dr. FOSTER. Senator Pastore, we don't agree that it is good for them. We think it is a mistake.

Chairman PASTORE. You think the Russians have made a mistake in defending themselves against nuclear attack?

Dr. FOSTER. Yes, Senator, I do.

Chairman PASTORE. Why?

Dr. FOSTER. Because their system will be defeated. We will send in on target as many warheads when their system is completed by simple exhaustion as we would have sent in if there had been no system.

Chairman PASTORE. Could you not say the same thing about the Chinese?

Dr. FOSTER. The difference, Senator Pastore, was explained by Secretary Nitze in his opening statement.

Chairman PASTORE. Just the element of time?

Mr. NITZE. In my opening statement, I said that the first ICBM deployed by the Chinese would be of relatively primitive technology, and small in number. That kind of offensive force could certainly be handled by the system that we are installing up through the 1970's. As I said, with foreseeable improvement to the system, we believe our system will be capable of damage denial into the 1980's.

Chairman PASTORE. I merely make this point.

I remember visiting you, Dr. Foster, at Livermore, and you were very much concerned about an antiballistic missile that was paraded around in the May Day parade in Russia.

If you were concerned then, why are you less concerned now?

Dr. FOSTER. Senator, I do not mean to indicate I am not concerned. I am concerned every day about what the Soviet are doing, because Mr. McNamara has made clear we must provide an assured destruction capability. We must be assured that we can destroy the Soviet Union, if they attack us.

Now, when you say you must be assured, that assurance has to come from a careful and detailed study of everything they have, and everything you have got. So you have to be concerned over what they do, and what they have.

Senator JACKSON. Senator Pastore, maybe this is a good point at which we ought to get a matter clarified, because you have raised an excellent point.

It seems to me, Dr. Foster, you might be able at this point in the record to divide this issue; namely, first indicate to the extent you can in open hearing the number of missiles that the existing state of the art can handle; second, indicate what the program is with reference to the problem beyond that.

Beyond what we now contemplate or talk about with the thin system it is my understanding that we are continuing to invest a half billion dollars a year in research and development, and that for the problem posed by the kind of missile attack the Soviets can mount, and later on even the Chinese, really it is in the hands of the scientists and engineers to come up with effective tools and techniques, if they can.

Have I stated this generally correctly?

Dr. FOSTER. I believe you have, Mr. Chairman.

Senator JACKSON. Could you enlarge on this, and indicate what the state of the art is at the present time, and the general figures as to how many missiles the system can handle, and beyond that, what happens?

Dr. FOSTER. Let me try to do that for you, sir.

We have a capability today, demonstrated by field experiments, to intercept intercontinental missile warheads with high assurance. That makes it a numbers game, in part.

Suppose we have deployed a thousand missiles capable of intercepting incoming objects, and radar defended by short-range Sprint missiles, so that deliberate attacks on those radars are not likely to knock them out.

If we make a decision to deploy such a system with, say, a thousand interceptors, the point is that the Soviets, who are now about the business of deploying missiles in hardened silos, deploying some number that we don't know, let us call it n, the Soviets in a few years will have n missiles—if Mr. McNamara made the decision to deploy this ballistic missile defense that had 1,000 interceptors, the Soviets would look at that system and say, "Now, in 1975 the Americans will be able to intercept 1,000 of our missiles. If we are determined to have the capability that we decided we would have a few years ago, we must now deploy not n but n plus 1,000 missiles."

They make this decision. Then in 1975, or whenever it is, we might have such a heavier system deployed the Soviets would have n plus a thousand, and we would have a thousand interceptors.

If an exchange then took place, and we were very fortunate, in that our ABM system really worked, it could stop as many as a thousand of those incoming warheads, and n would fall and devastate the country.

That is, unfortunately, the status of the current numbers game, as far as the technology is concerned.

We don't see a simple way to put up a defense that is within our technology and economy that cannot be defeated by the Soviet technology and economy.

We do see, however, a way within our technology, and certainly within our economy, to deploy a defense system that is several generations ahead in technology of the first-generation ICBM that the Chinese would put up.

So, with the Soviet Union, it is a matter of economy and technology, and with the Chinese, the difference is very large.

Does that help, Mr. Chairman?

Senator JACKSON. Yes.

In other words, as we look to the future, we have to rely on research and development and the scientists to develop the tools, if they can, that could give us an effective defense against a Soviet-type missile attack.

This is why the move to develop a thin system can be fully justified from a technical point of view. It can be effective to the limit announced by the Secretary and as you have outlined it here today.

But when you get beyond that, the state of the art is such that the validity of the thin system cannot be automatically projected on out either arithmetically or in any other way, saying that with an increase in such-and-such numbers you can continue to provide a defense against such a threat as the one posed by the Soviet Union.

Chairman PASTORE. Just assume you did have this thousand plus n, and it was fired either by the United States or by Russia, concurrently on both sides. What would be the status of the world, in your estimation? Would you not have destroyed the major part of the world?

Dr. FOSTER. Senator Pastore, the n missiles which landed would cause terrible destruction, and the destruction, as I indicated, would be the same with or without ballistic missile defense.

Now, in regard to what the future might hold, we have, as you know, been carrying on a vigorous research and development program in ballistic missile defense. This has amounted to over a half billion dollars a year.

It has consisted not only of a very aggressive effort trying to push the Nike X and area defense components as hard as we can, but in addition, over a hundred million dollars a year in the advanced projects research agency has attempted to investigate the most advanced ideas that the minds of scientists in this country can provide.

Looking into the future, with the deployment of the Sentinel system, we still have three major jobs to do. The first one is to make sure that this system, once deployed, remains viable for at least a decade against the Chinese threat.

No. 2, continue research and development in the hope that it will be possible to find a means whereby we can provide defense of this country against all-out Soviet attack, a means that is clearly within our technology and economy, but not within theirs to defeat.

The third purpose of the advanced research and development will be to make sure that we put into the field in actual hardware, equipments which are as advanced as we can provide in the way of the state of the art in ballistic missile defense.

The purpose of these equipments is to be able to see exactly what our offensive threat looks like through the eyes of the most advanced ballistic missile defense system we can devise.

So it is both to keep open the possibility that we may be able to not only keep the Sentinel system alive, but technologically that we may be able to defend the country as well as to provide us the assurance that we can penetrate the Soviet Union as we continue research and development.

Senator JACKSON. Congressman Hosmer.

Representative HOSMER. We mentioned the matter a moment ago of possible orbital treaty violations. How about the limited test ban treaty?

I am referring to the January 15, 1965, Soviet tests which vented nuclear material which was detected both by the United States and the Japanese Governments.

I believe Mr. William Foster, Director of the Arms Control and Disarmament Agency, once stated that it may have been a technical violation of the treaty.

Mr. FOSTER. Mr. Hosmer, there is no doubt that radioactive debris was found on land away from the Soviet Union.

I imagine there are those who would find that in a very narrow technical view this could constitute a violation.

At the same time, however. it is pretty clear to me, and I hope to everyone else, that both countries have made major efforts in an attempt to minimize the possibility that radioactive debris vented from underground explosions do not go off our own territorial limits.

Representative HOSMER. Would it not be simpler to write the Soviets a letter and tell them that we picked this up in areas outside their boundaries, and we knew it was impossible to keep from getting it out, and we did not consider it a violation of the treaty, and we were going to proceed under the same ground rules?

Dr. FOSTER. Mr. Hosmer, we have talked with the Soviets, and in addition, we have had our own accidents, and debris has been released from underground explosions.

Representative HOSMER. We are not quarreling about minor amounts of releases of radiation constituting violations of that treaty, then?

Dr. FOSTER. No, we are not, Mr. Hosmer.

Representative HOSMER. In your explanation of this ABM system you laid emphasis on the fact that it is designed to protect people in cities, and not our retaliatory capability, did you not?

Dr. FOSTER. I indicated, as I recall, that it does provide protection for the Minuteman, and that in addition it is possible to add Sprint missiles and missile site radars in the Minuteman field to provide additional protection to the silos.

Representative HOSMER. As I understood the rationale of the system, since it is supposed to be limited to the Chinese, it is that it is designed to protect people, and not to protect our retaliatory capability.

Dr. FOSTER. Mr. Hosmer, there are two separate purposes. One purpose is to attempt to provide a cover over all of the United States against ICBM's launched from China. That is the Sentinel system that I described.

The second capability is being able to add additional Sprints and radar as necessary in order to provide still additional coverage of the Minuteman silos against attempts by the Soviet Union to knock out those silos.

Representative HOSMER. That confirms the suspicion of some people, at least, that this is really the first stage of an anti-Soviet ABM, as well as an anti-Chinese ABM. Is that right?

Dr. FOSTER. It is certainly not so, and I had not intended to convey that impression.

Representative HOSMER. From the answer you gave, could it be at least in the nature of a building block, if somebody later decided to build upon it to make a full system, rather than a thin system?

Dr. FOSTER. Mr. Hosmer, this is not being deployed as a building block for some heavier system.

Representative HOSMER. I am not asking if it is. I am asking if it were possible, if we changed from thinking thin to thinking thick, that we could build on.

Mr. FOSTER. The thinking may be thick, but it is not that way.

Our components, as I indicated previously, are such that if one did want to put batteries around specific cities, one certainly could do that.

However, as I have indicated, I believe, as the Secretary does, that the Soviet reaction would be automatic, and we would not be able to end up providing that protection.

Representative HOSMER. We would have to start over again, then?

Dr. FOSTER. Pardon, sir?

Representative HOSMER. We would have to start over again?

Dr. FOSTER. Well, if we did not start, we would not have to start over again.

Representative HOSMER. I meant if we wanted to go to the full system.

Dr. FOSTER. If you went to the full system, Mr. Hosmer, the Soviets, I believe, would react.

Representative HOSMER. I am not talking about their reaction. I am talking about our capability to go to the full system.

Dr. FOSTER. Certainly we have the capability economically to go to a full system.

Representative HOSMER. You alleged that this FOBS, which used to be SCRAG before Mr. McNamara announced it——

Mr. NITZE. I believe not, Mr. Hosmer. I believe what was referred to as SCRAG was a device which was exhibited in a parade in Moscow which was undoubtedly quite different than the FOBS.

Representative HOSMER. In what way? Is not SCRAG the delivery vehicle for FOBS?

Mr. NITZE. No, I believe not.

Representative HOSMER. In any event, Dr. Foster, you described FOBS as capable of taking out some of the stuff like B–52's, and so on. On what are you working there, 2 pounds per square inch over pressure? Two to three?

Dr. FOSTER. No, Mr. Hosmer, I think it would require more than that, and we could supply more than that. It would not have the accuracy to take out a Minuteman site.

Representative HOSMER. I am talking about the soft stuff right now. On the Rand damage effect computer I get a 99-percent chance of destroying an airplane with 2 pounds per square inch overpressure with a 10,000-foot CEP.

If you go up to a little higher than that, to three, it gets down to 8,000 feet CEP.

Five, it gets down to 6,000 feet CEP.

Is that about the range you are thinking of in terms of the accuracy of FOBS?

Dr. FOSTER. Yes, that is correct, Mr. Hosmer.

I have indicated that FOBS could cause very serious damage to our airfields. The important point, however, I think, is that so can an ICBM, and we have warning against either, and if either comes in, the B-52's will be off and flying.

Representative Hosmer. That is one way of looking at it.

Aside from being just an airplane wrecker, I kind of wonder if this FOBS is not a couple of steps ahead in the form of an anti-antiballistic missile weapon, in the sense that you have these various radars, and so on. I don't know how far they are hardened, but I suppose that if their warheads carried a big enough wallop, the other side's first strike tactic would be to throw in FOBS and knock out the ABM system, and then follow it up with more accurate, powerful ICBM's on the missile site.

Dr. FOSTER. Mr. Hosmer, are you thinking of the Soviet destroying the Sentinel system, or are you talking about the Chinese destroying the Sentinel system?

Representative HOSMER. Right now I don't think the Chinese have the capability, so I must be talking about the Russians.

Dr. FOSTER. Mr. Hosmer, we give the Russians credit for being able to take it out. It is not deployed to protect us against the Russians.

Representative HOSMER. We are doing like we do on a penny, "In God we trust"?

Dr. FOSTER. No, sir. We depend on our retaliatory capability to make sure that the Soviets will not launch FOBS or ICBM's or bombers.

Representative HOSMER. I quote Mr. McNamara, who says it just about the same: "Our deterrent rests on our ability to absorb any surprise nuclear attack and to retaliate with such strength so as to destroy the attacking nation as a viable society."

Now, that means that our retaliatory capacity must in some manner be protected against the first-strike surprise attack.

Mr. NITZE. That is correct.

Representative HOSMER. We are not going to protect it by ABM?

Dr. FOSTER. We can protect the Minuteman.

Representative HOSMER. But Mr. McNamara says "no," we are not going to use the ABM to protect our ——

Dr. FOSTER. We have the option to deploy.

Mr. NITZE. In his September 18 speech he said, "Moreover, such an ABM deployment designed against a possible Chinese attack would have a number of other advantages. It would provide"—wait a minute—"further, the Chinese-oriented ABM would enable us to add as a concurrent benefit a further defense of our Minuteman sites against Soviet attack, which means at a modest cost we would in fact be adding even greater effectiveness to our offensive force and avoiding a much more costly system." (See app. 4, p. 105.)

Representative HOSMER. We are, in fact, using this as a protection against Soviet first surprise attack as well as against Chinese?

Mr. NITZE. What this says is we have this capability, and we may very well exercise it, adding the Sprint missiles to the defense of the Minuteman farms, which would be a defense for those missiles against the Soviet attack.

All that has been said is that we do not have the capability of assuring protection for our populace.

Representative HOSMER. In order to do an adequate job of that, I have heard that the cost of this system would have to go up from something around $5 billion to something around $40 to $60 billion.

Mr. NITZE. In order to defend the Minuteman sites in addition to the defense against the Chinese capabilities, that was all included within the estimate of $5 billion that was made on September 18. That included both.

Representative HOSMER. It would not protect the Minuteman very well against them.

Dr. FOSTER. It cannot guarantee that no Minuteman will be knocked out.

Mr. NITZE. It will give a guarantee that a larger number will survive than if it were not there.

Representative HOSMER. Good. I am glad to hear that.

Do we have any quantitative estimates?

Mr. NITZE. We can give you those in classified testimony.

Representative HOSMER. Now, this business of Mr. McNamara's about always retaining this capability of retaliation with sufficient strength, that is what gets so many of us wondering, simply because we don't really have it backed up with much of anything.

We see, do we not, without regard to what the rate is, some increase annually in the number of Soviet intercontinental ballistic missiles, and now Scrag, at the same time our number of retaliatory weapons is remaining steady?

Mr. NITZE. I believe not. I believe it would be true if you said launchers.

Representative HOSMER. Certainly launchers, then.

Mr. NITZE. As I described when I was going through the Polaris-Poseidon decision, this does not increase the number of launchers, but it greatly increases the number of weapons.

Representative HOSMER. That is correct, but their launchers are being increased?

Mr. NITZE. What you are really trying to do is to have systems which can survive, and which then can accurately and effectively penetrate to targets through the defense that one must anticipate.

Representative HOSMER. We still have two weaknesses from this. The first is that the more bombs you have on the end of a missile, if it is destroyed before it gets out of the ground, the more weapons resting within it you destroy.

The second is the other side, not being stupid is probably going to the same kind of multiple reentry vehicle.

We could not talk about that until 4 weeks ago, when Mr. McNamara used the MIRV phrase.

We are going to have them doing the same thing, so we are all even, are we not?

Dr. FOSTER. Mr. Hosmer, I think it is quite right, when we put multiples on to the missiles, it means not only that when the enemy knocks out a silo, he knocks out more warheads, but it means more warheads survive when he does not knock them out.

Representative HOSMER. He has more chances to knock out more warheads?

Dr. FOSTER. But for the number that are surviving, we then have more warheads to penetrate the defense.

What we do is keep track of this arithmetic. We keep track of his capability today, and project his capability in the future to knock out our silos.

If we think the combination of his yield and his accuracy and his numbers of missiles could seriously reduce the number of Minutemen that will survive, then we must take action.

Today, for instance, we look into the future and see that it is possible for a number of Minutemen to be knocked out, and therefore we have options. The options are to defend the Minuteman, build more fixed silos, build stronger silos. There are a number of options we can do just within the fixed-site Minuteman approach.

Representative HOSMER. As I gather, you have adopted one of the options, which is the ABM.

Dr. FOSTER. No, Mr. Hosmer. The deployment of the Sentinel system permits us any time within a year to make a decision on whether or not we want to defend the Minuteman silos.

Representative HOSMER. You have not yet?

Dr. FOSTER. We have not taken that step, no.

Representative HOSMER. Dr. Foster, you gave considerable testimony during the Senate Preparedness Committee and the Senate Foreign Relations Committee hearings in relation to the ratification of the test ban treaties.

What you have just said leaves two more strings dangling. In connection with these multiple birds, they have to get over there and penetrate. Now you told the Foreign Relations Committee this:

Suppose the USSR were to develop a defense such that our ability to penetrate might depend on a saturation attack. For this application, specially designed hardened warheads might be required. Considerable progress on such warheads can be made by underground test, but under the treaty, atmospheric experiments to determine if the warhead actually has the necessary hardness against combined radiation and shock effect would be prohibited. We might thereby be denied assurance of such a penetration capability.

Without saying why, can you be any more reassuring about the situation today than you were in 1962 or 1963, whenever it was?

Dr. FOSTER. 1963.

Yes, Mr. Hosmer. I did indeed indicate that the important sets of experiments that one would not be allowed to do without atmospheric tests was the actual testing of the reentry vehicle to nearby nuclear explosions in the atmosphere.

Subsequently, we have made very aggressive efforts in our underground program, and I believe that in executive session I can convince you that this is no longer a problem.

Representative HOSMER. Why? We get back to the reassuring statement.

If you can, I will back you up.

Dr. FOSTER. I will give you the facts and leave it to your judgment.

Representative HOSMER. The next thing also arises from one of your statements during the 1963 period, when you were discussing the yield of Soviet weapons. This is what you said about their test:

Looking over the hundreds of shots that have been fired in the past, and analyzing in detail to the extent that we can, we find that progress has been reasonably well correlated with experience. Now, to date the Soviet have had several times the experience of the United States in yield above one megaton.

I quote that to you in relation and in context with the issue I brought up about the size of their warheads.

Dr. FOSTER. Mr. Hosmer, I think I can help you on that.

Representative HOSMER. I suppose you will say we have an intelligence estimate that shows they are not interested in those higher yields.

Mr. FOSTER. Mr. Hosmer, I think two things have happened since then. No. 1, our understanding of the way, at least the way the United States is going to have to respond to the Soviet capability in order to be able to provide our assured destruction capability indicates that we will have to go to smaller, not larger, yields.

The Soviets, as well, since that period, have gone to smaller, not larger, yields.

Representative HOSMER. Are you basing this on what they have told you?

Dr. FOSTER. I am basing this on intelligence. I will be glad to give you the details in executive session.

Secondly, I still believe that the best estimate of how well one is doing in fabrication of warheads that we have available, had then and do now, is the number of tests.

I believe you realize that the United States, through its vigorous underground test program, has had an opportunity to perform far more tests than has the Soviet Union since 1963.

Representative HOSMER. I realize that. I also realize that in the 1961–62 test series the Soviet Union had the opportunity, and availed themselves of it, to do a great deal more testing in atmospheric and exoatmospheric environments, as to both offensive and defensive warheads.

Is that not correct?

Dr. FOSTER. Yes, Mr. Hosmer; they had an opportunity to do a great deal of testing, as did the United States.

Representative HOSMER. I understand my time is about up.

I hope that in your reply to this estimate of mine, Mr. Secretary, which I brought out actually to elicit or challenge you to give us something more specific than Mr. McNamara's constant reiteration of this business that he can always retaliate with assured destruction, something that the American people can grab onto and feel a little bit more confident that this Nation can accept a first strike and actually will have a capability thereafter to do the kind of damage job on the Soviet Union which it is readily apparent to them would constitute assured destruction, because it is they, not us, who must have that feeling.

Thank you.

Senator JACKSON. Senator Aiken.

Senator AIKEN. I have only a few questions.

Is our retaliatory power considered an effective defense against nuclear war with Russia?

Mr. NITZE. We believe it is. There is always some danger, but we believe it is effective.

Senator AIKEN. You believe it is effective?

Mr. NITZE. Yes, sir.

Senator AIKEN. You believe it would not be effective against China?

Mr. NITZE. Mr. McNamara's statement was that he thought it would probably be so, but there was this consideration which I elaborated in my opening statement, that an offensive force——

Senator AIKEN. I did not get your opening statement.

Mr. NITZE. It was in my opening statement that I made the point that the Chinese ICBM capability in its first stage, in its first generation, will be both small in number and vulnerable, and that there are certain considerations which affect the possessor of a small, vulnerable force in a crisis situation, and that consideration is that in a crisis it either has to use that force first in a surprise attack, or else he runs a very great danger that it will be eliminated before it can have any effect whatsoever.

That pressure could make people who are not by nature reckless undertake more reckless acts.

If we have a defense which can deny him any capability for damage to the United States, then that pressure on him will diminish or be totally removed.

Senator AIKEN. The reason I asked the question is that I could not quite understand how our retaliatory power would be effective against the strongest nuclear power on earth, with the exception possibly of the United States, but not effective against a weak power that might not have, say, over a hundred missiles.

Mr. NITZE. Mr. McNamara went into this question at greater length both in his September 18 speech and in his response to questions in a Life magazine article. (See app. 4, p. 105, and app. 5, p. 113.)

I think it is fair to summarize his conclusion that he believed that our deterrent power against China would probably be effective, but you could not be sure that this other effect might not make even a cautious people more reckless.

Marginally, therefore, he thought this was a decision that we should take vis-a-vis China.

Senator AIKEN. Suppose China acquires 10, 20, or more weapons, and says that instead of directing these weapons toward the United States, it will direct them toward the allies of the United States, maybe Australia or Thailand or friendly nations like Canada or Mexico.

Do we have any plans for protecting them, or are we just going to protect our own territory with the ABM system, and let the rest of the world go by?

Mr. NITZE. The President has made it clear that we would propose to assist other countries that might be threatened by nuclear blackmail in resisting that blackmail. We would back them up.

As I said in my opening statement, the fact that the Chinese would not be able to threaten our cities we thought would give an added indication of our determination to back them up against such nuclear blackmail.

This was not just for the protection of the United States, but would put us in a better position not only to back up our allies, but would make more credible the fact that we were in such a position.

Senator AIKEN. That, in effect, would be retaliatory power, would it not?

Mr. NITZE. The very fact that we could not be threatened by China, we think, would increase the assurance of our assurance to the other Asian nations.

Senator AIKEN. I heard Dr. Foster refer to the possibility of the Russians being mistaken in their evaluation. Don't they have the same factors to make their evaluations by that we do, of these various systems planned?

Mr. NITZE. We have our technology, and I think they work at it very hard, indeed. They sometimes come to different conclusions than we do. We think we have been sound in our conclusions.

Senator AIKEN. It does not seem reasonable that, using the same factors for evaluation, they would be wrong so much more than we were.

I do not know. I am just seeking some elementary information. I think that is enough to last me for today.

Senator JACKSON. Senator Gore.

Senator GORE. I think Chairman Jackson and Chairman Pastore, also the administration, are to be congratulated on finally having public hearings on this subject, so that the whole people whose civilization is threatened may become better informed.

I have only three questions, Mr. Chairman.

One, to attempt to place into perspective this recent publicity about orbital missiles. I think it may be unfortunate that that preceded these hearings.

As I generally understand it, the threat of nuclear attack can come from these five sources: intercontinental ballistic missiles with nuclear warheads, landbased; intermediate missiles, which might be landbased or might be fired from submarines off our shores; from planes carrying nuclear weapons; from sabotage placement such as weapons hidden within holds of ships coming in our harbors, or surreptitious placement of smaller weapons at strategic places within the United States; and five, weapons in orbit.

Now, there may be others, but from my study of the matter it seems that those are the five general categories for delivery of missiles.

Is that correct, Dr. Foster?

Dr. FOSTER. Yes, I believe it is, Senator Gore.

Senator GORE. Now, I am not qualified to list them in the order of danger and degree of threat, but would you disagree with the order in which I have listed them?

Dr. FOSTER. I would rule the last two out, as serious military capabilities, at least as we understand the technology.

Senator GORE. Now, the first three you have left are ICBM, intermediate range, either landbased or from submarines, and from planes.

The United States possesses this capability itself, all three methods of delivery, and in your view in ample quantity?

Dr. FOSTER. Yes, sir, it does.

Senator GORE. Now, the second question—I think you may want to clarify the use of the word "exhaustion." I am not sure how far one can go with the multiple warhead technology, but you have used that term three times, and I am not sure it is generally understood.

Dr. FOSTER. Yes, sir.

In formulating our plans for the development and subsequent deployment of systems in the mid and late 1970's, we have to be sure that the system then in being will be able to cope with Soviet ballistic missile defense.

Now, clearly there are a number of ways to attempt to defeat ballistic missile defense. In truth, we use all of the ones that seem to make good sense. We do use chaff and decoys and electronic jammers, all manner of things, but a number of these cannot be said to be of high confidence. That is to say, the enemy may in that time be able to figure out a way in order to find the reentry vehicle that you have among the chaff, and so the chaff would not disturb him, and he would be able to deal with the reentry vehicle.

So we have tended to go to one other measure, and that is a very conservative measure, the use of multiple reentry vehicles. These are many different, separately aimed warheads in reentry vehicles, each of which is capable of causing enormous destruction, each of which then must be engaged by the defender.

We plan, then, to put over in nearly the same time so many individual objects that he must shoot at for his own defense that they require all the defenses he has, and then some more.

This is what I have referred to as exhaustion.

Senator GORE. In other words, you think that the United States through use of multiple warheads, through a number of warheads, diversity of attack, and the splitting of warheads, even in flight, into many missiles, to use another phrase, could overwhelm any defense that the Soviet Union might have, or in the future might have?

Dr. FOSTER. I believe that is true, Senator Gore.

Senator GORE. I have one other question, and then I shall desist.

This is directed to you, Mr. Secretary. Perhaps it is a geopolitical question.

It seems to me that in the future our real vital national interest rests with the equation between the three major world powers. Now you have expressed the opinion that the Soviets were deploying more out of fear of the United States than fear of Chinese nuclear development.

I am not sure that you said that exactly. That is what I understood you to say.

Mr. NITZE. I was referring to the Moscow system. What I was suggesting was that I thought they probably deployed the Moscow system in order to give the hope of some measure of defense of Moscow against the potentialities of the United States, rather than those that they foresaw at that time from China.

I did not mean to suggest that in the future they would not also count on their capability vis-a-vis the Chinese.

Senator GORE. That comes to the point. I am coming now to the——

Mr. NITZE. Because they certainly are concerned.

Senator GORE. From their statements, I thought they were more concerned with the immediacy of a threat from China.

Of course they recognize our superior capability, but I doubt that they think that the United States is going to launch a nuclear attack against Russia. I hope they don't, anyway.

I am coming to the question of the ABM negotiations. Perhaps I will be pardoned if I say that despite our own deployment of the thin system, and despite the Russian development, I think it is imperative that we persist in achieving a nonproliferation agreement, and if possible an agreement to check the arms race in ABM deployments.

Mr. NITZE. We agree with that, Mr. Gore. I think the last paragraph of my introductory remarks bore on that question.

Senator GORE. Now that the United States has initiated deployment of a so-called thin ABM defense in response to the Chinese threat, does not this prejudice the opportunity of reaching an agreement with the Soviets?

Can we really expect the Russians, who are closer to the Chinese, and who have a longer history of hostilities and animosities with the Chinese, to desist, themselves?

How does this affect our chances of achieving an ABM agreement, and secondly, what is the status of the negotiations, if they have started?

Mr. NITZE. Insofar as they might feel that they need an ABM defense against China, it would seem to me—I cannot read their minds, but it would seem logical that they might be interested in some thin defense against China.

In that event, probably their negotiating position might be that we both maintain a thin defense.

Certainly it would be better from our standpoint if it were possible to negotiate an agreement by which we could have high assurance. It could enable us and them to limit the extent to which the armament race might otherwise go.

Senator GORE. Thank you.

Now will you go to the second question: what is the status of the ABM negotiations?

I don't know whether we can call it negotiation yet, but an attempt on our part to negotiate.

Mr. NITZE. I don't think I can add much. The President and Mr. McNamara tried hard to get such discussions going. They did not mature.

I think the situation is about in that condition at this time.

Senator GORE. Thank you, Mr. Chairman.

Senator JACKSON. Senator Pastore.

Chairman PASTORE. I merely want to clarify one point.

Do I understand you now, Dr. Foster, it is the policy of the Defense Department to establish an ABM system which has been characterized here as a "thin system" only against the Chinese threat at the present time?

Am I correct in that statement?

Mr. NITZE. I think Mr. McNamara outlined three purposes. One was against the Chinese capability. The second purpose was that we could add thereto a defense of the Minuteman field. A third was that such a system would give protection against an accident.

Chairman PASTORE. The point I want to establish is this: When we talk about a thin system, we are not talking about politics. We are talking about the number of Sentinel emplacements. Is that correct?

Mr. NITZE. That is correct.

Chairman PASTORE. Therefore if we had a development vis-a-vis Russia, where the future would dictate that we expand the system, we could easily do so. It would only be a question of money.

Is that not so?

Dr. FOSTER. Yes, we could do so.

Senator JACKSON. Let me just see if we can wrap this up on three or four points here that I think should be made very clear.

First, I take it that both of you gentlemen agree that as to whether or not we go beyond the thin system depends on research and development progress.

Mr. NITZE. That is correct, Mr. Chairman.

Senator JACKSON. Now, second, I take it it is the position of the administration that, having spent since 1956 about $3 billion in research and development to make possible the system that you are now proposing to deploy as a thin system, you plan to continue a vigorous research and development program in antiballistic missile defense concurrent with the effort that you are making in deploying the thin system.

Mr. NITZE. We like to call this the Sentinel system, rather than thin, because vis-a-vis——

Senator JACKSON. To a fat man, I guess everything is thin these days.

Mr. NITZE. Vis-a-vis the Chinese threat, this is a really high-performance system.

Senator JACKSON. What is the answer?

Mr. NITZE. The answer is "Yes."

Senator JACKSON. You propose that you continue to invest in research and development around a half billion dollars annually—that amount is in the budget currently, we have appropriated the money—and that you are going to prosecute this program with vigor and determination.

I think the American people want to know this.

Mr. NITZE. This is correct.

Senator JACKSON. This is correct, is it not?

Mr. NITZE. Yes.

Senator JACKSON. I also take it as a part of that effort that you are going to continue to push hard on a good detection system. You mentioned the over-the-horizon radar, and this is a part of the administration effort, is it not?

Mr. NITZE. That is correct.

Senator JACKSON. In addition, I also take it that you will want to have whatever kind of antisatellite capability is necessary to deal with situations that might develop in the future that would affect the security of the United States.

We have an antisatellite capability at the present time?

Dr. FOSTER. Yes; Mr. Chairman.

Senator JACKSON. If it is necessary to push and improve that capability; you are going to do it?

Mr. FOSTER. I will be glad to give you the details of the programs that are proposed in executive session.

Senator JACKSON. I think it is fair to say that you can tell the public at least that we now have a certain capability of dealing with the antisatellite problem and that we will try to make sure, will we not, that in the future that capability will be adequate to deal with any foreseeable threat.

Mr. NITZE. I think that is correct.

Senator JACKSON. The answer is "Yes"?

Mr. NITZE. Yes.

Senator JACKSON. Now let us turn to the intercontinental ballistic missile problem.

Is nuclear superiority over the Soviet Union, or nuclear parity, our goal?

Can you comment on this, because this question is being raised from time to time. There has been a lot of discussion in various circles about this problem. I think the American people need some reassurance on this question as to our basic policy and our basic objective.

Mr. NITZE. Mr. Chairman, our policy obviously is to have fully adequate deterrent power, which means our offensive capability would be able to survive any kind of attack that the enemy might launch, and give us the necessary assured destruction of the other side.

And I think that is the more important thing, but with respect to superiority, which is hard to measure, we believe that we know all the relevant criteria of such superiority, we have that superiority now, and we propose, during the full period that we can estimate, to maintain superiority on what we believe to be the relevant criteria.

That does not mean necessarily some one criterion, such as megatonnage, which I have described, but taking the whole complex together.

Senator JACKSON. Dr. Foster, do you have any comment on that?

Dr. FOSTER. No, I don't, Mr. Chairman.

Senator JACKSON. Now, this means that you will move in the field of missiles as may be required in light of the progress that the Soviet Union appears to be making now and may continue to make for the foreseeable future, to improve qualitatively and quantitatively both our sea-based and our land-based systems.

Mr. NITZE. That is correct, Mr. Chairman.

Senator JACKSON. I think it is important that these statements be made.

I personally want to say I feel reassured by what Secretary Nitze and Dr. Foster have had to say in response to these questions. I think it goes to the heart of the problem. It goes to the great concern that the American people have, in the light of the developments, especially the progress being made by the Soviets, both quantitatively and qualitatively, in ICBM's, ABM's, and now the so-called FOBS system.

Senator Pastore, do you have any questions?

Chairman PASTORE. No.

Senator JACKSON. The Chair wants to thank you gentlemen very much for your statements and your responses to the questions.

Since your statement was broken up by questioning from the committee, Dr. Foster, we will place your prepared statement in full in the record at this point.

(The prepared statement of Dr. John S. Foster, Jr., Director of Defense Research and Engineering, follows:)

Dr. FOSTER. Mr. Chairman, it is a pleasure to appear before you today. Before describing some technical features of deployment, I would like to amplify Secretary Nitze's remarks on the history of our experience with ballistic missile defense.

The original need to provide a defense against ballistic missiles came in the 1940's with the introduction of the German V–2 short-range ballistic rocket, and the experience subsequent to World War II with this class of weapon. By the middle 50's the potential threat to the United States had become serious because of the extension of missile ranges to intercontinental distances. The ICBM presented a unique threat because of its speed and thermonuclear warhead. Traveling at four miles a second, it would reach this country in 30 minutes compared to the hours previously required by enemy bombers.

For almost a decade, the ICBM was considered by many to be the ultimate weapon against which no defense was possible. However, by the mid-50's a concept had evolved that we hoped would be an effective defense.

In 1956, the NIKE ZEUS development program was started. Its design resembled in many respects that of its predecessors, NIKE AJAX and NIKE HERCULES. Radars were used to detect and track incoming targets, and a rocket interceptor equipped with a nuclear warhead was launched and guided to the target. A system was installed and tested at Kwajalein in the mid-Pacific Ocean. Successful intercepts were made against actual ICBM targets launched from California in the early 1960's.

The ZEUS system used a family of mechanically slewed radars and consequently its traffic handling capability was severely limited. The only way to add the capability of handling simultaneous targets was to increase the number of radars; consequently, the larger cities required as many as 30–40 radars total of four different types. Even with this large number, the system could still be easily overwhelmed by the enemy's use of multiple objects such as decoys or balloons since each of them would have to be taken under fire.

These defects were corrected in 1963 by the iniation of the NIKE X concept. Phased array radars were introduced which steer their beams electronically in a few millionths of a second. The traffic-handling capability was thus vastly improved. Also, the SPRINT missile, a very high acceleration interceptor, allowed launches to be delayed until after the cloud of objects had reentered the atmosphere. The atmosphere slowed down the pieces of chaff and balloons, and the radar could discriminate them from the warheads which did not slow down until much lower altitudes.

In spite of these improvements, the system, when measured against the Soviet threat, had grave problems. As Mr. Nitze stated, NIKE X was originally conceived as a terminal defense system operating at moderate range. A battery at the most could defend one city; in the larger cities, more than one battery was required. The deployments were consequently very expensive even if one were to attempt to defend a few of our cities. The cost to defend only 25 cities was about $10 billion investment; to defend 50, about $20 billion, and any reasonable deployployment would still leave hundreds of cities unprotected. (There are more than 200 cities above 100,000 population.)

But system cost has not been a major factor. The major factor is that the Soviets could, if they chose, concentrate on one or more cities and by the simple process of exhausting the interceptor force, penetrate the defense. This could be done either by using many individual ICBM's or by using missiles carrying many multiple warheads. It was possible, therefore, for the Soviet economy and technology to defeat the defense by buying more or better offensive weapons.

Finally, in 1965 we introduced area defense. The basic additions were the PAR (Perimeter Acquisition Radar) and the long-range SPARTAN missile. Because of its long range, a relatively few batteries can protect the entire country.

Area defense removed one of the defects of NIKE X by providing coverage to all U.S. cities instead of certain selected ones. However, by its very nature, it could still be penetrated by heavy or sophisticated attacks such as the Soviets could mount with their advanced technology.

In 1966, a new threat appeared—the probability that the Chinese Peoples' Republic (CPR) were developing an ICBM. This is obviously vastly different from the Soviet threat. It will not materialize until the early 1970's, and when it does it will be small in numbers and relatively unsophisticated. As Secretary Nitze has just said, against this threat we have high assurance of providing damage denial for the whole country. Furthermore, we think we can maintain this capability against a growing Chinese threat at least until the 1980's.

The Chinese oriented deployment is called SENTINEL. Let me describe it in some detail.

The four principal components used in SENTINEL are two radar types and two missile types. (Chart No. 1, see p. 10.) The first radar is a Perimeter Acquisition Radar called PAR, and the second is a Missile Site Radar (MSR). The two missile interceptors are called SPARTAN and SPRINT.

The PAR radar is used for long-range detection and acquisition. It is a large phased array type, which as I said, means that its beam can be moved from one direction in the sky to another in a few millionths of a second. Chart 2 (see p. 11) is a photograph of such a radar. This particular radar is installed at Eglin Air Force Base, Florida, for satellite observations. The large concrete building houses the transmitter, receiver and associated electronics. The antenna elements are embedded in, and actually form part of the structure of one of the walls of the building. The PAR will be of similar construction. It will operate at a relatively low frequency and is particularly adapted to long-range detection and tracking. I will come back to this point later.

Chart 3 (p. 12) shows a cut-away view of the Missile Site Radar. This phased array radar is at a higher frequency. It is designed to track targets at shorter ranges than the PAR, and is also used to guide and track our missiles, the SPRINTs and SPARTANs, to the intercept point. Because of its electronic scanning capability, it can handle a large number of intercepts simultaneously.

This next chart (No. 4, p. 12) shows the two interceptor missiles. The larger of the two is actually our old ZEUS missile, not the SPARTAN, but closely resembles the SPARTAN. Because the SPARTAN is somewhat larger than the ZEUS, it can operate out to ranges of several hundred miles. You will see the importance of this when I discuss the area defense concept. This missile has three stages, uses solid propellant, and is launched from an underground silo. It will carry a nuclear warhead having a yield in the megaton range, and is designed to intercept above the atmosphere.

The SPRINT, shown here, is a smaller but very high-performance interceptor. It has two stages, uses solid propellant, and is launched from an underground silo. It also carries a nuclear warhead, but because it is designed to make intercepts within the atmosphere, the yield is in the kiloton range. As I stated before, the SPRINT can wait until threatening objects reenter the atmosphere, which aids greatly in filtering out harmless objects so that only those which are likely to be dangerous need be attacked. It can wait because its very high acceleration allows it to climb thousands of feet in a few seconds. Because of its limited range (compared to SPARTAN) it is essentially a terminal defense component and is, therefore, particularly well adapted to defending point targets such as Minuteman silos or radars. Recently we have had several very successful tests of the SPRINT at White Sands Missile Range.

Now let's put these components together and see how they work. Chart 5 (p. 13) shows an engagement, obviously not to scale. First, the long-range PAR picks up the attacking warhead as it comes over the horizon. It tracks it for a minute or two establishing its ballistic trajectory. You will appreciate that this is a job for an associated computer. A SPARTAN is then launched to the computed intercept point. It is guided by the MSR, and at the point of closest passage, the SPARTAN warhead detonates. Because the SPARTAN has a high yield warhead, the lethal radius is large compared to the distance between the warhead and the incoming object, thus destroying it. As mentioned above, multiple intercepts can be made simultaneously, that is, several SPARTANs can be on their way toward various targets.

The next chart (No. 6, p. 14) gives some idea of the coverage provided by a single SPARTAN battery. The elliptical area, called a "footprint", is the area defended by one battery—all cities lying within that area will be protected. The area extends a little farther to the south from the battery than to the north because ICBMs aimed at points south of the battery must pass over the battery on their way to the impact point.

Let us look at the whole country. A few PARs are deployed close to our northern border. The next chart (No. 7, p. 15) shows how any missile coming from the north must pass through the PAR detection fans.

From the following chart (No. 8, p. 15) we see that the whole country is covered. The batteries are so located that their footprints, when combined, essentially cover the whole country. No one is left unprotected.

Now I must emphasize that this type of defense is practical against small and relatively unsophisticated attacks. A massive attack can simply target as many ICBMs at a city as are necessary to exhaust the SPARTANs within range. Then there is no defense. A sophisticated attack can destroy the radars and negate the defense. There are many options open to an offense to attack the defense. We know them well because we must know what is necessary to penetrate any Soviet ABM. But in the case of small and unsophisticated attacks, a defense such as this is very effective.

I turn now to a question often raised regarding the effect on our population if this ballistic missile defense were to be used.

There are three main effects to consider: the flash, the blast, and the radioactivity. (Chart No. 9, p. 16.) When the warhead explodes there will be a bright flash of light. Most of the population underneath would barely notice it. If any were looking at that part of the sky, the flash could temporarily blind them. There would be no serious after-effects.

Because the high yield bursts take place above the atmosphere, there would be little or no blast. It would be like a sonic boom.

There would be no significant fallout from the radiation emitted at the time of the explosion. If dozens of defensive bursts occurred, they would deposit radioactivity in the atmosphere. There would be no harmful short term effect and the long term effect would be very similar to that experienced from our late atmospheric test series in 1962. Consequently, there is no need to greatly increase our fallout shelter program.

Although the SPRINT warhead would explode in the atmosphere, it would not cause damage because of its low yield.

Finally, what level of fatalities can we expect This last chart (No. 10, p. 17), indicates the fatalities we could suffer from various numbers of enemy missiles. Also shown is the situation with the SENTINEL system deployed. As you can see, in the event of a Chinese attack, we will have high assurance of no losses for many years. Later, if the CPR threat grows in numbers and sophistication, there could be some increase in the probability of fatalities. To obviate this, we intend to continue to pursue a vigorous R&D program to improve our defense. In this way, we can prolong the period over which we have high assurance of preventing damage to the U.S.

Mr. Chairman, thank you very much for the opportunity to describe this system. I would be pleased to answer any questions the Committee may wish to ask.

Senator JACKSON. The Chair will state that we will recess now until tomorrow morning at 10, at which time the committee will resume its public session in this room.

Our witnesses will be Dr. Philip E. Mosely, director of the European Institute at Columbia University, former director of the Russian Institute, Columbia University; Dr. Thomas W. Wolfe, senior staff member of the Rand Corp., member of the faculty of the Sino-Soviet Institute, George Washington University; and Mrs. Alice Langley Hsieh, senior staff member of the Rand Corp., and analyst, Communist China's external political and military policies.

Dr. Mosely will be heard first in the morning, and we will then go to Dr. Wolfe and then to Mrs. Hsieh.

Thank you again for your testimony, gentlemen.

(Whereupon, at 4:30 p.m., the subcommittee recessed, to reconvene at 10 a.m., Tuesday, November 7, 1967.)

STATEMENT BY DEPUTY SECRETARY OF DEFENSE PAUL H. NITZE, IN RESPONSE TO STATEMENT BY CONGRESSMAN CRAIG HOSMER MADE AT THE BEGINNING OF THE SUBCOMMITTEE HEARING

Mr. Hosmer's statement makes two inferences: that numbers of launchers or megatons are a useful measure of the capabilities of a nation's strategic forces, and that the capabilities of the U.S. strategic forces to survive a Soviet attack and deliver an overwhelming blow in return is in question.

The best single measure of strategic nuclear capability is the amount of damage a force can inflict on the enemy This is to some degree related to the number of launchers and of megatons in the force, but more important factors are the number of warheads, reliability, survivability, and accuracy.

Let me illustrate why total launchers or megatonnage, as such, are inadequate indicators of force effectiveness, with an example. One possible U.S. missile could carry ten separately aimed 50 kiloton warheads for a total of one-half megaton. If we wanted to, we could design the same missile to carry one 10 megaton warhead. The effectiveness of these two possible missiles in destroying targets is compared in the following table:

COMPARATIVE EFFECTIVENESS OF 2 HYPOTHETICAL MISSILE PAYLOADS

[Number of targets destroyed]

Type of target destroyed	10 50-kt. warheads	1 10-mt. warhead
Airfields	10	1.0
Hard missile silos	1.2 to 1.7	1.0
Cities of 100,000 population	3.5	1.0
Cities of 500,000 population	0.7	1.0
Cities of 2,000,000 population	0.5	.6
Total megatonnage	0.5	10.0

The single 10 megaton warhead yields 20 times the megatonnage of the 10 50-kiloton individually targetable warheads. However, the missile armed with the 10 50-kiloton warheads could destroy—
10 times as many airfields, soft missile sites, or other soft military point targets;
1.2 to 1.7 times as many hard silos; and
3.5 times as many cities of 100,000 population.
While a force armed with the 50-kiloton warheads destroys only 70% as many undefended cities of 500,000 population, and 80% as many unprotected cities of 2,000,000 population as a force armed with the 10 megaton warheads, we have enough larger warheads in our forces to hit cities of these sizes if they are undefended. If the cities are defended, the Multiple Independent Re-entry Vehicles (MIRV) force the defense to shoot ten times as many interceptors, once again showing the superiority of the multiple small warheads.
Therefore, the MIRVs provide much more effective payloads for our missile boosters than single large-yield warheads by every relevant criterion of military effectiveness, even though they deliver much less total megatonnage. This example shows how misleading it is to compare forces by counting megatons or launchers.
Mr. Hosmer notes that the decisions made by one Administration affect the choices available to the next. But on this question of megatons there has been continuity between the Eisenhower, Kennedy and Johnson Administrations. For instance, in the 1950s we built a large number of very high yield weapons for our bombers. During the Eisenhower Administration it became clear that those weapons would not be deliverable against defenses anticipated in the '60s, and the Eisenhower Administration planned to phase down those high yield weapons. This was done during the Kennedy Administration.
If we were really primarily interested in megatons, it would have been possible to keep those in the inventory, adding some ten thousand megatons over and above what was kept in the inventory.
Instead, we put into the inventory weapons which were deliverable, which were much improved weapons and which had a much higher target kill capability.
The second major inference of Mr. Hosmer's statement is that the U.S. might be unable to maintain its second-strike capability. Although the question of time is essential to this analysis, the year in which our Assured Destruction capability is alleged to fail appears nowhere in his statement. Today the Soviets could put less than 500 reliable ICBMs over the U.S., each carrying one weapon. Soviet warheads average less than half the 10–30 megatons cited by Mr. Hosmer. (There is no disagreement between Secretary McNamara and his Joint Chiefs of Staff on this—we all use the same estimates.) We estimate they could destroy about 100 Minuteman. This would leave almost the entire Minuteman force, as well as our alert bombers and sea-based missiles to attack the Soviet Union in retaliation. The more than 2,000 surviving, alert weapons could destroy almost half the population of the Soviet Union.
If we look towards the end of the time period discussed in Mr. Hosmer's statement—1973—the picture does not change significantly. By that time we expect the Soviet ICBM force to grow. (We cannot be sure what is the precise purpose of the Soviet strategic nuclear forces. Although most evidence seems to point to a decision on their part to build an Assured Destruction force, to be prudent we do protect ourselves against a possible Soviet first-strike goal.) But by 1973 we will have MIRVs on many Minuteman, and the Poseidon program with its MIRVs

will be well along, greatly increasing the ability of our systems to penetrate a Soviet ABM even after suffering a first strike. We estimate that Soviet numbers and accuracy will increase to the point where they could destroy about 300 Minuteman in this time frame instead of 100. Although they will have a large ICBM force by that time, more than half their force will consist of lower yield, less accurate SS–11s which will probably have little capability against Minuteman. But here are the main points that Mr. Hosmer misses in his statement. First we are taking steps to protect Minuteman against much better Soviet offenses than we actually expect. Secondly, even if any two of the three elements of our second-strike forces—our land-based ICBMs, our submarine-based Polaris and Poseidon, and our strategic bombers—were rendered useless by some unforeseeable disaster, the remaining element could by itself inflict unacceptable damage on the USSR.

I have gone through Mr. Hosmer's calculations to clarify where his numbers come from, and where we disagree with his data.

First, he considers a case where we and the Soviets have parity, and the Soviets are assumed to have an accuracy of about 2,000 feet which is not correct. He calculates a destruction probability of 92% for some combination of yield and hardness, although 25% is closer to the fact. Moreover, he neglects reliability and alert rate. Even using his combination of yield and accuracy, but taking a combined alert and reliability rate of say, 65% we get 1,054 x .65 x .92 = 630 ICBMs destroyed, or 424 remaining, not 84 as Mr. Hosmer calculates. (The actual number remaining would be more like 700.) To 424 we can add the 300 Polaris/Poseidon missiles Mr. Hosmer calculates, for a total, using his factors, of approximately 700 missiles. But how many weapons do these provide? By the time the USSR could *have* an ICBM force anywhere nearly as effective as Mr. Hosmer posits, we will have an average of several weapons per missile, leading even after applying appropriate reliability factors, to thousands of weapons, plus decoys and other devices capable of overwhelming a Soviet ABM. Several hundred of these weapons successfully delivered to Soviet cities could destroy 30% of the total Soviet population. Mr. Hosmer's calculations assume that we stretch our weapons so thinly over the Soviet Union that if only half get through, half the targets escape unharmed. In actual fact, there is considerable overlap in the targeting. Rather than the 150 missiles he calculates as reaching target, some ten or twenty times that number of weapons would reach target.

Mr. Hosmer's treatment of many of the major elements of the strategic power equations is questionable. He says, for instance, that Soviet MIRVs would cancel out the advantages of our MIRVs. But, to take an extreme example, no number of Soviet MIRVs could destroy our Poseidon (submarine-based) MIRVs. He glosses over the strategic bombers, the third component of our forces, although we have no intention of phasing out the B–52 G/Hs and are adding FB–111 bombers with SRAM missiles to the force.

SCOPE, MAGNITUDE, AND IMPLICATIONS OF THE UNITED STATES ANTIBALLISTIC MISSILE PROGRAM

TUESDAY, NOVEMBER 7, 1967

Congress of the United States,
Subcommittee on Military Applications,
Joint Committee on Atomic Energy,
Washington, D.C.

The subcommittee met at 10 a.m., pursuant to recess, in room 1202 New Senate Office Building, Senator Henry M. Jackson (chairman of the subcommittee) presiding.

Present: Senators Pastore and Jackson: Representatives Holifield, Morris, Bates, and Anderson.

Staff members present: John T. Conway, executive director: Leonard M. Trosten, staff counsel: George F. Murphy, Jr., national security affairs, and Francesco Costagliola, staff consultant.

Senator JACKSON. The committee will come to order.

Today we continue our public hearings on the problems of missile defense.

These problems, of course, cannot be understood except in a broad economic, social, political, and ideological context. In the present world, the devising of proper Government action depends on the contribution of many types of experts—not just one. The broad viewpoint offers the best chance for wise decisions on weapons programs—just as it does on other Government plans of action.

We are privileged to have as our witnesses today three outstanding scholars and analysts who will testify on the issues before us from their differing perspectives and backgrounds. Our witnesses are not only scholarly observers of affairs—they are also persons with substantial Government experience at home and abroad. The views they will offer are a product of that experience combined with their study and analysis.

We are honored to have as our first witness this morning the distinguished student of Soviet affairs, Prof. Philip E. Mosely. Now director of the European Institute of Columbia University and professor of international relations at Columbia, he has an enviable record of publications on Russian history and on the internal and foreign policies of the Soviet Union.

From 1942 to 1946, Professor Mosely was an officer of the Department of State, in charge of an intensive program of planning for the postwar settlements, and active participant in the wartime negotiations with the Soviet Union. Between 1946 and 1955 he was professor of international relations in the Russian Institute of Columbia University, and served as its director, 1951 to 1955. From 1955 to 1963, Dr. Mosely was director of studies at the Council on Foreign Relations, New York.

Dr. Mosely, we are delighted to have you with us this morning. You may now proceed in your own way.

STATEMENT OF PHILIP E. MOSELY, PROFESSOR OF INTERNA-
TIONAL RELATIONS AND DIRECTOR OF THE EUROPEAN INSTI-
TUTE, COLUMBIA UNIVERSITY; FORMER DIRECTOR, RUSSIAN
INSTITUTE, COLUMBIA UNIVERSITY

Dr. MOSELY. Thank you very much, Mr. Chairman, for this warm
welcome and for this opportunity and privilege of appearing before the
subcommittee.

In accepting this invitation to appear before the subcommittee I am,
of course, expressing my own analyses and opinions, not those of any
institution or group.

THE PRESENT STATUS OF THE COMMUNIST GROUPING

The ruling Communist Party of the Soviet Union celebrates today
the 50th anniversary of the founding of the Soviet regime. It does so
in the midst of problems, doubts, and challenges that have not been
foreseen by its founders or explained by its dogmas. The past 10 years
in particular have been marked by numerous challenges, both bitter
and subtle, to the international leadership of the Soviet ruling party.

The diversity of trends and ambitions that has emerged within the
smaller Communist regimes in Eastern Europe means that communism
today is defined and applied within a broad range of approaches, some
of them more "liberal" and others more Stalinist. The bitter contest
between the leaderships in Moscow and Peking has shaken to its roots
the concept of international Communist solidarity and unity of action.
These differences have profoundly undermined the illusion of "omni-
science" and of an inevitable advance in power which formerly inspired its followers to believe in and act on Communist claims to bring
about the establishment of an alledgedly harmonious, universal, and
united Communist system throughout the world.

The disarray of the Communist governments and parties arises
from many causes, of which only a few major ones can be briefly
listed here. One principal cause has been the rapid recovery of the free
world economy after World War II, the remarkable rates of growth
achieved by the major industrial countries, and many innovative
improvements in the flow of trade, investment, and development aid
in the non-Communist world. Still another cause has been the vigorous
movement for European economic integration, despite the failure, so
far, to extend it beyond the Six. The postwar economic competition
between the modern capitalist system and the still rigid and dogmatic
Communist system has turned out very differently from what the
Kremlin and its supporters predicted in 1945.

A second major cause has been the revulsion against the extreme
suppression of individual and intellectual liberty under Stalinism.
The recurrent waves of "de-Stalinization" have introduced currents
of empirical and rational thought into the Soviet system and have
opened the way to improve its functioning in many, many ways.
People everywhere must welcome any and all improvements in the
daily life of the Soviet and other Communist-ruled countries. But
de-Stalinization, which was indispensable to the better functioning of
the Soviet system, has also opened the way both to fresh experimenta-

tion in the smaller Communist regimes of Eastern Europe and to the hysterical reaffirmation of Stalinist concepts and methods in Communist China.

A third major cause of disarray has been the failure of the Communist forces to continue the momentum of expansionism that they had achieved through Soviet military victories at the end of World War II. Except for Yugoslavia and mainland China, none of the new Communist regimes came into power by their own efforts, and the predictions of continued and rapid Communist advance, which gave high morale to Communist parties immediately after World War II, have been discredited. Instead, Communist expansionist efforts have suffered several major setbacks in the past 10 years. These failures have been due to the great efforts and sacrifices of many countries, but they have been due primarily to the determination of the American people to maintain a margin of superiority in overall deterrence.

Khrushchev's attempts, between 1958 and 1962, to pry West Berlin loose from the protection of the Atlantic powers were defeated and have so far not been renewed by his successors. The Soviet attempt in 1960, to exploit the vulnerabilities in the Congo was rebuffed. Castro's abortive attempts to build a federation of Communist states around the Caribbean have strengthened the solidarity of the Americas and have caused grave embarrassments to Moscow's more cautious approach to Latin America.

The Kremlin's adventurous attempt, in 1962, to implant its nuclear-missile power in the Western Hemisphere led to a serious loss of prestige and influence. It showed that Moscow was using the smoke-screen of "peaceful coexistence" to gain new positions of nuclear power and blackmail. The retreat from an overexposed salient showed that it was not prepared, in terms of the existing ratio of strategic power, to back up its adventurous ambition.

After all the propaganda talk was swept away in the first nuclear confrontation, one basic fact stood out clearly: The ultimate safeguard of peace is the strategic superiority of U.S. power. If the balance in 1962 had stood in favor of the Soviet Union, the scenario and the outcome of the Cuban missile crisis, and its consequences in all continents, would have been vastly different.

SOVIET AMBITIONS IN EUROPE

Many of our friends and allies in Europe hold a very complacent view of the Soviet Union and its policy today, and this difference of view is at the root of most of the recent difficulties of the Atlantic alliance. President Charles de Gaulle can safely assert, under the umbrella of American nuclear superiority, that the only danger to Europe now rests in American "hegemony." He has the enthusiastic approval of both Moscow and the French Communist Party in his efforts to weaken NATO, to remove the U.S. presence from Western Europe, and to prevent the broadening and strengthening of the European community into a powerful political entity. President de Gaulle, in my opinion, has not given objective and realistic attention to recent restatements of Soviet ambitions toward Western Europe.

These ambitions have recently been set forth by Leonid Brezhnev, General Secretary of the Communist Party of the Soviet Union. He has done this in a major policy statement of April 24, 1967, to a Conference of European Communist and Workers' Parties on the Question of European Security, held at Karlovy Vary, in Czechoslovakia. In his address Mr. Brezhnev called for a sweeping change in the strategic role of Western Europe. He called for the dismantling of NATO in 1969, the removal of all U.S. forces from Europe, and the removal of the American Sixth Fleet from the Mediterranean.

Brezhnev said, and I quote:

In weighing the opportunities opened up by developments in Europe, we cannot ignore the fact that within two years the governments of the NATO countries are to decide whether or not the North Atlantic Treaty is to be extended. In our opinion it is very right that Communists and all progressive forces are endeavoring to make use of this circumstance in order to develop in ever wider scale the struggle against preserving this aggressive bloc . . .

Mr. Brezhnev said further:

There is no justification for the permanent presence of the U.S. Navy in waters washing the shores of Southern Europe . . . The time has come for the demand that the U.S. Sixth Fleet be withdrawn from the Mediterranean to ring out at full strength.

The Soviet party leader went on to recommend neutrality, not to any members of the Communist grouping, but to the countries of Northern Europe:

For a host of countries, including those in Northern Europe, neutrality could be an alternative to their participation in the political-military groupings of the powers . . . The Soviet Union would be prepared to meet halfway any undertakings which serve this purpose.

Even when it has been in a state of admitted strategic inferiority to U.S. power, the Soviet Union has periodically pressed forward policies designed to advance its direct political interests and to undercut the security of the West. This restless ambition has been illustrated in the problems of Berlin and the Cuban missile adventure, and most recently in the strong encouragement it has given to the militant Arab forces in the very serious Near Eastern crisis of June 1967.

In each of these probings the strategic inferiority of Soviet power has set definite limits to the extent of the risks that the Soviet policymakers were willing to run. It is painful and disturbing to contemplate the far wider range of risks which the Kremlin might have accepted if it had been confident of possessing an equality or a superiority of overall deterrent strength.

SOVIET AMBITIONS OUTSIDE EUROPE

Until now the Soviet Union has concentrated its efforts on maintaining massive conventional forces and building an extremely powerful nuclear-missile force. It has not devoted many of its resources to building small, long-range, mobile forces which might exert a decisive influence in local situations at a distance from its own borders. There are many signs that Soviet strategists and planners are aware of the potential advantages of developing this additional capability for small-scale but effective intervention in distant regions of the world.

In recent years the Soviet Union has developed very large long-range aircraft, capable of reaching into Central Africa without intermediate stops. It has revived the tradition of seaborne and airborne infantry, armed with great firepower. It is planning to build helicopter carriers, suitable for small-scale offshore interventions. The current Soviet capability in this field is small, but present initiatives suggest that the Soviet Union may have a substantial range of power in this field by the early 1970's. Such small-scale forces could bring important gains, but only provided that those gains could be exploited under the protection of overall nuclear equality or superiority.

THE OUTLOOK

How one defines nuclear-strategic "inferiority," "equality," and "superiority" is a matter that I must leave to others more expert in this field. What I do emphasize is the political side of the question, to which I have devoted much thought of my own.

In a period of nuclear inferiority, the Soviet leadership, under Khrushchev and his successors, has persisted in its three-pronged effort: To maintain or reestablish its unitary leadership over the increasingly diverse and disobedient Communist countries; to weaken and divide the West and thereby to open Western Europe to the impact of increased Soviet pressure and to isolate the United States; and, finally, to seek targets of political opportunity in the less developed parts of the world.

In any future period in which it might attain either nuclear equality or nuclear superiority, however that may be measured in terms of the ratio between offensive and defensive systems, we would be prudent to assume that Soviet policy would be tempted to undertake a more extensive, more acute, and more dangerous range of risks in order to pursue its declared long-range ambition to reshape the world according to its own dogma.

I wish to thank you, Mr. Chairman, for this opportunity to present some of the findings that I derive from my research on international affairs.

Senator JACKSON. Thank you, Dr. Mosely, for a very valuable contribution to our discussions. Certainly your interpretation of the significance of Western superiority in military power is among the most convincing and significant that I have heard.

The Chair would like to suggest that we go on now to hear our other two witnesses and then we can put questions to all three of them, if there is no objection to that procedure.

Chairman PASTORE. The only thing is that I have to leave to make a quorum of the Appropriations Committee and then I have to be at the White House at 11:15. I would like to ask Dr. Mosely, it might not be completely relevant to the statement you made, Dr. Mosely. I regret very much I have been called out two or three times to answer the telephone and therefore I was not here to read your entire statement, but I think I got the tone from what I have heard. I would like to ask this question: How much in your opinion has the schism between Moscow and Peking affected this very dogmatic attitude of the Soviet Union and its leaders? Do you have an opinion on that?

Dr. MOSELY. Yes, Senator. The rift between Communist China and the Soviet Union goes very deep today. It has forced the Soviet Union to assert the right of each Communist regime and each Communist Party to decide its own interests. But it insists they must do so under the general purpose of communism as an international movement.

Here there is a disagreement. For example, at the meeting of last April the Rumanian Communist Party refused to attend and also the Yugoslav party, and from Western Europe the parties of Norway, the Netherlands, and Iceland also refused to attend because they felt that this might commit them to a common statement of obedience to general Soviet demands and principles. They were unwilling to do this.

Today the Soviet Union has to accept the definition of policy by each Communist Party within the broad framework of the general aims of the movement. Now in the future the Soviet leadership hopes to bring about a restoration of close cooperation with Communist China. They believe that within Communist China, when Chairman Mao has passed from the scene, he will not be able to pass on his power intact to the small group to which he has been trying to transfer it in the past 2 years.

They believe that within the Chinese Communist system there will be people who will take a sober view of what China can do in separation from the Soviet Union; that in the field of industrial development there will be people who remember with regret how much aid China received from the Soviet Union through the system of deliveries, contracts over several years and easy terms of repayment, and that they will want to turn again to the Soviet Union.

They believe that in the military establishment of Communist China there are people who realize that Communist China cannot be a truly modern power except perhaps with respect to a small number of nuclear weapons, but in other fields of military power they will be very backward without Soviet cooperation, Soviet military industry, and they believe that Communist China will see that it cannot afford to be on the worst possible terms with the Soviet Union and the United States, the two most powerful countries in the world today, and there will be a gradual movement in the Chinese regime toward a restoration of cooperation through joint decisions. When that happens, the situation in Asia will be very different from what it is today.

Chairman PASTORE. In other words, what you are actually saying is that the prospects are much more disappointing for the free world after the death of Mao?

Dr. MOSELY. Yes, sir, Senator.

Chairman PASTORE. Do you envision the coming together, of better amenability between Moscow and Peking?

Dr. MOSELY. Yes, sir.

Chairman PASTORE. With the passage of the present leadership in Red China?

Dr. MOSELY. Yes, Senator, I feel that the Soviet leadership in particular feels that Mao is—well, he is in his dotage, that he is controlled by his wife and a few other leaders who are ambitious to gain power for themselves and to hold it against their rivals within the leadership. These rivals, however, still occupy important positions in the political, military, and economic establishment, and the Soviet analysts feel, many of them, that there will be a swing around. Maybe it will take 2 or 3 or 5 years after Mao's death because the prestige of Peking has been committed to a separate line based on hostility to the Soviet Union.

But they believe there will be an underlying impulse that will bring Communist China back into cooperation with the Soviet Union.

Not obedience, because Communist China, in my opinion, has been making its own decisions right along since before 1949, but toward the actions in fields of common interest.

That will make for a very different situation in Asia where today the Soviet Union is cultivating good relations with India, Pakistan, and Japan as an offset to the present uncertainties regarding what the present Communist leaders may do.

Chairman PASTORE. Let me ask you another question.

In 1963 I had occasion to speak to President Kennedy with reference to the upthrust of Red China as a nuclear power. I asked him the question, "What will we do once Red China develops an atomic or hydrogen bomb?" He said to me at that time, "We will have to reappraise the balance of power in the world." Now, Professor Mosely, how far away from that reappraisal would you say that we are?

Dr. MOSELY. Senator, I would say that we are about 10 years from that. In other words, it will probably take about 10 years for Communist China to have a really strong nuclear force, with which it could threaten the United States with some degree of destruction. That is my layman's guess based on a careful reading of what is available.

Chairman PASTORE. Would you say that America is much more realistic in appraising the apparent danger of Russian communism than the European community?

Dr. MOSELY. Yes, Senator; on balance I think it is, because the United States has the main responsibility for deterring Communist expansion. We naturally have many groups who disagree, but as a people we do take a very sober view of the strength of the Soviet Union, of this repeated and restless stirring of their ambitions even when they have been at a strategic disadvantage as in the past 10 years.

I think that in Western Europe there are several reasons why people generally take a more complacent view. In the first place they believe that the United States will take care of the problem of overall strategic deterrence, and there is not really very much that they can do or need to do about it. Then, because we are so powerful, they also like to exercise their feeling of criticism, of resentment about some of our policies. It gives them a certain satisfaction in view of the relative decline of their power positions in the world to be able to criticize us, to complain, and, of course, we listen in a very friendly way, because they are our friends.

Then there is the factor that they live under the threat of Soviet intermediate missiles and have for some 13 years. They realize that they cannot change that situation and therefore they prefer not to think about it.

So, it is a mixture of these various pyschological factors that makes them say, "Well, you Americans are simply hipped on the idea of the Communist menace. Look, we can travel as tourists to Bulgaria and Rumania, everything is very peaceful." They are no longer watching the overall strategic factor the way we have to because we have the main responsibility.

Chairman PASTORE. Could I ask you a hypothetical question?

If America chose—and I am not suggesting that it do so—if America chose to withdraw its troops from Western Europe, do you think that De Gaulle would be a different kind of man?

Dr. MOSELY. Senator, I would have to go into several hypothetical conditions.

Chairman PASTORE. I think you more or less brought that out in your statement about this umbrella. Here is a man who has insurance without having to pay a premium.

Dr. MOSELY. Right.

Chairman PASTORE. Now if we remove the insurance, would he have to buy his own policy? That is what I mean.

Dr. MOSELY. The insurance, Senator, depends on all the NATO countries and France is a member of the alliance. I think it is extremely unwise and it is resented by many people within France that De Gaulle refuses to make any orderly contribution and goes his own way.

On the other hand, our presence in Western Europe defends all of Western Europe, including France, and we cannot separate the defense of France from that of Germany, the Low Countries, Britain, Italy, and other members of NATO. In that respect, then, De Gaulle can do what he likes; we have to make the adjustments which we have made in the disposition of forces. On the other hand, the reappraisal of NATO by the other members except France has led to a reaffirmation of basic NATO strategy and of the great need to have a U.S. presence in Europe.

Whether we will need a particular size of force on the ground is another question which will undoubtedly be reviewed from time to time, but the question of the U.S. presence as a stiffening, as an incentive to European cooperation among our European allies, too, is very important.

Chairman PASTORE. May I ask you one final question?

Is it your judgment then that the long-range adversary of Russia, according to Russia's opinion, is the United States, and not Red China?

Dr. MOSELY. Yes; in the Soviet view Communist China is a country which has gone off the rails in the past few years, and through resentment of Soviet preponderance within the Communist movement it has thrown its whole propaganda and political influence against the Soviet Union.

But looked at in the longer range, the Soviet leaders are confident that they will be able at some stage to restore cooperation with China. The idea of inevitable conflict seems to them not a good guide. If the Soviet Union and Communist China begin to coordinate their policies in Asia and the Middle East, why then we will be in for a very, very difficult time.

Chairman PASTORE. In other words, you see the amenability of Moscow going to Peking sooner than that will come to Washington?

Dr. MOSELY. Not today, but looking beyond the death of Chairman Mao, there will be new leaders in Communist China. It is not at all clear that Mao has succeeded in reshaping his regime into this militant regime run by gangs of teenaged Red Guards, and so on, into anything that will last very long after his death or his incapacitation.

Chairman PASTORE. Thank you very much.

Senator JACKSON. To follow up on the matter which Senator Pastore has raised, we should not be surprised to wake up some morning in the foreseeable future and find that a regime has come to power in China that is on good terms with the Soviet Union?

Dr. Mosely. Yes, Senator. The recent changes within China suggest that the military are playing a more and more important part in the internal management of the system. At the recent National Day on October 1 I understand that possibly 50 percent to 60 percent of the people placed on the reviewing stand were military men.

One effect then of this turmoil of the Red Guards since the summer of 1966 has been in the end to strengthen the role of the military who have their own system of communications, who have ultimate responsibility for order in different parts of the country, who are keenly interested in keeping up industrial production, exports, and agricultural production, because that is the basis of stability for the whole system.

So, perhaps over the past months Mao has really discredited the Red Guards' militant approach which he tried. We don't know exactly why Mao tried this experiment. The longer term effect may be to strengthen the role of the military who in turn rely strongly on securing an adequate food supply from agriculture and on industry.

Senator Jackson. In your judgment, is the Soviet leadership giving high priority to encouraging the emergence of a regime in China that will be friendly to them?

Dr. Mosely. Senator, I doubt there is very much they can do. But until a few months ago, the Soviet spokesman frequently referred to "sober forces," "forces of reason," within China, and I am sure that they had in mind many people with whom they had worked during the period of close Soviet-Chinese collaboration. Soviet advisers have previously worked in the military establishment, in industry, in setting up many parts of the Chinese operating system. So Moscow is not thinking in the abstract of individuals who would be sober, reasonable, and inclined to cooperate with the Soviet Union, but of perhaps tens of thousands of people, experts, party managers and military planners with thom they had worked. Many of those people are still at their posts in China.

There has not been, as far as we can see, any large-scale physicial elimination of the people that Mao has described and denounced as his opponents. So those people are presumably there. There doubtless will be a regrouping of the party's power after Mao passes from the scene. As long as he is there, he can keep up the pressure because he has been in power so long, he has built the power, but perhaps some other group more favorable to cooperation with the Soviet Union will someday simply capture him as a symbol without waiting for his death or incapacitation.

Senator Jackson. Looking ahead, I take it that if we are to be prudent in planning to meet our strategic weapons requirements we should take into consideration the possibility of facing not only the continuing threat of the Soviet Union but also the new threat from China which could constitute a combined, not simply a separate, strategic threat. Is that a fair conclusion?

Dr. Mosely. Yes Senator. This is speculating ahead, but after all, we have to do it. For example, if the Soviet Union and Communist China agreed on a course of action, and if the Soviet Union felt by that time that it had nuclear equality or superiority with the United States, the Chinese deterrent could be used to exert political blackmail on neighbors of China while the Soviet Union would hold the ring against the U.S. major deterrent. That would be a form of combined political use of the two deterrents, the small one of China and the very large one of the Soviet Union. This is what the Chinese would like to do.

Senator JACKSON. It would, in fact, convert Chinese medium-range missiles in a way for political blackmail purposes, assuming they might deploy such missiles first, thus giving them blackmail capability over their neighbors backed up with ICBM's from the Soviet Union which would be used to hold the United States at bay. Such a combination of military forces could have enormous political consequences not only in Asia but elsewhere in the world, if we did not have an adequate deterrent during this period. Is that a fair conclusion?

Dr. MOSELY. Yes, Senator. That is a fair conclusion.

Senator JACKSON. I have other questions. I will defer them until later.

Representative HOLIFIELD. Dr. Mosely, I was interested in your statement, if I understood correctly, that you gave a time period of about 10 years for the development of the cohesive force and, as I understood it, a military capability of Red China to become a threat to the Western World. Did I understand you? If not, will you clarify that?

Dr. MOSELY. That is my view, Congressman.

Representative HOLIFIELD. Now that depends of course upon two things. The political change in China which has been referred to as being a possibility or even a probability, and it also would pertain to advancement of their technology for delivery vehicles, is that not true?

Dr. MOSELY. Yes, sir.

Representative HOLIFIELD. Now, in the event of a withdrawal of influence from Asia by the United States, and by that I mean pulling back from their commitments, commitments we have at present and that we are active in upholding in Vietnam, also our commitments to other entities in Asia, and assuming for the moment that that occurred and the technology and the industrial capability of Japan would fall under the domination of Red China, would we not be faced with an acceleration of the 10-year period to something below that, possibly 6 or 7 years?

Dr. MOSELY. Yes, we would, Congressman. By that time the Communist Chinese regime would be using its relatively small but effective deterrent to try to drive Japan into neutrality and to bring about the withdrawal of U.S. strategic power from that area.

It would use pressure to try to create a spirit of helplessness in South Korea, which we are pledged to defend. It would exert strong pressures and increase internal political pressures on the Philippines. It would, in other words, try to use politically its growing, although still small, strategic power.

The fact that it is an Asian power and has the first Asian deterrent would have a strong psychological factor, much in the way in which Japan's defeat of Russia in 1904-5 brought about an upswing of pride and nationalism and anti-Western uprising in many parts of Asia. So the effects politically would be very extensive.

Representative HOLIFIELD. It is well known that Japan is now the third greatest industrial nation in the world. I think it passed Western Germany recently in its capability and production. They also are a nation without any military defense, having been precluded from building up a military capability by a treaty.

If their capability in electronics and airplanes, shipping, shipbuilding, and that sort of thing was incorporated by domination by the Red Chinese, and if at the same time a political rapprochement was obtained with the Soviets, we would be faced in an area where 2 billion people live with almost certain domination of that area, manpower, and resources, if the presence of the U.S. military strength was withdrawn or if we lost face in Asia. Is that not true?

Dr. MOSELY. Yes, Congressman, that would be an extremely serious situation because Communist China's manpower and other resources could then be developed at a more forced pace with the help of Japanese industry. China would be the dominant partner within a very short time.

Representative HOLIFIELD. So that the stake that the United States has in Asia is far greater than the struggle that is now going on in Vietnam?

Dr. MOSELY. It is. In my opinion we are in a very difficult situation in Vietnam. Whether this was the best place, in terms of local conditions and social and political conditions, to make the stand, is a problem we are going to have to face in this country. In my opinion if we have to give up in Vietnam, if we should decide not to carry on this type of struggle beyond a certain point, the effects will be extremely serious.

For one thing, many countries are helping us. Thailand is providing an increased number of troops and is already under strong political attack because it is cooperating so fully and generously with our strategic position in Vietnam, through the use of their airfields and in many other ways.

There is already a political grouping on Chinese Communist soil which says that it is the pro-Communist Government of Thailand of the future and there is a radio system broadcasting into Thailand urging the people to overthrow their authorities, abandon the U.S. alliance, and line up with Communist China. It would be relatively not too difficult to bring about a new civil war in Malaya where it went on for 8 years, even though there were only 2,000 or 3,000 guerrillas, but they were able to keep 50,000 British, Malayan, and Gurkha troops pinned down for several years.

Singapore is now under a reformist or moderate regime. The only alternative to it in case of a swing in Southeast Asia toward Communist China would be a Communist government in Singapore. So that the situation is not a strongly balanced one in our favor.

The acceptance of surrender or abandonment of Vietnam would have very serious consequences. If it ever should be decided on political or other grounds that we cannot achieve the goals that we have gradually developed in our effort in Vietnam, we would have to consider extremely costly and persistent and long-lasting measures elsewhere in the area in order to avert this domino effect.

Representative HOLIFIELD. That is all, Mr. Chairman. Thank you, Dr. Mosely.

Senator JACKSON. Congressman Morris?

Representative MORRIS. I have no questions at this time.

Senator JACKSON. Congressman Anderson?

Representative ANDERSON. I have one question, Mr. Chairman.

Certainly the thrust of your statement, Dr. Mosely, is that the Soviet Union does have the desire and fixed goal of altering the present strategic ratio of power in the world, but why do you think they have that goal? Is it imperialism? Is it simply a fetish for defense and defense-mindedness, or is it basically ideological, which causes them to have this goal and desire?

Dr. MOSELY. Congressman, there are many factors and you touched on all the important ones.

One factor is a sense of defense-mindedness which makes them feel they are never safe until they are stronger than the potential opponent. Instead of feeling that a country can have enough defense at any given time, they have a feeling that they must have superiority, and this is very deep seated in their popular psychology and is therefore accepted by their people in terms of the sacrifices that they know that they are making for strengthening their defense.

A second feature is that they are very conscious of power. Historically they look back on many periods when Russia was invaded, because it was weaker than a neighbor. They go back to the Mongols and 200 years of their direct rule over Russia and another 200 years in which the Tartars, the successors to the Mongols, were able to take Moscow, burn cities, carry away slaves, and sell them. They think in very concrete terms.

They can tell you in Russian villages what happened in the year 1241, for example. They remember the invasions. Of course, they are very conscious of the invasion by Napoleon, the invasion of their territory in World War I, and the very deep penetration by Hitler's forces in World War II.

So, for them as people, to be told: "Now we are one of the two great powers, and no one would dare to attack us," this is a matter of deep psychological satisfaction to individual Russians.

Representative ANDERSON. Thus far what you have said, if I may interrupt, certainly explains their concern about their own border and why they would want to maintain a satellite system of the Eastern European countries. What about the fact you mention in your statement that they seem to be moving now in the direction of seeking to improve their capability for intervening in situations which are very far from their own shores?

Dr. MOSELY. Yes, that is the next step. The defensive psychology of the people supports great sacrifices for military power. That is a domestic psychological base of this great strategic power and other forms of military power that they are building.

Going beyond that, they have a great pride in Russia as a great power. As Khrushchev has said and Brezhnev has said repeatedly since 1964, there is no question in the world in which the Soviet Union will not have an important voice. So, instead of concentrating on the immediate periphery around the Soviet Union and trying to expand further as Stalin tried in the case of Berlin, Greece, Turkey, and so on, his successors since 1955 have pursued a policy of leaping over the barriers and trying to build up groupings, clients, or supporters in areas a little further away, as in the Arab world and as they hope to do in parts of Africa, but they have found it is rather complicated to try to get hold of that situation.

Thus, the Soviet Union believes that power is extremely important to it, and they are making great sacrifices to build this and they have great scientific and technological capacities and these fields.

Finally, the third psychological factor is the belief that the Communist system has the answers to all ills in the world and that when it has triumphed throughout the world, then there will be universal harmony, fraternity, universal prosperity, and an end to all wars. From the Soviet point of view, the danger of war increases as communism increases its strength and expands the areas it rules. In other words, the greatest danger of war, in view of Soviet ideology, arises as their power expands and as their capacity to exert power increases.

So, from their point of view, the growth of their power, the fact that no one would attack them today, that they have a secure deterrent of their own and could destroy any other country in the world today, this does not give them the sense of relaxing. It makes them feel the next stage is the most dangerous one and that they must have the maximum power organized and ready to use at that time. That does not mean that they have a precise plan or a schedule. They don't operate that way. They have broad purposes and then they take the opportunities that they see opening up, often through the weaknesses of other countries.

Representative ANDERSON. Thank you.

Senator JACKSON. Dr. Mosely, I have several questions but I will defer and call the next scholar.

Our second witness is Dr. Thomas W. Wolfe, able analyst of Sino-Soviet affairs and strategic problems, who is senior staff member of the Rand Corp. and member of the faculty of the Sino-Soviet Institute, George Washington University.

Dr. Wolfe served from 1942 to 1962 in the U.S. Air Force, his last assignment before retirement was Director, Sino-Soviet Region, Office of Assistant Secretary of Defense, ISA, 1960–62. Former journalist with the Cleveland Plain Dealer from 1936 to 1941, he is coeditor and author of authoritative books and articles on Soviet nuclear strategy and the military technical revolution.

Dr. Wolfe, we are delighted to have you with us this morning. You may now proceed in your own way.

STATEMENT OF THOMAS W. WOLFE, SENIOR STAFF MEMBER, THE RAND CORP., MEMBER OF THE FACULTY OF THE SINO-SOVIET INSTITUTE, GEORGE WASHINGTON UNIVERSITY, WASHINGTON, D.C.

Dr. WOLFE. Thank you, Mr. Chairman, for the privilege of being here.

It scarcely needs saying that in the past few years the question of deploying antiballistic missile—ABM—defenses has taken its place among the more controversial issues of the nuclear missile age.

My remarks on this subject will fall generally under four broad headings:

    (1) A brief history of the Soviet ABM program.

    (2) Soviet attitudes toward ABM limitation.

    (3) How Soviet ABM activity relates to the overall Soviet strategic posture.

    (4) Political implications of a changing United States-Soviet military balance.

Today the Soviet Union is 50 years old, as we are all reminded by the anniversary celebration taking place in Moscow at this moment. How old the Soviet ABM program may be today is somewhat less precisely known, but in all likelihood its origins date back some 10 to 15 years.

Early public indications that the Soviet Union was interested in the possibility of antimissile defense go back to the midfifties, at which time a Soviet officer wrote that "technically, creation of a potent defense system against ballistic missiles is fully feasible." (1)

In 1961, Khrushchev told an American journalist that development of Soviet intercontinental missiles and means of defense against missiles had been initiated simultaneously (2), which would suggest that Soviet research efforts in the ABM field began some time in the early fifties.

The first specific claim of Soviet success was not heard, however, until Marshal Rodion Malinovskii at the 22d Party Congress in October 1961 reported that "the problem of destroying missiles in flight * * * has been successfully solved." (3)

Khrushchev himself in July 1962 made the much-quoted boast that the Soviet Union had developed an antimissile missile that could "hit a fly in outer space," (4) and thereafter public allusions to Soviet progress in the ABM field multiplied rather rapidly.

The first public display of a Soviet weapon for which an ABM role was claimed came at a Red Square parade on November 7, 1963 — just 4 years ago. This missile was given the identifying nickname of "Griffon" by Western officials.

According to Western estimates, it was a two-stage vehicle with an altitude of 25 to 30 miles, a slant range of about 100 miles, a speed of mach 3 to 5, and could probably be fitted with either a TNT or nuclear warhead. (5)

Whether it was actually capable of intercepting ICBM's remained a matter of considerable doubt, however, and some experts suggested that it may have been developed primarily as a counter to high-performance bombers armed with air-to-surface missiles (ASM), such as the B-58 or the then projected B-70. (6)

A second and more likely candidate for the ABM role was first paraded by the Soviets a year later in November 1964. This missile, nicknamed "Galosh," was described by Soviet commentators as capable of intercepting ballistic missiles at long distances from defended targets (7), suggesting that it was an exoatmospheric weapon designed to take on incoming missiles several hundred miles above the earth.

Although Galosh has always been sheathed in a protective canister when displayed in public, a demonstration firing of the missile was once included in a documentary film shown on Moscow television.

The display of ABM-associated hardware such as the Griffon and Galosh missiles in the 1963-64 period did not in itself go very far toward answering the prime question whether the Soviet Union had achieved an operationally satisfactory ABM system which it was prepared to deploy on a serious scale.

Speculation in the Western press and discussion in the U.S. Senate in April 1963, dwelt on the possibility that the Soviets had already begun deployment of first-generation ABM defenses around Leningrad, (8) but the evidence relating to such deployment remained inconclusive.

At the time of Khrushchev's ouster in the fall of 1964, despite occasional prior Soviet references to inclusion of antimissile defense in the overall "antiair defense" system, (9) ambiguity persisted as to the precise status of the Soviet ABM program.

Apart from the standard barrier of Soviet secrecy, several factors helped to becloud the ABM situation while Khrushchev was still in office. The state of the art in the 1963–64 period was still such as to make deployment of ABM defenses a technologically uncertain course; therefore, Khrushchev may have hesitated to approve going ahead with large-scale investment in a first-generation system employing Griffon, especially if an improved second-generation system was already well along in development.

There is, indeed, some indication that a Griffon defense complex may have been initiated around Leningrad in 1962 and then halted because of technical problems. (10)

Furthermore, very large resources would be required for an ABM deployment program, and in the latter years of Khrushchev's tenure the problem of resource constraints had grown quite severe, contributing, indeed, to Khrushchev's desire for detente, and perhaps persuading him that major new expenditures in the ABM field had best be postponed.

At any rate, it seems a reasonable conjecture that, for whatever reasons, Khrushchev left the final decisions on operational deployment of a Soviet ABM system to his successors, although he must have sanctioned most of the preparatory steps for doing so.

It was only after the new Brezhnev-Kosygin regime assumed power that it gradually became clear that the Soviet leadership had definitely committed itself to a deployment program.

The first official U.S. cognizance of considerable evidence that the Soviet Union was deploying an antiballistic missile defense system was given by Secretary of Defense Robert S. McNamara in an interview on November 10, 1966, (11) following several months of increasing speculation on the subject in the press.

As numerous accounts now publicly available indicate, the Soviet Union has installed a second-generation ABM defense system, employing the Galosh missile, around Moscow. (12)

How extensive further ABM deployment throughout the Soviet Union may be is still a matter of debate, which turns on the reportedly unsettled question whether a second defensive system also currently under construction and covering a larger geographical area—the so-called Tallin system—is designed primarily for long-range defense against aircraft or is also part of the ABM deployment program. (13) At the moment, the former view seems to have gained ground.

Whatever the ultimate answer to this question may prove to be, it may be noted that Secretary McNamara told the Congress early this year when presenting his 1967 military posture statement that:

* * * we must, for the time being, plan our forces on the assumption that they will have deployed some sort of an ABM system around their major cities by the early 1970's. (14)

Just as the deployment status of Soviet ABM defenses remains subject to conflicting interpretation, so the effectiveness of these defenses also is a matter of some debate.

This arises less around the capabilities of the Soviet defensive system at its present stage, which most experts would consider quite inadequate to cope with the kind of attack that could be mounted against the U.S.S.R. than around its future potential.

Given further advances in the state of the art, together with possible Soviet exploitation of such phenomena as the X-ray effects of large-yield nuclear explosions above the earth's atmosphere, (15) some competent observers have felt that the techniques of defense against missile attack might be improved to the point of negating many of the hitherto preponderant advantages of offensive delivery systems, even in the face of further offensive improvements such as penetration aids and multiple warheads.

Obviously, the complex interaction of many technical and operational variables is involved here. Indeed, the uncertainties attending the ongoing duel between offensive and defensive systems are such that it would be rash to try to predict in the abstract which will gain the upper hand, let alone trying to predict specifically how successful Soviet efforts to erect effective missile defenses may prove to be.

What can be said at this juncture is that Soviet spokesmen themselves have failed to express undiluted confidence in their country's ABM efforts to date.

Publicly advanced Soviet claims of ABM progress in the past few years have varied from outright assertions that the Soviet Union has solved the ABM problem to more guarded statements like that of Marshall Malinovskii at the 23d party congress in April 1966 that Soviet defenses could cope with some but not all enemy missiles. (16)

Again early this year several prominent Soviet military leaders voiced differing views on this subject. Generals P. F. Batitskii and P. A. Kurochkin took the optimistic position that Soviet ABM defenses could reliably protect the country against missile attack, while two other senior officers, Marshals A. A. Grechko and V. I. Chuikov, offered the more sober view that the Soviet Union did not yet possess defenses capable "in practice" of intercepting all incoming enemy planes and missiles. (17)

If nothing else, these conflicting assessments in February 1967 would seem to suggest that professional military opinion within the Soviet Union itself was by no means agreed, up to that time at least, upon the effectiveness of an ABM program in which something on the order of $4 to $5 billion worth of resources already had been invested. (18)

It should be added, however, that although Soviet military men may differ as to the present capabilities of the country's ABM defenses, none have questioned publicly the desirability of building such defenses.

Let me turn next to the question of Soviet attitudes toward limitation of ABM deployment, a question which has come to the forefront of the ABM dialog during the past year or so, and one which bears closely upon the subject of these hearings.

To begin with, during the period preceding Soviet decisions to embark on ABM deployment, the Soviet leadership was not visibly impressed by arguments widely raised in the West that "first deployment" of an ABM system was a step likely to destabilize the strategic environment and set off a new round in the arms race.

Although Soviet delegates at various international meetings, including the Pugwash conferences, were frequently exposed to such arguments, no public discussion of the pros and cons of ABM deployment comparable to that in the West emerged in the Soviet Union.

Indeed, one of the few Soviet figures to address this question in print, Maj. Gen. Nikolai Talenskii, argued in October 1964 that ABM would not disturb the stability of mutual deterrence, and that an appropriate combination of offensive missiles and ABM defenses would be a wise policy for a "peace-loving" country like the Soviet Union, compensating for any imbalance that might exist in strategic delivery forces. (19)

Despite a generally unreceptive Soviet attitude toward the notion of holding off the deployment of ABM in order to avert another cycle of strategic arms competition, it seemed plausible to some students of Soviet affairs that such a decision might be stayed by economic and other considerations.

In particular, in light of the earlier examples of the "missile gap" of Khrushchev's day which greatly stimulated U.S. missile programs and had the net effect of placing the Soviet Union in a relatively unfavorable position with respect to strategic forces, it was supposed that the Soviet leaders might think twice about stirring up Western concern over an ABM gap.

However, Soviet predilection for building strategic defenses, combined with the possible overcoming of earlier technical obstacles in ABM development, evidently prevailed over the economic costs and the risks of stimulating a strategic arms race in the judgment of the present leadership, which has gone ahead with deployment of ABM defenses.

Whether this decision will continue to hold up in the face of American efforts to persuade the Soviet Government to reconsider its ABM policy remains to be seen.

U.S. hopes of persuading the Soviet Union to agree to a mutual freeze of some sort on ABM deployment were voiced by President Johnson in his state of the Union message on January 10, 1967, and shortly thereafter exploratory soundings were initiated looking toward the possibility of negotiations on ABM limitation, linked perhaps with limitations on strategic offensive systems.

The general Soviet tone, set by Kosygin in an interview in London on February 10 and again during his visit to the United States in June 1967 (20), has been on the cool side, although the Soviets have not closed the door to possible negotiations.

During the first 8 months or so after the American invitation to discuss an ABM moratorium, nothing concrete emerged from the diplomatic soundings toward this end, except perhaps a few signs that the U.S. initiative may have aroused an ABM policy debate within the Soviet Government.

Among such signs was publication of a Pravda article on February 15, 1967, in which Kosygin was made out to be more receptive to the idea of an ABM moratorium than his actual remarks in London a few days before warranted.

Two days after the Pravda article, written by F. Burlatskii, Western news agencies in Moscow reported that the article had been privately repudiated by Soviet sources who claimed that the regime's position on ABM negotiations was negative, as would be made clear in a new article.

However, a corrective article did not appear, suggesting that internal policy differences may have arisen over the question of negotiations.

In March, a strong statement by a military spokesman of the case for continuing with an ABM deployment program appeared in a Red Star article stressing the importance of strategic defense measures along with the value of a powerful offensive posture. (21)

Both the article and its timing again suggested that an internal ABM policy controversy might be going on, with various parties seeking to influence the debate.

It has been conjectured that the existence of internal policy differences in Moscow may help to explain why the Soviet Government was in no hurry to get on with talks about a mutual freeze on ABM deployment, and that Soviet footdragging might be brought to an end by the latest U.S. initiative (22) namely, Secretary McNamara's announcement in San Francisco on September 18, 1967, that the United States has decided to go forward with a "relatively light" and "Chinese-oriented" ABM deployment. (23)

To date, however, this move has had no perceptible effect in spurring the Soviet leadership to reconsider its ABM deployment policy or to enter negotiations on the subject.

The Soviet response to Mr. McNamara's San Francisco announcement and his subsequent elucidation of the rationale behind the "light" or "thin" ABM system in an interview with Life magazine (24) has been somewhat restrained but certainly not sympathetic.

The few Soviet commentaries to date—and no high-echelon Soviet leaders have yet spoken to the move—have asserted that the deployment decision was taken to appease pressure from "hardline" political opposition and from the U.S. arms industry for which it will create huge profits; that it will not help to bring the arms race under control; that it may be an impediment to concluding a nuclear nonproliferation treaty; and that it will not satisfy advocates in the United States of a "heavy" deployment costing $40 to $50 billion. (25)

There has been no Soviet comment on the military effectiveness of the "light" system, nor—interestingly enough—on its presumed orientation against China.

Indeed, one has the impression that the Soviets consider the "light" system merely the first step in a more extensive deployment aimed at the Soviet Union, which the China rationale simply serves to camouflage.

One further noteworthy omission to date in Soviet response to the U.S. deployment decision has been failure to comment upon its effect on possible ABM negotiations between Moscow and Washington.

By contrast with Moscow's silence on the Chinese and the negotiatory aspects of the ABM decision, commentary in various East European countries has been a good deal more outspoken on both subjects.

The explanation that the U.S. system is intended for defense against China, for example, was dismissed in a Czech account as "artificial." (26)

As for the matter of negotiations, a Polish commentator wrote that the American decision amounts to "openly blackmailing" the Soviet

Union by saying "either immediate negotiations or an armaments race." (27)

A Bulgarian writer took a slightly different tack, asserting that "the Soviet ABM defense has spoiled" the U.S. missile strategy built on "the concept of a surprise first strike," and that is why the United States "has been making a lot of noise about its readiness to negotiate a mutual refusal to use the defensive ABM." (28)

In only one case, an editorial in a Warsaw newspaper, has East European comment been critical of both sides. Observing that "creation of antiballistic systems means more than just a new stage of the arms race and a new wave of military expenditure on both sides," the editorial warned that ABM systems can upset the relative stability of mutual deterrence by restoring the operative role of nuclear weapons, "because an aggressor will assume that he is no longer exposed to destruction by retaliation." (29)

While it is interesting that East European commentators have not uniformly followed the Soviet cue in discussing the U.S. deployment decision, the question at hand is not what the East Europeans think about the move but how the Soviet leadership may react to it.

During the earlier phases of the ABM controversy, the view was sometimes advanced that the Soviet leadership might undertake a token deployment of ABM as leverage to force the United States into negotiations on overall strategic forces, without necessarily intending to carry out widespread ABM deployment within the Soviet Union.

The tenability of this view seems to have progressively declined over time, as Soviet reluctance to rise to the opportunity for negotiations has manifested itself—most lately, in response to the U.S. "light" deployment decision.

One certainly cannot rule out a change of Soviet attitude, particularly if the leadership should become persuaded that the prospects of improving the Soviet Union's relative power position would be better served by negotiations calculated to cut off a new cycle of U.S. strategic programs than by banking simply on unilateral Soviet efforts to alter the strategic balance. However, it would appear that the Soviet leaders thus far do not see it that way, perhaps because they genuinely believe in the efficacy of their ABM system to the point that negotiating it away seems to make no sense, or perhaps because they feel that American interest in an ABM moratorium grows mainly out of the economic pressures of the Vietnam war and will be superseded by a new round of strategic programs when the war ends, in which event Soviet interests would be best served by avoiding a negotiatory pause and pressing on with an ABM program which already enjoys a headstart.

I should like to turn next to the matter of how Soviet ABM activity relates to the overall Soviet strategic posture.

Let me say first that there is a rather widespread and somewhat oversimplified impression in the West that the Soviets have a deep seated traditional preference for defense over offense, and that this defense mindedness serves as a sufficient explanation for the effort devoted to an ABM program.

While it is true that Soviet military thinking attaches great value to strategic defense forces for protection against air and missile attack, it does not do so at the expense of the offensive aspect of military forces.

On the contrary, Soviet military philosophy emphasizes, to quote a recent statement on the subject, that "the decisive mode of military operations always has been and remains the offensive." (30)

In short, a concept of balanced forces, both offensive and defensive, governs the Soviet outlook.

The point to be made here is that the efforts of the Brezhnev-Kosygin regime to repair the Soviet Union's strategic posture, which at the close of the Khrushchev period remained clearly second best to that of the United States, have not been confined to the ABM field but have reflected the concept that a complementary "mix" of strategic offensive and defensive forces should be sought.

When Khrushchev's successors first came to office, it was by no means clear, however, how vigorously they would seek to improve the Soviet Union's strategic position vis-a-vis the United States.

Their initial approach did indicate, if nothing else, a determination to strengthen the technological base upon which any effort to alter the strategic balance would ultimately depend.

Appropriations for scientific research were stepped up (31) and, as made evident by public display of new families of offensive and defensive weapons (32) the Soviet military research and development program was pushed even more energetically than before.

It was only after the new leaders had been in power a year or two, however, that it gradually became apparent that they had committed themselves to a substantial buildup of Soviet strategic delivery forces.

As indicated by informed accounts which began to appear in the U.S. press in the summer and fall of 1966, an accelerated program of Soviet ICBM deployment had been set in motion in the Soviet Union. (33)

By the beginning of 1967, the number of operational ICBM launchers reportedly had reached around 450, with deployment proceeding at the rate of 100 to 150 a year (34) and according to some accounts, the operational ICBM total today approaches 700. (35)

These figures may be compared with a total deployment of fewer than 200 ICBM launchers during the entire Khrushchev period.

Not less significant than the rapid growth of numbers was a shift to new types of missiles in dispersed and hardened sites, in contrast with the ICBM force of the Khrushchev period, much of which consisted of early generation missiles of "soft site" configuration.

Meanwhile, as emphasized in the late Marshal Malinovskii's report at the 23d Party Congress in April 1966, "special importance" has been attached to developing mobile land-based missiles for the strategic missile forces, (36) a step which would further diversify the Soviet Union's strategic delivery potential.

The same report pointed out that the Soviet Union continues to count upon the additional contribution to its strategic delivery capabilities provided by long-range bombers equipped with air-to-surface missiles for "standoff" attacks against enemy targets and by missile-launching submarines. (37)

What the ultimate size and character of the Soviet strategic forces may be remains uncertain. But the large investment in the strategic force buildup of the past few years along with concurrent deployment of ABM defenses, does testify to the apparent determination of the Brezhnev-Kosygin regime to erase the image of a Soviet Union strategically inferior to its major adversary.

Two further items bearing on the Soviet strategic posture deserve mention. One is the active interest shown in development of an orbital or fractional orbital delivery system, as evidenced by statements of Soviet military officials, by a testing program, and by parade display of a large missile (SCRAG), claimed by the Soviets to have "orbital" capability. (38) This development is currently very much in the news, following Secretary McNamara's statement on the subject a few days ago.

The other has been renewed Soviet emphasis on civil defense preparations, accompanied in January 1967 by reorganization of the civil defense system. (39)

Steps to bolster the Soviet strategic posture, one should note, have been paralled in the past few years by measures to improve the maritime-air-logistic elements of power needed to project Soviet military influence into distant areas without having to invoke the threat of immediate nuclear holocaust.

In a sense, these measures might be described as an attempt to extend the "reach" of conventional Soviet military power.

Although this aspect of Soviet military policy under the Brezhnev-Kosygin regime lies outside of the scope of the present discussion, it is relevant to say that it represents part of a process through which the Soviet Union seems to be striving to bring its military posture into line with its growing global obligations and commitments.

At the very least, the Soviet leadership is providing itself with wider options for global intervention than it has hitherto possessed.

Taken together with changes underway in the Soviet strategic offensive and defensive forces, attainment of a longer "reach" by Soviet conventional forces could help to bring about a significant transformation of the familiar situation of the past two decades in which the United States enjoyed not only marked strategic superiority over the Soviet Union, but also went virtually unchallenged in its capacity to project mobile military power into distant conflict situations around the globe.

This observation brings me to the final portion of my statement, in which I shall try to offer a few but I fear, inadequate, remarks on some of the political implications for the future of a changing United States-Soviet military balance.

Let me emphasize first the contingent and precarious nature of any assumptions about the future military balance itself.

The precise character of any new correlation of forces that may emerge in the next decade or so is not predictable.

It may well be that we shall witness a reversal of trends that have been gradually narrowing the measurable margin between U.S. and Soviet power, as has been suggested, for example, by those who see in the U.S. program for MIRV and the initiation of an ABM system responsive steps which promise to wipe out whatever gains the Soviets may make. (40)

On the other hand, depending in part on what the United States chooses to do in part upon the willingness of the Soviet leaders to raise the ante and the capacity of their economy to stand the strain, a situation of acknowledged "parity" of perhaps even some margin of strategic "superiority" might be attained by the Soviet Union.

In this connection, it is worth noting that a recent Czech commentary on the MIRV program offered some reverse arithmetic on the effect of multiple warheads upon the balance of forces.

Referring to the larger payload capacity of Soviet missiles which would presumably permit them to carry more multiple warheads than U.S. missiles, the Czech writer claimed, to quote him, that "with the introduction of multiple warheads, the change in the number of warheads which can be transported by American and Soviet rockets will alter the balance of forces from the now claimed American superiority of 3 to 1 to a Soviet superiority of 4 to 2." (41)

This exercise in the arithmetic of superiority is cited not as an earnest of what may happen, but simply to underscore the point that "superiority" is itself an elusive concept.

A great deal of controversy attends the question of what constitutes "parity" or "superiority"; indeed, the level at which it becomes militarily meaningless to exceed a major nuclear adversary in numbers of weapons, megatonnage, deliverable warheads, or other attributes of strategic forces is something on which views differ widely not only in the United States, but apparently in the Soviet Union as well. (42)

Likewise, the contribution which an ABM system might make to attainment of strategic superiority is a disputed question, influenced, as mentioned earlier, by many technical and operational variables.

The weight of offense over defense in the strategic force equation doubtless remains great enough today to assure against any dramatic shift of superiority based on the introduction of an ABM system alone.

As for the future, it might be argued that the prospect of gaining the upper hand could become more feasible in military terms under certain circumstances, such as, for example, a situation in which an aggressor possessing an appropriate combination of offensive and defensive forces were to launch a first strike that would leave only disorganized residual counterblows to be dealt with by ABM defenses.

This is not to say that Soviet military planners necessarily see superiority within their grasp on the basis of such a scenario, nor that they can expect to make a sufficiently airtight case on military grounds to tempt the political leadership to risk putting it to test.

However, despite the military uncertainties that seem likely to persist in tomorrow's world and to continue acting as a restraint upon deliberate resort to war, any substantial shift in the previously recognized strategic balance can hardly help having a far-reaching impact upon world politics.

Like popularity in politics, strategic superiority may be difficult to define, but when it shifts, those concerned are likely to be sensitive to the change.

In the present instance, a prime question is: How would Soviet conduct on the international scene be affected by an acknowledged shift in the power balance favoring the Soviet Union? One can only offer a speculative answer.

The least likely, but worst case, in my opinion, would find the Soviet leadership so heady from the unaccustomed novelty of no longer playing second fiddle on the world stage that it might, during some major crisis, try to press its advantage too far and set off a devastating war.

Given the unadventurous temperament of the incumbent collective leadership and the reinforced conviction that it would probably feel that history was running its way anyhow, the chances that it would blunder into war in this fashion seem to me rather low.

An almost equally unlikely, but certainly far better case, would be one in which the Soviet leaders would shed their ingrained suspicion of the Western World, feeling secure at last from external danger and inclined to play a more responsible "status quo" role in international politics.

This alternative rests on premises of marked transformation in the world outlook of the Soviet ruling elite. Despite the process of societal change at work within the Soviet Union, the Soviet leadership, it seems to me, has not come round to a view that counsels lasting accommodation with the present world order, and in an atmosphere of success for its system remains unlikely to do so.

In a third and more likely case—but one hardly pleasing to us—the Soviet leadership, it seems to me, would try to test the new strategic relationship, seeking such political gains as the traffic might bear.

This in itself may seem no more than a replaying of past Soviet performance. But operating from a more favorable correlation of forces, the Soviet leaders would probably attempt to reopen various stalemated issues and to seek fresh advances in the third world, thus introducing new elements of turbulence into international relations, and even enhancing the chances of converting the situation into the worst case which I mentioned first.

If the assessment is at all close to the mark, it is difficult to escape the conclusion that U.S. interests would suffer in a strategic environment in which American primacy is widely questioned, even though the Soviet Union may not clearly have gained the upper hand.

U.S. diplomacy would enjoy a much less comfortable freedom of action than in the past, and the element of uncertainty in crisis situations would probably become much more severe.

The answer may seem to lie simply in making sure that American preeminence is maintained. But a difficult dilemma, not to be easily brushed aside, arises here, for the economic, political, and social costs of maintaining U.S. preeminence seems likely to go up steadily with the passage of time as the other side also seeks preeminence from its own growing power base.

In such an environment, many of the issues thrust to the surface of American life by the Vietnam war may well become more embittered.

In closing, let me return for a moment to the ABM issue, which has been the catalyst, so to speak, of this rather somber image of a future with which we may find it necessary to cope.

Seen in the perspective of an evolving United States-Soviet strategic relationship, it seems to me that time and events have left behind any reasonable prospect of precluding the progressive deployment in both countries of ABM defenses on a fairly substantial scale.

While the military merits of ABM systems may or may not come to fully justify their deployment, these systems have probably become already too potent a symbolic element in the strategic equation to be readily discarded.

Once started down the ABM road, neither superpower can afford to forgo a means of defense which might afford a meaningful measure of protection and which at the same time helps to symbolize its rank order as a superpower and sets it off from lesser powers.

Certainly, this is one sense in which it is true that in starting down the ABM path, the Soviet Union and the United States have not only been eyeing each other, but China as well.

Having registered doubt that further attempts to forestall or limit
ABM deployment are likely to succeed, let me also register my
sympathy with the efforts that have been made to date by the U.S.
Government to do so, and why.

First, it seems likely to me that ABM deployment will lead to
higher levels of offensive and defensive armaments, the resource costs
of which are serious indeed.

Second, ABM may well restore the premium on a first strike and
destablize the deterrent balance that we have come to take more or
less for granted.

Third, tensions generated by such instability and by the shifting
structure of strategic relationships are not likely to lead in the direction of reasonable settlement of issues between the world's contending
powers and coalitions.

Fourth and finally, in the event nuclear war should occur either
deliberately or by accident, the presence of ABM systems would
probably have the effect of increasing rather than minimizing the
release of megatonnage, and there are, of course, deep-seated human-
itarian and biological reasons for wanting to avoid this situation,
which could despoil the biosphere we are all obliged to share.

Thank you, Mr. Chairman.

Senator JACKSON. Thank you, Dr. Wolfe, for a most useful addition
to our hearing record on the Soviet ABM development and the Soviet
approach to military issues.

(The following are the explanatory notes to Dr. Wolfe's statement:)

1. Major F. Kriksanov, "The Problems of the Interception of Intercontinental
Ballistic Missiles," *Voennaia Znaniia*, No. 7, July 1957, pp. 15–16.
2. Interview with C. R. Sulzberger, *The New York Times*, September 8, 1961.
3. *Pravda*, October 25, 1961.
4. *The New York Times*, July 17, 1962.
5. See *The Soviet Military Technological Challenge*, Center for Strategic Studies,
Georgetown University, Washington, D.C., September 1967, p. 88.
6. *Ibid.*
7. *Pravda*, November 8, 1964. See also *Krasnaia zvezda*, November 10, 1965.
8. See John P. Thomas, *The Role of Missile Defense in Soviet Strategy and
Foreign Policy*, Research Analysis Corporation, McLean, Virginia, March 1965,
p. 1.
9. See Thomas W. Wolfe, *Soviet Strategy at the Crossroads*, Harvard University
Press, Cambridge, Mass., 1964, p. 309, footnote 20.
10. See Hedrick Smith, in *The New York Times*, January 29, 1967.
11. *The New York Times*, November 11, 1966.
12. See, for example, Hanson W. Baldwin, in *The New York Times*, November
27, 1966; Henry Gemmill, in *Wall Street Journal*, December 14, 1966; *The Soviet
Military Technological Challenge*, p. 90.
13. See Hanson W. Baldwin, in *The New York Times*, February 5, 1967; Anne
M. Jonas, "Strategic Deterrence in the 1970s: Five Problems for U.S. Policy,"
Air Force and Space Digest, July 1967, pp. 32–33.
14. *Statement . . . before a Joint Session of the Senate Armed Services Committee and the Senate Subcommittee on Department of Defense Appropriations on the
Fiscal Year 1968-1972 Defense Program and 1968 Defense Budget, January 23, 1967*,
mimeographed, p. 41.
15. For a discussion of this question, see *The Soviet Military Technological
Challenge*, pp. 91–97.
16. *Krasnaia zvezda*, April 2, 1966.
17. See Thomas W. Wolfe, *Soviet Military Policy at the Fifty Year Mark*, the
RAND Corporation, RM–5443–PR, September 1967, p. 21.
18. *Ibid*, pp. 21–22.
19. Major General N. Talenskii, "Anti-Missile Systems and Disarmament,"
International Affairs, No. 10, Moscow, October 1964, pp. 15–19.
20. *The New York Times*, February 10, June 26, 1967; *The Washington Post*,
February 18, 1967; *The Soviet Military Technological Challenge*, p. 101.

21. Lt. General I. Zavialov, "On Soviet Military Doctrine," *Krasnaia zvezda*, March 31, 1967.
22. See Stephen S. Rosenfeld, in *The Washington Post*, October 15, 1967.
23. *The New York Times*, September 18, 1967.
24. *Life*, September 29, 1967, pp. 28 a, b, c.
25. *Pravda*, September 24, 1967; *Izvestiia*, October 4, 1967; *Literaturnaia gazeta*, No. 41, October 11, 1967, p. 9.
26. Jiri Hochman, "Rockets, Antiballistic Missiles, and Politics: On McNamara's Speech in San Francisco." *Rude Pravo*, September 23, 1967.
27. Warsaw domestic broadcast, September 26, 1967, FBIS *Daily Report, USSR & East Europe*, September 27, 1967, pp. FF–1, 2.
28. G. Naydenov, "Antimissile Advertisement," *Rabotnichesko Delo*, September 24, 1967.
29. Editorial, "The Other Nike," *Slowo Powszechne*, September 21, 1967.
30. Zavialov, in *Krasnaia zvezda*, March 31, 1967. See also *Soviet Strategy at the Crossroads*, pp. 193–196.
31. Published Soviet allocations for scientific research have risen as follows: 1963—4.7 billion rubles; 1964—5.2; 1965—5.4; 1966—6.5; 1967—7.2
32. Accounts of Red Square displays of new equipment may be found in: *Pravda*, November 8, 1965; *Krasnaia zvezda*, November 10, 1965; *The New York Times*, November 8, 1964, May 9, 1965, November 8, 1965.
33. *The New York Times*. June 9, July 14, November 13, December 18, 1966. See also The Military Balance, 1966–1967, Institute for Strategic Studies, London, September 1966, p. 2.
34. Richard J. Whelan, "The Shifting Equation of Nuclear Defense," *Fortune*, June 1, 1967, p. 87; George C. Wilson, in *The Washington Post*, April 19, 1967.
35. *The New York Times*, October 30, 1967.
36. *Krasnaia zvezda*, April 2, 1966.
37. According to recent Western estimates, the Soviet Union possesses about 200 heavy bombers (M–4 "Bisons" and TU–95 "Bears," some of which are used as tankers), and about 35 submarines capable of firing an average of three ballistic missiles each. In addition, about 40 submarines are equipped to fire cruise-type winged missiles, which could be used against land targets but which probably have a primary mission against naval forces. See *The Military Balance*, 1966–1967, pp. 3, 5.
38. See *Soviet Military Policy at the Fifty Year Mark*, p. 25; Evert Clark, in *The New York Times*, October 17, 1967.
39. Marshal V. Chuikov, "The Soviets and Civil Defense: The Business of All and of Each," *Izvestiia*, June 15, 1967. Raymond H. Anderson, in *The New York Times*, November 23, 1966.
40. See William E. Griffith, *The United States and the Soviet Union In Europe: The Impact of the Arms Race, Technology and the German Question*, Center for International Studies, Massachusetts Institute of Technology, Cambridge, Mass., October 1967, p. 9.
41. Jiri Hochman, in *Rude Pravo*, September 23, 1967.
42. For a recent U.S. example of such controversy, see account in *The New York Times*, July 12, 1967, of a study by The American Security Council sponsored by the House Armed Services Committee, together with an answering statement by the Department of Defense. In the Soviet case, long-standing doctrinal commitment to the goal of both quantitative and qualitative superiority has sometimes been at odds with the view that amongst major nuclear powers "Superiority has become a concept which has no bearing on war." See G. Gerasimov, "Pentagonia, 1966," *International Affairs*, No. 5, May 1966, p. 28.

Senator JACKSON. Our third witness is Mrs. Alice Langley Hsieh, noted analyst of Communist China's external political and military policies, who is senior staff member, Social Science Department, the Rand Corp.

From 1945 to 1954, Mrs. Hsieh was an officer of the Department of State, dealing primarily with political-military problems in the Far East. From 1955 to 1958 she was consultant to the Rand Corp., and has been a member of the senior staff at Rand since 1958. She is a member of the Department of State's Panel of Advisers for East Asia and Pacific Affairs, author of "Communist China's Strategy in the Nuclear Era" (1962), and of many articles and studies, particularly on the role of the military in Communist China's external policies.

Mrs. Hsieh, we are delighted to welcome you to the committee.

STATEMENT OF ALICE LANGLEY HSIEH, SENIOR STAFF MEMBER, THE RAND CORP.

Mrs. HSIEH. Mr. Chairman, members of the committee, I am complimented by your invitation to testify at these hearings. The views expressed in this statement as well as any made in response to questions are my own.

They should not be interpreted as reflecting the views of the Rand Corp. or the official opinion or policy of any of its governmental or private research sponsors.

You have asked me to testify at a time when the Chinese Communists in detonating six nuclear devices since October 1964, including a thermonuclear device in the megaton range—June 17, 1967—and the testing of a missile with a nuclear warhead—October 27, 1966—have visibly demonstrated their intent to become a nuclear power, but also at a time of continuing upheaval and disarray on the Chinese mainland consequent to Mao Tse-tung's insistence on pushing forward the so-called great proletarian cultural revolution.

As a result of the latter, students of Chinese Communist affairs have been forced to revise radically, if not reverse, many of their earlier assessments of the political cohesion and stability of the Chinese Communist regime.

However, to date, I have seen little evidence that the cultural revolution has affected China's nuclear missile progress.

Nor have I seen any evidence that the cultural revolution has changed the basic premises underlying China's military strategy.

Persistent in the thinking of many Americans is the image of China as a militarily reckless, adventurous regime.

Some observers have predicted that the Chinese, when in possession of a nuclear-delivery capability, would not be hesitant to threaten Tokyo, Bangkok, et cetera, with nuclear destruction.

Others for some years have been warning of a massive Chinese ground intervention in Vietnam.

During the past year, some people have argued that Lin Piao would seek to consolidate his power as heir-apparent to Mao by engaging in an external military adventure.

Far from conforming with this public image of warlike bellicosity, China's external military policies in pursuit of her long-term foreign policy objectives—great power status, hegemony in Asia, removal of U.S. power and influence from the Western Pacific—have been characterized by a considerable degree of caution.

These policies reflect a realistic assessment of the military situation and the careful calculation of risks that dominate China's military doctrine.

Current doctrine is an outgrowth of traditional Chinese Communist doctrine on the use of force. China's strategy as reflected in the writings of Mao Tse-tung evolved pragmatically in response to concrete problems and experience in the course of the Chinese Communist conflict with both the Kuomintang and the Japanese.

Because of the vast inferiority of Chinese Communist military equipment and skilled manpower to those of the enemy—whether the Kuomintang or the Japanese, Mao developed a view of war as a protracted struggle that relied heavily on the use of political, psychological, economic, and diplomatic techniques in addition to purely military means.

The key to Mao's thinking lies in the primacy he grants to the political element. What he did was to then establish an integrated doctrine whereby a weak force could hope to succeed against a militarily stronger enemy.

Despite the fact that the Chinese Communists have detonated six nuclear devices, despite the fact that within a few years they may acquire a nuclear delivery capability, for a long time to come they will be confronted with the same problem: How to make political gains from a position of military inferiority.

But current Chinese military doctrine is a mixture of the old and new. Traditional doctrine has felt the impact of advances in military technology, both conventional and nuclear.

While these have outdated the applicability of many of Mao's strategic concepts and tactics for conflict situations involving high level of violence—but not necessarily for lower level conflicts—they have at the same time confirmed the relevance of the key factor in Mao's military thinking; that is, the primacy of the political element.

The Korean war brought home to the Chinese the importance of conventional modernization—their disadvantage when compelled to engage in positional warfare and when confronted with superior firepower and modern airpower.

By 1953–54 at the latest, one or more of several factors contributed to China's increased appreciation of the implications of nuclear war—the more open debate on military doctrine among Soviet military leaders, the enhanced U.S. striking power in the Far East, and the continued advances abroad in military technology; for example, the development of thermonuclear weapons and tactical nuclear weapons.

Equally relevant to the evolution of Chinese doctrine has been Peking's evaluation of both the material aid it could expect—or not expect—from the Soviet Union and the role of the Soviet nuclear shield in deterring a nuclear attack.

The massive Soviet assistance of the Korean war period had been continued but at a reduced scale during the remainder of the fifties.

By the late fifties, this also probably included some Soviet provision of short-range missiles for experimental and training purposes.

Soviet assistance apparently included aid in the construction of nuclear facilities.

While it is doubtful if this assistance went beyond help in the peaceful uses of nuclear energy, what help was provided created a basis from which the Chinese could develop their own military nuclear program.

Substantial Soviet assistance seems to have been premised on Soviet control over key elements in China's military establishment—a condition the Chinese refused to accept.

Peking's evaluation of the U.S.-U.S.S.R. military balance has likewise had important implications for Chinese doctrine. There is reason to believe that by 1957–58 the Chinese were confident that Soviet nuclear power deterred an unprovoked U.S. attack on China.

Otherwise, it is extremely doubtful if they would have felt free to reject the Soviet bid for military control or to challenge the Soviet Union in the international Communist movement.

The point at issue between Peking and Moscow was not whether Soviet power deterred the United States from an unprovoked attack on China but whether the Soviet Union was prepared to use its power to back up China's external objectives and to support effectively revolutionary activity in underdeveloped areas.

Two other factors obviously influence the content of Chinese doctrine. First, there is China's vast military inferiority in relation to the United States—as well as to the Soviet Union—its present lack of advanced weapons despite its testing programs, and the economic underdevelopment of the mainland.

To a considerable extent these weaknesses are offset by the fact that the Peking regime exists in a dynamic, constantly shifting world context.

Peking is thus in a position to exploit the suspicions that newly independent countries have of the former imperialist powers, the internal economic and political instability of new countries, and the rivalry and incipient conflict that characterizes the relationship among many of the newly emerged states, whether in Southeast Asia, south Asia, Latin America, or Africa.

In view of these several considerations, it is not surprising that pragmatic rather than doctrinaire considerations dominate China's military thinking.

Chinese doctrine is based on four realistic and shrewd assessments—

(1) Of China s military capabilities and vulnerabilities;
(2) Of U.S. military capabilities and intentions;
(3) Of the extent of the assistance and support that China can expect—or not expect—from the Soviet Union; and
(4) Of the opportunities for exploiting China's limited military power at low risk.

Despite charges that the Chinese minimize the destructiveness of nuclear weapons, for well over a decade Chinese military literature has acknowledged the destructiveness of nuclear weapons and recognized the key implications of nuclear weapons for modern military operations and strategic concepts.

China's military leaders apparently believe that if war should occur, it might well take the form of a surprise nuclear attack against the mainland.

China's military leaders appear to be particularly aware of the danger of a strategic surprise attack for a country with no strategic or retaliatory capability of its own.

They have acknowledged the vulnerability of their military targets, industrial complexes, and communications centers to destruction by nuclear attack.

Furthermore, in admitting that the effectiveness of their defense against a surprise attack is the key to their effectiveness in the next phase of the war, the Chinese have come close to acknowledging the decisiveness of the initial phase of a nuclear war.

However, their image of a future war is sketchy. Because they have little alternative, China's military leaders have on a number of occasions evoked the image of a protracted war on China's soil requiring large conventional forces in which space is traded for time.

In brief, Chinese thinking concerning a nuclear war with the United States has been and remains, despite the detonation of six nuclear devices, entirely defensive.

However, despite their admissions of technological-military inferiority to the United States, the Chinese continue to emphasize the important asset they possess in their capability for ground combat.

China's military leadership clearly considers the capability for ground combat as a deterrent to invasion. They probably do not see these forces as enabling them to engage in prolonged high-level actions that would require extensive logistic support and involve high risk of U.S. counteraction.

Rather, they probably view them as an instrument—political as well as military—that can be used to intimidate weak neighbors such as Burma, Cambodia, and Nepal, and to influence certain crisis situations by threatening ground intervention, as forces in being that can be used in limited types of operations—the Sino-Indian border—and as a readymade labor and supply organization that can be employed covertly in support of Communist-inspired uprisings in contiguous areas.

China's recognition of the implications of nuclear warfare, of her vulnerability to nuclear attack, of her military-technological inferiority to the United States, and of her inability to count on Soviet military backing in support of her external objectives is strongly reflected in Peking's intention to avoid any military initiatives that might lead to a direct confrontation with U.S. forces, conventional or nuclear.

This does not mean that in the course of an evolving crisis situation China may not believe her vital interests, in particular her own security or the preservation of neighboring Communist regimes, as for example in the case of Korea, so directly affected that she will avoid a confrontation with the United States at any cost.

Nor does it rule out a possible miscalculation of U.S. intentions under similar circumstances. It does mean that where the initiative remains with Peking, China's preferred strategy will be a low risk one.

There has been considerable concern about the possibility of a massive Chinese ground intervention in Vietnam when in fact China's policy toward Vietnam since the Tonkin Gulf incident in August 1964 has been one of very low risk, increasing caution, and a growing generalization of her commitment in the area.

Close analysis of Chinese statements since mid-1964 suggests that the pace and level of military operations in South Vietnam are being set not by Peking but by Hanoi; that the Chinese, despite their continued opposition to any negotiations, would prefer to see a moderation in the pace and level of military operations because of the possibility of further escalation on the U.S. side (in fact, in the course of 1965 after the initiation by the United States of the bombing of North Vietnam, the Chinese were genuinely concerned about the possible spillover of the bombing from North Vietnam to the mainland—a concern that was revived to some degree in August of this year when the United States initiated attacks within 10 miles of the Chinese border); that the Chinese are not likely to go out of their way to intervene in Vietnam and thus face the possibility of a direct confrontation with the United States; and that much of what the Chinese have to say publicly is geared to their competition with the Soviet Union for Hanoi's loyalty and to their desire to impress American public opinion.

As indicated earlier, this does not mean that situations could not arise where the Chinese believed their national interests so threatened that they would forgo the use of military power.

The Chinese clearly could not tolerate U.S. action that directly threatened the security of China or a persistent pattern of U.S. actions which changed their perception of U.S. strategic intentions toward China.

Nor could the Chinese probably permit a substantial threat to the preservation of the North Vietnamese regime.

I have gone into this detail on China's past and present military doctrine and strategy, because it is only against this background that we can consider the uses to which the Chinese are likely to put their emerging nuclear missile capability.

The Chinese have demonstrated a high level of technological-scientific knowledge and skill in detonating six nuclear devices, including a thermonuclear device in the megaton range and the testing of a missile with a nuclear warhead.

As to delivery vehicles, so far as offensive delivery systems are concerned, the Chinese have probably decided to give priority to the development of a missile capability and to downgrade the development of an advanced aircraft delivery capability.

The provision by the Soviets of short-range missiles in the 1958–59 period and the prestige associated with missile development no doubt provided the basis for China's thrust in this direction.

There have also been reports that China is constructing a Soviet-type G–2 class submarine, that is, conventionally powered and capable of firing three missiles with a range of about 400 miles.

At the moment, however, it is still difficult to determine whether the Chinese will give priority to an intercontinental missile capability or concentrate on an operational regional capability.

For a number of political and military reasons, the latter appears the more likely. There is little doubt that at some point the Chinese will choose to test an ICBM.

That the test firing of an ICBM or even any token capability to threaten the U.S.Z.I. will have important political and prestige payoffs goes without saying.

However, we cannot rule out the possibility that because of political and technological considerations the Chinese will opt to launch a satellite before testing an ICBM.

The launching of a satellite would emphasize the peaceful, not military, uses of China's missile development. It could not be interpreted or condemned as a military threat.

A scientific and technological space feat of this order would have the advantage of proving to the rest of Asia that despite the chaos and turmoil that have characterized the mainland of China during the past 2 years in the course of the great proletarian cultural revolution, Communist China retains the economic, educational, scientific, and technological base prerequisite to great power status.

To what extent the Chinese will give priority to the deployment of an ICBM system as against a MRBM capability is again an open question.

To a considerable degree the value to the Chinese of an ICBM system as an instrument for crisis management and aggrandizement in the Asian theater represents an ambitious and dangerous use of such a capability, the success of which can be questioned on various grounds.

It could well make the achievement of China's regional objectives more difficult.

Thus, for a number of reasons, the Chinese may attach higher value and priority to securing a theater missile capability than an intercontinental missile operational capability.

The Chinese may well see more concrete political-military gains emerging from the "hostage" type threat a theater missile capability would give them against non-Communist countries as well as against U.S. bases in the western Pacific.

As a deterrent to U.S. conventional intervention or escalation to the nuclear level, a regional Chinese retaliatory capability—against U.S. forces in Asia and against U.S. allies—may appear to the Chinese far more credible and hence more useful than an intercontinental threat to the U.S.Z.I. whose use or threat of use would only invite overwhelming U.S. retaliation.

While it is impossible to predict with any degree of certainty the long-term future, there are no indications to date that when China is in possession of a nuclear delivery capability, whether regional or intercontinental, she will be more prepared than at present to engage in a high-risk military policy.

So long as China is not certain of Soviet military support for her objectives, and provided the United States remains prepared to make the risks of overt Chinese military operations extremely high, the Chinese—whatever type of leadership emerges over the next few years—are likely to continue to avoid military initiatives that might invite massive U.S. nuclear retaliatory strikes against the mainland.

Rather in accordance with Peking's preferred foreign policy style, the Chinese are likely to make a new low-risk and subtle use of their nuclear delivery capability along political-military and propaganda lines with a view to achieving inter alia the following objectives:

1. The enhancement of China's international political stature;
2. The imposition of restraints on U.S. military policies in the area and the undermining of the United States-Asian alliance and base system;
3. The inhibition of Asian nations self-defense efforts; and
4. The fostering of internal instability and national liberation movements in the area.

The play that Peking has accorded its several nuclear detonations, in particular its insistence that the nuclear powers reach agreement on the no first use of nuclear weapons, reaffirms the importance China accords to placing restraints on U.S. military policies in the Far East with a view to limiting U.S. freedom to use nuclear weapons or to threaten the use of nuclear weapons to deter Chinese political-military initiatives.

It is interesting to note that in its reaction to Secretary of Defense McNamara's announcement of the U.S. decision to build an anti-ballistic missile system against China, Peking reiterated its position, first enunciated in October 1964, that "in no circumstances will China be the first to use such weapons."

The U.S. decision was stated to be "an important step * * * taken by the U.S. imperialists to continue with their nuclear blackmail and nuclear threat against China after the U.S.-Soviet nuclear monopoly was shattered by the development of China's defensive nuclear weapons; at the same time, it is another anti-China measure adopted to intensify the administration's collusion with the Soviet revisionist leading clique."

A "hostage" type theater capability would enable the Chinese to claim—with what plausability is another matter—that the U.S. nuclear deterrent was canceled out or neutralized and that her superior conventional forces tilted the regional balance of military power in her favor.

In any event, Peking would hope thereby to exploit Asian fear of involvement in a nuclear war, Asian anxiety that the hosting of U.S. bases would attract a nuclear strike, and concern that any U.S. confrontation with a nuclear-armed China would escalate into nuclear if not general war.

Peking would hope to encourage U.S. allies—

(1) To question the reliability and desirability of U.S. security arrangements;

(2) To impose restraints on U.S. military policies in the area by attempts to reinterpret or modify the terms of the alliance and by restricting the use of American bases or extracting from the United States a greater return for the use of such bases;

(3) To pressure the United States to avoid a confrontation with China at any level; and

(4) To seek to persuade the United States to seek some rapprochement with China, if necessary, on Chinese terms.

As noted earlier, the Chinese continue to emphasize the role of their conventional ground forces. The Chinese, in the little they have had to say about arms control arrangements, have avoided any reference to the reduction of conventional forces, specifically ruling out arrangements that might include such forces.

In fact, the position that the Chinese have taken on the no-first use of nuclear weapons suggests that China may see in the possession of a nuclear capability a means of enhancing the role of their conventional forces.

The Chinese may believe that the threat of China's conventional involvement under a nuclear umbrella may make the United States reluctant to intervene in local crisis situations for fear either of ground confrontation with the Chinese or escalation to the nuclear level.

Equally, if not more important, the Chinese may calculate that fear of escalation would lead Asian nations to assert pressures on the United States to avoid any confrontation with China—conventional or nuclear.

However, in her use of a nuclear capability, China's efforts will have to be carefully balanced. A too militant effort would be likely to invite adverse reactions in the form of instigating U.S. allies in Asia to strengthen their security ties with the United States and encouraging Asian neutrals to seek nuclear guarantees from either or both the United States and the Soviet Union.

Or undue Chinese bellicosity might encourage Asian nations, capable of doing so, to develop their own nuclear weapons.

In sum, provided the United States keeps high for the Chinese the risks of overt aggression, past and current Chinese military doctrine and policies argue against China's adoption of incautious military initiatives at a time she acquires a nuclear delivery capability whether of an intercontinental or regional character.

The probability is low that there will be any major change in Peking's military doctrine or style of risk-taking in military policy as a result of acquiring operational nuclear capabilities.

A nuclear-armed China is likely to find ample opportunity to advance toward her long-term objectives of great power status and hegemony in Asia through reliance on low-risk political-military and propaganda uses of force, and the exploitation of the political and economic instability that characterizes most of the underdeveloped areas of the region.

However, I do not mean to minimize the challenge China is likely to pose to the United States in the future.

Because the challenge and problems will not be clear-cut military ones, adequate responses to them on the part of the United States are likely to be difficult, particularly insofar as U.S. relations with its Asian allies and Asian neutrals are concerned.

To the extent a nuclear-armed Peking succeeds in imposing greater restraints on U.S. military policies in the area, in undermining the United States-Asian alliance and base system, in inhibiting Asian military cooperation with the United States, and in fostering internal instability and revolutionary movements in the area, China may be able to make effective U.S. responses to her military actions more difficult.

Thereby, Peking will increase somewhat the range of military options open to it; military initiatives once regarded as unacceptably risky may then be considered viable courses of action.

But the increased room for maneuver this foreshadows should stop well short of reckless Chinese behavior which accepts the risk of uncontrollable escalation to all-out war with the United States.

Thank you.

Senator JACKSON. We are grateful to you, Mrs. Hsieh, for an excellent presentation and helpful interpretation of the Communist Chinese approach on military issues. I am particularly intrigued by your discussion of whether the Chinese nuclear program will, at the start, emphasize IRBM's or ICBM's, and the chance you see that the Chinese may move to submarine-launched missiles.

How would you interpret the political significance of a Red Chinese decision to emphasize IRBM's? You dealt with this in part in your statement.

Mrs. HSIEH. It would be my evaluation that they would get far more political-military mileage from the development of an IRBM system, a medium-range ballistic missile capability, in terms of their objective in the area. If they emphasize this type of capability rather than making a major thrust in the direction of ICBM's they could use this regional capability to exert subtle political influences on allies in the area so that our allies will put pressure on the United States to limit our military responses in the area. This is an indirect use of a capability.

Senator JACKSON. In other words, they could use it indirectly against our base structure in the Far East by blackmailing our allies with whom we make such arrangements.

Mrs. HSIEH. Yes.

Senator JACKSON. Would there be any basis for an interpretation, in the event they deploy IRBM's, that this was also to deter the Soviet Union?

Mrs. HSIEH. I would not want to rule this out. One thing we have overlooked is that the Soviet homeland is going to become a target of the Chinese nuclear delivery capability long before the United States homeland does, that is, the target of a medium-range or intermediate-range ballistic missile capability. I think it would be an interesting question to watch the deployment of the ABM system in the Soviet Union as well as to watch the evolution of Chinese deployment of SA-2's. In time, we may get information on this score.

Senator JACKSON. It might have some bearing as to what is going on ideologically in the respective countries.

Mrs. HSIEH. Yes.

Senator JACKSON. Let me just follow through on this point. I would like to have your comment on Professor Mosely's reference to the possibility in the foreseeable future, looking ahead, of a regime in Communist China that would be friendlier to the Soviet Union and more cooperative with Moscow.

Mrs. HSIEH. I would like to preface my remarks first by saying that this is speculation, of course, but my own feeling is that over the next 2 to 5 years we are likely to see a more—I hate to use the word "pragmatic" but it is the one that seems best to describe the type of non-Maoist leadership in China. I would say there seems to be in the cards a more pragmatic, sober, responsible leadership, perhaps concentrating more on internal development than on ideological issues.

I would then say that this type of evolution in China offers opportunities to both the Soviet Union and to the United States. It is very possible that the Soviet Union is sitting back at this moment waiting the situation out in China despite the besieging of their Peking Embassy and the attacks in Moscow and that there is a good likelihood of a limited rapprochement between Peking and Moscow at some later date.

I do not see this, however, as any restoration of the monolithic type of situation which never really did exist at all. I think we might see increased Soviet economic assistance and military assistance, particularly in terms of defensive weapons, to China. But I have rather grave doubts whether the Soviet Union, unless they have reached such a point of strategic superiority toward the United States, would be any more willing at that time to back China's external objectives in the Far East than they were, let us say, at the time of the Quemoy incident in 1958.

Senator JACKSON. In other words, during this period you would see the Soviets being rather leery of new adventures on the part of the Chinese outside their borders.

Mrs. HSIEH. They would want the war to be of their own timing and choosing and not of the timing and choosing of Peking.

On the Chinese side I see some difficulties in this restoration of a very tight relationship because the Chinese have never been overly enthusiastic; in fact, they refused to subordinate their military establishment to that of the Soviet Union. This goes back to the period of 1959 when they accused the Soviet Union at an earlier date of demanding unreasonable control over the Chinese Military Establishment. Limited arrangements, assistance, but I cannot see the close monolithic type of military arrangement.

At the same time, I would like to add, though, that this new type of situation offers opportunities also to the United States that we might want to keep in mind. A time might come when some type of limited relationship between ourselves and the Chinese might be possible with a new pragmatic regime.

Senator JACKSON. Would this be a time when we might consider recognition?

Mrs. HSIEH. It would depend on some extent, we might at that time want to consider recognition. A good deal, of course, would depend on whether the Chinese were willing to live with perhaps an independent Taiwan regime, whether they would be willing to overlook this fact. But a more pragmatic inner looking regime might be willing to. In any event, they might perhaps be less hostile to the United States.

Senator JACKSON. When the various Communist Parties meet during this period, what will be the ideological situation so far as the attitude of Communist China toward leadership of the Soviet Union?

Mrs. HSIEH. I am not sure if the ideological considerations are likely to be the major ones. I would say each party will be increasingly looking toward its own national self-interest.

Senator JACKSON. Would there be the same kind of vituperation and bitterness on the part of the Chinese toward the Soviets that has been evident now since 1959? Would this continue?

Mrs. HSIEH. In a new situation I would say this would probably be downgraded.

Senator JACKSON. But they would not be willing to agree to the dominance of the Soviet Union worldwide so far as Communist policy is concerned?

Mrs. HSIEH. There might be a papering over, perhaps, of this type of question at that time.

Senator JACKSON. It would be a fuzzy period.

Mrs. HSIEH. It would be a fuzzy period; yes.

Senator JACKSON. I wonder if you could comment on or give us an interpretation of the political significance of a Red Chinese decision to build missile-carrying submarines.

Mrs. HSIEH. I have only seen one indication of this. I think this again is in terms of prestige, international stature, the possibility that they would be in a position to attack the U.S. homeland, giving them the prestige of this. I do not see them, however, making a reckless use of this capability. I emphasize this because there have been a number of scenarios devised recently which emphasize recklessness and miscalculation on the part of the Chinese. All of these add up to one thing, that the Chinese are prepared to commit suicide.

In my analysis in the years I have studied Chinese military policy I have seen no suicidal tendencies on their part. There exists the strong deployment of nuclear weapons that we maintain in the Western Pacific—the Polaris, to be followed eventually by the Poseidon, the sea-based aircraft of the 7th Fleet, and the land-based aircraft. With these weapons we have the capability of completely devastating the mainland of Communist China. I think it is important, very important, that we maintain this capability in the Western Pacific because it is this capability that keeps the risk to the Chinese of any overt military activity on their part extremely high. They are very well aware of what this means to them. They are very sensitive to our deployment in the Western Pacific.

Senator JACKSON. Now if the Chinese go the intermediate range ballistic missile route, where does that leave our ABM thin defense program, which is designed to deal with the ICBM threat from Red China? I really have been fascinated by your observations about the IRBM program. It makes a lot of sense to me. I am now trying to carry it the next step.

Mrs. HSIEH. I am quite willing to carry it the next step. I don't think the U.S. deployment of a light ABM system against this hypothetical Chinese attack is going to make any basic difference to China's military strategy, whether they have either an intermediate range ballistic missile or a modest intercontinental missile capability. I think it could possibly further underline their thrust in the direction of a medium-range ballistic missile capability. This is one that would cover the U.S. bases in the area, Japan, Korea, Philippines, Southeast Asia, possibly South Asia.

I would say that in making this decision we have given considerable credibility to a threat that has not yet even been tested. In fact the Chinese are going to have in the future considerable difficulty in making credible their deployment of either a medium-range ballistic missile capability or an ICBM capability. It is not so easy to do.

Again I would like to add that the decision has had some unfavorable effect in areas of the Far East, particularly in Japan. The Japanese Government has been diplomatic enough to say that this does mean a plus in the U.S. deterrent posture but foreign ministry spokesmen have asked will this give rise to further discussions in Japan about the difference between defensive and offensive nuclear weapons. One of the most popular journals in Japan, Asaki, has indicated this is going to give rise to further and new discussions on the desirability of deploying a regional ABM system in the area. One of the newspaper commentators has suggested that rather than instilling Japan with confidence in the U.S.'s deterrent posture this could possibly leave the Japanese in a position of doubting the credibility of the U.S. commitment: that the United States might only act if the U.S. homeland were threatened; that this would then mean that Japan will have to review the question of the development of a regional ABM system, preferably in conjunction with the United States. He added Japan may also have to review the whole question of nuclear weapons. This has very important implications for the nonproliferation of nuclear weapons treaty.

Senator JACKSON. That is all very interesting.

Dr. Wolfe, I have one question that I want to ask. I found of particular importance your discussion of the Soviet offensive buildup. Would you discuss this trend and also explain further the Soviet defensive buildup?

Incidentally, if you have any comments on Mrs. Hsieh's remarks or on any views that have been made here—and I say the same to Dr. Mosely—I think they will be very helpful for the record.

As I see it, Mr. Khrushchev has not been criticized for putting missiles in Cuba in 1962. He has been criticized, however, for having failed in his enterprise—for biting off more than he could chew. I am interested in getting your further comments on the growing buildup of the Soviet offensive ICBM capability.

Dr. WOLFE. Mr. Chairman, I would suppose that after the Cuban experience there was a period of very serious, if we can call it, agonizing reappraisal, within the Soviet leadership, even before Khrushchev was removed from power. If one looks at the programs which have materialized in the period since Cuba it is obvious that many of the decisions relating to these programs were taken while Krushchev was still on the scene. So I would feel that there probably was a kind of consensus within the Soviet leadership along the following lines: The Soviet Union simply cannot make its way in a world where it suffers the kind of imbalance which was so graphically demonstrated in the Cuban experience; if the Soviet Union is going to prosper abroad, to pursue the kind of foreign policies it sees necessary, something has to be done about the strategic situation. The decision must have been at that time to commit fairly substantial resources to this enterprise, resources upon which there were many important demands from other sectors of the Soviet economy. One might also say that the new regime itself became committed at the outset to important programs of economic improvement, and restoration of the declining rate of economic growth, so that the strategic decisions were hard ones to take in the light of the regime's own internal priorities as well.

I think it likely that the change in the situation in Southeast Asia from 1965 on also helped create a climate in which strengthening of the Soviet strategic posture seemed desirable. Successive, sequential decisions by the Soviet leadership indicate that it has moved steadily in the direction of bolstering its strategic posture.

As both Dr. Mosely and I pointed out, the Soviet attention to its military position has been part of a larger process than just worrying about ICBM or strategic forces alone. One must ask the fundamental question that I think Mr. Anderson did ask a little earlier: Why does the Soviet Union feel impelled to make commitments of its resources in this direction? The explanation that they are insecure in the face of our own posture in the world only goes part way, I believe, to explain what lies behind the Soviet drive.

I would be inclined to look at this question within the context of certain broad trends of the whole postwar period. The Soviet Union is improving its military posture, both strategic offensive and defensive forces and its military "reach" with conventional forces. It is doing so in a world that it also shares with the United States. What the United States does or may not do has enormous impact on Soviet policy-making. It is a fact, I think, that at this particular stage of the postwar period, some two decades after the end of the last war, the United States is showing a growing restlessness with its involvement in the outer world, there is a certain inward turning at this time.

It is worth recalling that after the last war the Soviet Union had some reason to expect that with Western Europe weakening, with the colonial world dissolving, that for the next decade there was great prospect for Communist advancement. As it turned out, although the Soviet Union made advances in Eastern Europe, significant ones, it gained no ground in Western Europe and it did not successfully exploit the dissolution of the colonial world, partly because the forces of nationalism were difficult to cope with but also partly because the policy of the United States in both Europe and the "third world" helped prevent the Soviet Union either from drawing the older weakened states, or the wobbly new ones, into the Communist orbit.

Now if some two decades later the Soviet leaders look out on the world and see the United States in a phase of inward turning or, if you will, in a sense abrogating the containment role it has maintained in the last two decades, at a time when Soviet capacities to intervene globally are increasing, the questions that are then posed, and very important ones it seems to me, are something like this: Does the Soviet Union see a prospect of moving into the areas that may become vacuums, as it were, created by retrenchment of American commitments? Is this a part of the explanation for Soviet interest in providing itself with options to operate more effectively in the world at large? Or one can pose a somewhat different question: Are the non-Communist states now strong enough, do they have enough sense of unity to make their own way largely without the kind of American support they have had in the past? If this is the case, then the prospects before the Soviet leaders of converting their improved military posture to political use appear in a different light.

To conclude, I think one might say that the Soviet leadership has a problem somewhat analogous to that of other leaderships: How in the nuclear missile age do you manage to convert military power, however imposing it may be, into useful political dividends? I think the Soviet leadership is going through a process of trying to learn how one does this just as other leaderships have been doing the same thing.

Senator JACKSON. Thank you, Dr. Wolfe, for your very able comment. I have a feeling that Dr. Mosely might like to make a comment or two with reference to Dr. Wolfe's comments, or Mrs. Hsieh's comments, or both.

Dr. MOSELY. Mr. Chairman, we have not consulted at all and we have arrived at very much the same points right down the line. That makes me more confident because I have followed the work of both these distinguished experts for a good many years.

The Soviet Union's programs, which they began during and right after World War II, are coming to fruition: the increase of nuclear strategic power, the versatility in the space program, the ability to try to influence the developments in the developing countries. They are learning from their mistakes as well as from a few successes. So for them this next decade is going to be one of considerable optimism that they can use the strategic power and their growing economic strength to achieve the goal of expanding their system.

I did not give a full answer to Congressman Anderson's very important question about why the Soviet leadership maintains this attitude in favor of expansionism. One reason is because of the way in which they choose their people for future leadership, passing them through ideological training, always reeducating them at each level as they rise up in the system, so that they are able to insure a firm ideological cohesion in the leading group. This is an attitude quite different from that of the mass of the people. The mass of the people think, as I explained earlier, in terms of "Well, it is great to be so strong that we are now assured of defense, of being one of two great powers in the world."

In order to rise to leadership future Soviet officials and leaders go through a system of party schools, party indoctrination, and this is how they maintain the dynamism of this ideocracy. "Ideocracy" means that the claim to rule is based on possession of and ability to apply a specific set of ideological ideas. Other systems rest on quite different systems of legitimate rule. In the free countries it is through free elections, the competition of parties, clashes of opinions of individuals and groups, all the other freedoms we take for granted. In the case of monarchy the claim to rule is based on the divine right of birth, and so on. Ideocracy is a new type of system in which the people who rule claim the right to rule and tell every man how to think and what to do on the grounds that they alone have a monopoly on the correct way of thinking. This belief remains strong in the Soviet leadership. This is the basis of their inner cohesion and it also leads them to make many blunders because they put on these ideological blinders and they proceed to assume that other countries and regimes in power are behaving the way they are supposed to behave, according to the Communist analysis, whether they do behave that way or not.

When outside nations don't behave in that predicted way, as happened in the Cuban missile crisis, for example, then they are up against it. They have no alternative lines of policy they have discussed as fallback positions because their rigid way of thinking leads them to screen out the other alternatives. Similarly, last June either the Soviet calculation was wrong regarding the crisis that was building up in the Near East or else they held a set of assumptions about the outside world that were completely inaccurate. So, they suffered a very serious loss of influence and prestige as a result of that crisis.

The only way we can understand how they arrived at those predictions and therefore the measures that they recommended and took is that they were simply excluding a truly objective or empirical analysis of the situation. That is part of the danger. The risk is not that they will decide that today is the day to spread communism throughout the world, but that they will make mistakes here, there, and other places, and the non-Communist powers have to build up the opposing force, a picture of the risks they will be running, to big billboard size so that they will see it, because they do not have a very subtle and informed way of analyzing the outside world.

Senator JACKSON. Thank you, Dr. Mosely.

I have many questions but I will turn now to my colleague, Mr. Holifield.

Representative HOLIFIELD. No questions.

Senator JACKSON. Congressman Bates.

Representative BATES. No questions.

Senator JACKSON. Congressman Anderson.

Representative ANDERSON. I have one question that I would like to ask Dr. Wolfe. We had testimony at the hearing yesterday from Dr. Foster, Director of Defense Research and Engineering, to the effect that the Soviet ABM system is a mistake and it is something that is doomed to be defeated.

Now do you think, Dr. Wolfe, that the Soviets believe that? Would they go ahead and allocate all of their resources, which are certainly limited, to an ABM system just to impress us if it did not possess some credibility for them, if they didn't believe themselves that it would work? Would they do it just to impress the United States?

The same question that Mr. Bates asked, you could ask the identical question with reference to fractional orbital bombardment systems.

Dr. WOLFE. With respect to surmising how the Soviets view the ABM system, there is a tendency, I suppose, to construct a rational model and then to try to fit the way people behave with the calculus of rationality. To some extent, out of our own experience we all know that we do not always act and perform according to this pure rational model, either in international politics or in defense or in our personal lives.

Now, if one were to look at some of the things that the Soviet Union has done in the past, particularly in the area of the strategic defense of the Soviet Union, one would find that Soviet behavior has not always conformed very well to criteria of rationality and optimum effectiveness.

Let me be explicit. During the long period when the Soviet Union was trying to construct strategic defenses against primarily the manned bomber threat from the United States, the Soviet Union devoted very large resources to building fighter aircraft and to maintaining a large conventional AA capability. At that time a strictly rational analysis of the threat would have shown that the kind of aircraft they had were day fighters not very capable of intercepting U.S. bombers which had moved on to a level of technical-operational capability where the threat was from high levels under all-weather conditions. The kind of fighters the Soviets had, the kind of AA they had at this time and into which they were putting their resources were not really meeting this threat in an adequate way. Nevertheless, they went on and did devote a lot of resources to them. Now, you can ask why?

I think the answer to this is complex. Partly it is a matter of bureaucratic interplay within the Soviet decisionmaking apparatus. Partly it is a matter of historical momentum. There is also the inevitable lag time in catching up with offensive developments. All these factors entered the picture. But certainly the Soviets must have been persuaded that from their point of view it was worth while making these efforts.

Now I do not want to infer that history necessarily repeats itself, but there is something of the same flavor to the way the Soviets have attacked the problem of trying to catch up with the offense in respect to ABM. Now, it may well be demonstrable, and I believe it is, on the basis of the kinds of analysis one can make of systems with their current capabilities, that the Soviets probably cannot expect to get great military dividends from the kind of ABM system they have today. However, I think the demonstration also could be made that under some circumstances in the future, given improvements in the state of the art, given a certain attitude by the United States itself toward its programs, the Soviet military planners might expect to do better. Specifically, they might persuade themselves that an effective combination of offensive and defensive forces under the circumstances that I pointed out, where the first strike would come from the Soviet side against our deployed defenses, might so reduce the weight of the counterblow, the retaliatory force that we could expect to mount, as to make it feasible in military terms for an ABM system to deal with the residual strikes. Those would be strikes from surviving fixed ICBM sites and from our seaborne forces.

Under some circumstances not all those forces would be in a position to react quickly, so that Soviet planners might have some expectation of being able to cope with them, if the Soviet Union makes the requisite effort.

I also indicated, and I emphasize again, that I doubt very much whether the Soviet military planners are in a position to make a very convincing case to the political leadership that the scenario can be so constructed that if the Soviet Union were to strike first it could expect to emerge with some level of acceptable damage in return.

I don't see in the immediate future any prospect that the Soviet Union will be in a position to do this. Nevertheless, we are facing the fact that the Soviet Union is making these efforts.

To turn to the fractional orbital question for just one moment, I think many of the same considerations probably apply here. Why would the Soviet Union go in this direction? One of the military reasons, on which I would agree with Dr. Foster yesterday, and the most logical and rational one that emerges from an examination of the situation, is that the Soviet Union was hoping to devise a backdoor capability to evade our ballistic missile detection systems in order to threaten soft-type targets. Our bomber system is a soft target. There are others that might also be attractive as a soft system. I would suppose, however, that this probably does not exhaust the reasons for Soviet interest evidenced in developing either an orbital or a fractional orbital system. Incidentally, I think it is premature, in a sense, to predict that this is necessarily going to be a fractional system, as distinct from a suborbital or eventually an orbital system. Certainly it can turn out to be any of these three.

Militarily, one can say that there are some other reasons why the Soviets might be attracted in this direction. These are purely speculative comments. For example, on military grounds one might speculate that the Soviet Union is looking at a situation at the outbreak of war in which they would expect U.S. counterforce strikes to take out most of the terrestrial-based Soviet delivery forces. In such a case, it might make sense to the Soviets to put aloft an orbital system during some period of crisis. The system would be ambiguous, for we would not necessarily know that it even had nuclear weapons aboard, hence our action against it might be hesitant. If the crisis then led to hostilities in which the United States took out most of the Soviet Union's terrestrial forces with counterforce blows, the Soviet Union would still have a residual destruction capability against the United States, deployed in space.

In other words, they would not be disarmed in a situation like this. This is one possible military use one might imagine the Soviet planners could be thinking about.

Now there are some other uses that are not so directly military. One would be to give a demonstration in some crisis of Soviet determination. Certainly this would complicate the U.S. position. If a relatively small force of these vehicles were put in orbit, they still could be ambiguous, for we would not know whether they were armed or not. What would be our threshold of toleration? How many of these things would we tolerate in orbit before we decided to act and, more specifically, how would we act in a crisis situation?

So, some calculation of use of this force under these circumstances might enter the Soviet motivation. I think there is also the point to be remembered that the Soviet Union has put great store on technological firsts, especially in space. It was the first sputnik which really dispelled the image of a technologically backward Russia and made the United States and the rest of the world conscious that the Soviet Union was really a serious competitor with the United States in military-technological strength.

Now, to build an image of a technologically advanced country which possesses novel weapons of a kind that not even the great United States has, this is a value which might—well, we might dismiss it ourselves and not feel it is necessary, but it might very well appeal to Soviet planners.

I think I have labored some of these points longer than I have a right to. Thank you.

Senator JACKSON. Thank you, Dr. Wolfe.

Representative BATES. Mr. Chairman, I would just like to say that we find ourselves in a position rather hard put to understand some of the very basic decisions that have been made.

Dr. Wolfe, you have indicated, first in the case of the fighter, then the question of large megatonnage versus the smaller megatonnage, the role that we took. Now we find it in ABM. Now we find it in FOBS. This is a tremendous effort on the part of the Soviets and a great strain on their economy but still they are going down these roads. We don't clearly understand why they are doing it. Logic seems to suggest, and military reasoning seems to suggest, an opposite course. Now they have been pretty effective in other respects in regard to technological advancements. So we don't find ourselves in a too-comfortable position when they take these opposite roads from the ones we are taking. Although I appreciate the efforts which Dr. Wolfe just made, the fact still remains that they are going to very unusual lengths, indeed, spending vast amounts of money on systems which we have discarded.

Dr. WOLFE. Those are the facts, so far as they speak for themselves, I would agree with you that many people have asked these questions. It certainly does not follow that all these decisions the Soviets have made are necessarily good ones. I would be inclined to agree with those who say that the Soviets have made poor use of their resources in many cases. On the other hand, I am also wary of fashioning our own response and also shaping our appreciation of what makes the Soviets tick solely in terms of the kind of rational model analysis to which I alluded in the first place. There are broader questions that arise.

It may well be that we need to understand better than we do what motivates decisions of these kinds in the Soviet case in order hopefully to be able to influence them in directions that are useful to us. For example, if the Soviets are going to spend a certain portion of their national product on defense anyway and if we—by what we do and by what our declaratory policies and our posture communicates to them—can influence the use of those Soviet resources in one direction rather than another, then this might be a good thing. To be specific, it might be useful to encourage the Russians to put more of their resources into the kind of weapon systems that pose the least threat to us. On the surface at least—although this gets more complicated as you develop a deeper analysis of it—on the surface it seems that it might be preferable to encourage the Soviets to use their resources in a defensive system rather than building offensive force which can attack us.

Senator JACKSON. I think this is one of the arguments in favor of an intercontinental bomber with supersonic speed which can come in on the deck. Obviously this would force the Soviets to invest a large part of their resources in order to provide an adequate defense. I have always advocated that one of the values of going ahead with a manned bomber system was that it would require them to invest in that way. Is there any merit in that, Dr. Wolfe?

Dr. WOLFE. Yes; in my view there is.

Senator JACKSON. We need a bomber system, but its impact in the way of a reaction on their part could be pretty well predicted, based on what they have done in the past.

Dr. WOLFE. My caveat here would be that it is obviously difficult to fashion one's own security programs in terms of criteria of how you want the other fellow to react. There is a limit beyond which you do not want to go in trying to fashion your own defense posture in terms of what you expect the impact to be on the other party. You may want to look first to your needs in terms of your needs as you see them.

My last word is that I do agree with your statement, Mr. Chairman, and I am sympathetic to a point, but I am not overoptimistic about our capability to manipulate the Soviet responses beyond a certain point.

Representative BATES. Mr. Chairman, the point I was trying to establish was this: In reference to these four roads that the Soviets took with respect to the fighter defense we did, of course, follow the same road, ourselves. Secondly, as far as the large megatonnage is concerned, the United States has not had sufficient tests to be absolutely certain of the effectiveness or the unusual characteristics of large megatonnage.

Thirdly, we are embarked on an ABM program and our R. & D. goes far beyond the thin defense against the Chinese threat, which also indicates our uncertainty because we are spending a large amount of money in R. & D. in that area. And, fourthly, we investigated FOBS although we discarded it. So it is not entirely clear in my mind that we are sure about the road to take and whether what the Soviet have in fact done is wrong in that respect.

Dr. WOLFE. Yes; I would agree with you that there are unanswered questions here and that we are all fallible so far as seeing well into the future goes, and that some of the decisions the Soviets have taken which look irrational in terms of our model today may turn out to be somewhat more productive.

One could even say in the case we have been talking about, although I am sure they did not foresee it, that it was fortuitous from the Soviet point of view that they maintained the interest they did in conventional AA artillery through long periods of time because it turned out that in a particular situation, that which has developed in North Vietnam, it has been very useful for the Soviet Union to have large stocks of AA artillery to be able to furnish to their client state.

If their military philosophy had been one that discarded all that equipment because it did not fit the requirements of the period we were talking about they might not have been in a position to furnish as much AA as they have. I emphasize again that this illustrates the fallibility of human foresight more than it does any uncanny foresight on the part of the Soviets.

Representative BATES. It reminds me that in 1950 in the Armed Services Committee we were told at that time we could never build a missile that could span the oceans or a bomb that would be small enough to be used for such purposes.

Dr. WOLFE. Yes. I think the conclusion——

Representative BATES. That was the scientific creed at that time.

Senator JACKSON. There is another example along about that same period. In 1949 every member of the General Advisory Committee of the Atomic Energy Commission opposed the United States going ahead with the development of the hydrogen bomb, on two grounds. One was that the Soviets certainly wouldn't go after this weapon and, secondly, what would you do with it anyway?

Representative HOLIFIELD. Mr. Chairman.

Senator JACKSON. Congressman Holifield.

Representative HOLIFIELD. On page 4, Dr. Wolfe, you mention the names of the four Russian generals and marshals. What is the background of Marshals A. A. Grechko and V. I. Chuikov?

Dr. WOLFE. Grechko, of course, is the successor to the late Marshal Malinovsky, as Soviet Minister of Defense. He is a man who has a kind of middle-of-the-road image. He was for several years the commander of the Joint Warsaw Pact Forces. He is the Soviet Union's most authoritative military spokesman at the moment. Marshal Chuikov is the incumbent head, the military head of the Russian Civil Defense Establishment. At one stage in his career he was head of the Soviet Ground Forces.

Representative HOLIFIELD. It is interesting to note then that Marshal Grechko takes about the same position that Secretary McNamara and Dr. Foster took in their presentations yesterday. It is also interesting to note that Chuikov, who is charged with the civil defense capability and is probably interested in complete protection or as good protection as is possible to obtain, also takes the position that the intercepting missiles are inadequate to do the job of protecting the Russian people adequately.

Dr. WOLFE. Yes. These contradictory views to which I have referred very briefly in this period, reflect internal differences in the Soviet Union which it was not possible to develop at length here.

There is abundant evidence that Soviet military men themselves do not all see precisely eye to eye on the relative importance and weight of offense versus defense and in their public statements, in particular, some are more wary than others of making all-inclusive claims as to the virtues of their particular systems.

One really has to look at these matters in the context in which the statements are made.

In connection with the 50th anniversary of the Soviet Union each of the prominent Soviet military leaders has had occasion to write or at least sign his name to commemorative articles.

One thing noteworthy about such articles is that each of these leaders has tended to be somewhat parochial, and it is quite natural, in stressing the virtues of his particular kind of force. Contradictions arise out of this. For example, Marshal Krylov, who is the head of the Soviet Strategic Rocket Forces, extolled the advantages of the mass use of strategic weapons, which he said could overcome defense systems.

He is thus taking a position that inherently contradicts the claims of other Soviet military leaders more associated with the active defense forces who have been claiming that these forces could, in fact, defend against missile attacks.

Representative HOLIFIELD. We have established the fact that there is a difference of opinion in the Soviet Union very similar to the difference of opinion that pertains here in the United States in regard to the degree of effectiveness of offense and defense.

Dr. WOLFE. Yes, I would say somewhat similar. I don't think it is as sharp a difference.

Representative HOLIFIELD. Could you or Mrs. Hsieh and Dr. Mosely give us your analysis of the degree of civil defense presently in the Soviet Union, and I am talking now not about offensive missiles but talking about so-called passive defense, and its relation to the degree of civil defense we have in the United States, keeping in mind the fact that at one time Secretary McNamara said that if we did deploy antiballistic missiles that we should have a parallel program of increased capability in passive defense, shelter, and so forth.

Dr. WOLFE. Do you wish me to comment?

Representative HOLIFIELD. Yes, I would like to have a comment from the three of you on that because I think that is part of the story that has not been told.

Dr. WOLFE. Since 1962 the Soviet Union has made explicit the recognition that civil defense makes a contribution to the overall strategic posture of the Soviet Union. They probably have gone further in making this kind of connection between passive civil defense and their country's overall strategic posture than we have.

A second difference is that the Soviet Union has carried out a more active program of indoctrination of its citizenry in the kinds of things you should do in a civil defense situation than we have in this country. That is partly owing to the difference in the societies.

The Soviet Union has various mass organizations which it is able to utilize for these purposes for which we have no counterparts in this country. Now the amount of exhortation that has accompanied the Soviet program through its history in itself suggests to the people who follow these things closely that probably the response of the citizenry has been less enthusiastic than the authorities would like. Otherwise there would not be such constant exhortation to get on with it, to take it more seriously and so on, but I think one can say that in this current period, and particularly since the reorganization which I mentioned of the civil defense system early this year, there has been a renewed Soviet emphasis on the importance of having a citizenry which is knowledgeable and knows how to handle itself under the various situations for which they are training.

In this respect the Soviet Union is, it seems to me, certainly in a different position than we tend to be in this country.

Representative HOLIFIELD. Dr. Mosely, do you care to comment on this point?

Dr. MOSELY. Thank you, Mr. Congressman.

The Soviet philosophy of passive defense is to prepare large numbers of local cadres and give them intensive training of up to 23 days at a time in actual practice exercises so then as cadres they can then control large masses of population in case of a crisis.

Also, there is a considerable preparation made, for instance in Moscow, through the use of the subway system which has been built deep underground like the London subway, cut through clay rather than chipped out of basaltic rock such as New York where I live, where the subway is just under the surface and it has little value as protection. In Moscow they have built it deep underground. They have very wide staircases so that as many as 20 people can go into the underground abreast at one time. They have special sections that are not in daily use, with steel doors, which would be closed off.

In other words, as far as Moscow is concerned, they have a very substantial preparation and they have prepared the cadres to organize the people who are also accustomed to being told what to do in a crisis. In that way they don't give much training to the general public but they do have several hundreds of thousands of people who have received specific and detailed training in civil defense. This certainly would in a time of crisis, in a situation of Soviet strategic equality, be an important factor psychologically in stressing their readiness to go to a higher level of risk than they have so far been willing to face.

Representative HOLIFIELD. Mrs. Hsieh.

Mrs. HSIEH. I see only occasional references in the Chinese literature about civil defense. There were a few in the late fifties and possibly early sixties. There was one time when I attributed to the militia, "the every man a soldier movement," some civil defense functions or missions. I have seen no immediate or major effort on the part of the Chinese to emphasize a civil defense capability because I do not think they envisage permitting a situation to arise where they would be subject to a nuclear attack.

As I indicated in my statement, their whole image of a future war is rather sketchy. If war should occur it is likely to take the form of an initial nuclear surprise attack, but that, then, the war would be a protracted one on Chinese soil where conventional forces would have to be engaged. Space would be traded for time. This is about all they can say at the present moment in view of their lack of a nuclear capability.

Representative HOLIFIELD. Thank you.

Senator JACKSON. Thank you, Mrs. Hsieh, Dr. Mosely, and Dr. Wolfe. We are indeed in your debt for your able presentations of your particular topic and your response to the questions that have been asked by the committee.

The Chair will state that we will stand in recess at this time until 10 a.m. tomorrow, when we will meet in executive session to hear from Mr. Richard Helms, the Director of the Central Intelligence Agency. Then tomorrow afternoon we will resume, and we will receive testimony from General Wheeler, Chairman of the Joint Chiefs of Staff.

Thank you very much.

(Whereupon, at 12:40 p.m. the committee was recessed, to reconvene at 10 a.m. Wednesday, November 8, 1967.)

APPENDIXES

Appendix 1.—Excerpt from the State of the Union Message by the President, Delivered Before a Joint Session of the Congress, January 10, 1967

". . . The Soviet Union has in the past year increased its long-range missile capabilities. It has begun to place near Moscow a limited antimissile defense. My first responsibility to our people is to assure that no nation can ever find it rational to launch a nuclear attack or to use its nuclear power as a credible threat against us or against our allies.

"I would emphasize that that is why an important link between Russia and the United States is in our common interest, in arms control and in disarmament. We have the solemn duty to slow down the arms race between us, if that is at all possible, in both conventional and nuclear weapons and defenses. I thought we were making some progress in that direction the first few months I was in office. I realize that any additional race would impose on our peoples, and on all mankind, for that matter, an additional waste of resources with no gain in security to either side.

"I expect in the days ahead to closely consult and seek the advice of the Congress about the possibilities of international agreements bearing directly upon this problem . . ."

Appendix 2.—Treaty on Principles Governing the Activities of States in the Exploration and Use of Outer Space, Including the Moon and Other Celestial Bodies, January 27, 1967

The States Parties to this Treaty,

Inspired by the great prospects opening up before mankind as a result of man's entry into outer space,

Recognizing the common interest of all mankind in the progress of the exploration and use of outer space for peaceful purposes,

Believing that the exploration and use of outer space should be carried on for the benefit of all peoples irrespective of the degree of their economic or scientific development,

Desiring to contribute to broad international co-operation in the scientific as well as the legal aspects of the exploration and use of outer space for peaceful purposes,

Believing that such co-operation will contribute to the development of mutual understanding and to the strengthening of friendly relations between States and peoples,

Recalling resolution 1962 (XVIII), entitled "Declaration of Legal Principles Governing the Activities of States in the Exploration and Use of Outer Space", which was adopted unanimously by the United Nations General Assembly on 13 December 1963,

Recalling resolution 1884 (XVIII), calling upon States to refrain from placing in orbit around the Earth any objects carrying nuclear weapons or any other kinds of weapons of mass destruction or from installing such weapons on celestial bodies, which was adopted unanimously by the United Nations General Assembly on 17 October 1963,

Taking account of United Nations General Assembly resolution 110 (II) of 3 November 1947, which condemned propaganda designed or likely to provoke or encourage any threat to the peace, breach of the peace or act of aggression, and considering that the aforementioned resolution is applicable to outer space,

Convinced that a Treaty on Principles Governing the Activities of States in the Exploration and Use of Outer Space, including the Moon and Other Celestial Bodies, will further the Purposes and Principles of the Charter of the United Nations,

Have agreed on the following:

ARTICLE I

The exploration and use of outer space, including the moon and other celestial bodies, shall be carried out for the benefit and in the interests of all countries, irrespective of their degree of economic or scientific development, and shall be the province of all mankind.

Outer space, including the moon and other celestial bodies, shall be free for exploration and use by all States without discrimination of any kind, on a basis of equality and in accordance with international law, and there shall be free access to all areas of celestial bodies.

There shall be freedom of scientific investigation in outer space, including the moon and other celestial bodies, and States shall facilitate and encourage international co-operation in such investigation.

ARTICLE II

Outer space, including the moon and other celestial bodies, is not subject to national appropriation by claim of sovereignty, by means of use or occupation, or by any other means.

ARTICLE III

States Parties to the Treaty shall carry on activities and the exploration and use of outer space, including the moon and other celestial bodies, in accordance with international law, including the Charter of the United Nations, in the interest of maintaining international peace and security and promoting international co-operation and understanding.

ARTICLE IV

States Parties to the Treaty undertake not to place in orbit around the Earth any objects carrying nuclear weapons or any other kinds of weapons of mass destruction, install such weapons on celestial bodies, or station such weapons in outer space in any other manner.

The moon and other celestial bodies shall be used by all States Parties to the Treaty exclusively for peaceful purposes. The establishment of military bases, installations and fortifications, the testing of any type of weapons and the conduct of military maneuvers on celestial bodies shall be forbidden. The use of military personnel for scientific research or for any other peaceful purposes shall not be prohibited. The use of any equipment or facility necessary for peaceful exploration of the moon and other celestial bodies shall also not be prohibited.

ARTICLE V

States Parties to the Treaty shall regard astronauts as envoys of mankind in outer space and shall render to them all possible assistance in the event of accident, distress, or emergency landing on the territory of another State Party or on the high seas. When astronauts make such a landing, they shall be safely and promptly returned to the State of registry of their space vehicle.

In carrying on activities in outer space and on celestial bodies, the astronauts of one State Party shall render all possible assistance to the astronauts of other States Parties.

States Parties to the Treaty shall immediately inform the other States Parties to the Treaty or the Secretary-General of the United Nations of any phenomena they discover in outer space, including the moon and other celestial bodies, which could constitute a danger to the life or health of astronauts.

ARTICLE VI

States Parties to the Treaty shall bear international responsibility for national activities in outer space, including the moon and other celestial bodies, whether such activities are carried on by governmental agencies or by non-governmental entities, and for assuring that national activities are carried out in conformity with the provisions set forth in the present Treaty. The activities of non-governmental entities in outer space, including the moon and other celestial bodies, shall require authorization and continuing supervision by the appropriate State

Party to the Treaty. When activities are carried on in outer space, including the moon and other celestial bodies, by an international organization, responsibility for compliance with this Treaty shall be borne both by the international organization and by the States Parties to the Treaty participating in such organization.

ARTICLE VII

Each State Party to the Treaty that launches or procures the launching of an object into outer space, including the moon and other celestial bodies, and each State Party from whose territory or facility an object is launched, is internationally liable for damage to another State Party to the Treaty or to its natural or juridical persons by such object or its component parts on the Earth, in air space or in outer space, including the moon and other celestial bodies.

ARTICLE VIII

A State Party to the Treaty on whose registry an object launched into outer space is carried shall retain jurisdiction and control over such object, and over any personnel thereof, while in outer space or on a celestial body. Ownership of objects launched into outer space, including objects landed or constructed on a celestial body, and of their component parts, is not affected by their presence in outer space or on a celestial body or by their return to the Earth. Such objects or component parts found beyond the limits of the State Party to the Treaty on whose registry they are carried shall be returned to that State Party, which shall, upon request, furnish identifying data prior to their return.

ARTICLE IX

In the exploration and use of outer space, including the moon and other celestial bodies, States Parties to the Treaty shall be guided by the principle of co-operation and mutual assistance and shall conduct all their activities in outer space, including the moon and other celestial bodies, with due regard to the corresponding interests of all other States Parties to the Treaty. States Parties to the Treaty shall pursue studies of outer space, including the moon and other celestial bodies, and conduct exploration of them so as to avoid their harmful contamination and also adverse changes in the environment of the Earth resulting from the introduction of extraterrestrial matter and, where necessary, shall adopt appropriate measures for this purpose. If a State Party to the Treaty has reason to believe that an activity or experiment planned by it or its nationals in outer space, including the moon and other celestial bodies, would cause potentially harmful interference with activities of other States Parties in the peaceful exploration and use of outer space, including the moon and other celestial bodies, it shall undertake appropriate international consultations before proceeding with any such activity or experiment. A State Party to the Treaty which has reason to believe that an activity or experiment planned by another State Party in outer space, including the moon and other celestial bodies, would cause potentially harmful interference with activities in the peaceful exploration and use of outer space, including the moon and other celestial bodies, may request consultation concerning the activity or experiment.

ARTICLE X

In order to promote international co-operation in the exploration and use of outer space, including the moon and other celestial bodies, in conformity with the purposes of this Treaty, the States Parties to the Treaty shall consider on a basis of the equality any requests by other States Parties to the Treaty to be afforded an opportunity to observe the flight of space objects launched by those States.

The nature of such an opportunity for observation and the conditions under which it could be afforded shall be determined by agreement between the States concerned.

ARTICLE XI

In order to promote international co-operation in the peaceful exploration and use of outer space, States Parties to the Treaty conducting activities in outer space, including the moon and other celestial bodies, agree to inform the Secretary-General of the United Nations as well as the public and the international scientific community, to the greatest extent feasible and practicable, of the nature, conduct, locations and results of such activities. On receiving the said information, the Secretary-General of the United Nations should be prepared to disseminate it immediately and effectively.

Article XII

All stations, installations, equipment and space vehicles on the moon and other celestial bodies shall be open to representatives of other States Parties to the Treaty on a basis of reciprocity. Such representatives shall give reasonable advance notice of a projected visit, in order that appropriate consultations may be held and that maximum precautions may be taken to assure safety and to avoid interference with normal operations in the facility to be visited.

Article XIII

The provisions of this Treaty shall apply to the activities of States Parties to the Treaty in the exploration and use of outer space, including the moon and other celestial bodies, whether such activities are carried on by a single State Party to the Treaty or jointly with other States, including cases where they are carried on within the framework of international inter-governmental organizations.

Any practical questions arising in connection with activities carried on by international inter-governmental organizations in the exploration and use of outer space, including the moon and other celestial bodies, shall be resolved by the States Parties to the Treaty either with the appropriate international organization or with one or more States members of that international organization, which are Parties to this Treaty.

Article XIV

1. This Treaty shall be open to all States for signature. Any State which does not sign this Treaty before its entry into force in accordance with paragraph 3 of this article may accede to it at any time.

2. This Treaty shall be subject to ratification by signatory States. Instruments of ratification and instruments of accession shall be deposited with the Governments of the United States of America, the United Kingdom of Great Britain and Northern Ireland and the Union of Soviet Socialist Republics, which are hereby designated the Depositary Governments.

3. This treaty shall enter into force upon the deposit of instruments of ratification by five Governments including the Governments designated as Depositary Governments under this Treaty.

4. For States whose instruments of ratification or accession are deposited subsequent to the entry into force of this Treaty, it shall enter into force on the date of the deposit of their instruments of ratification or accession.

5. The Depositary Governments shall promptly inform all signatory and acceding States of the date of each signature, the date of deposit of each instrument of ratification of and accession to this Treaty, the date of its entry into force and other notices.

6. This Treaty shall be registered by the Depositary Governments pursuant to Article 102 of the Charter of the United Nations.

Article XV

Any State Party to the Treaty may propose amendments to this Treaty. Amendments shall enter into force for each State Party to the Treaty accepting the amendments upon their acceptance by a majority of the States Parties to the Treaty and thereafter for each remaining State Party to the Treaty on the date of acceptance by it.

Article XVI

Any State Party to the Treaty may give notice of its withdrawal from the Treaty one year after its entry into force by written notification to the Depositary Governments. Such withdrawal shall take effect one year from the date of receipt of this notification.

Article XVII

This Treaty, of which the English, Russian, French, Spanish and Chinese texts are equally authentic, shall be deposited in the archives of the Depositary Governments. Duly certified copies of this Treaty shall be transmitted by the Depositary Governments to the Governments of the signatory and acceding States.

In witness whereof the undersigned, duly authorized, have signed this Treaty.

Done in triplicate, at the cities of Washington, London and Moscow, this twenty-seventh day of January one thousand nine hundred sixty-seven.

APPENDIX 3.—REMARKS OF U.S. SENATOR JOHN O. PASTORE AT THE LAUNCHING OF THE NUCLEAR SUBMARINE "NARWHAL" IN GROTON, CONN., SEPTEMBER 9, 1967

I have come to this day and moment with pride—pride in the workers whose skills have made this splendid nuclear submarine possible.

Pride in the mobility of purpose of the crew—men of courage who will guide this ship through the silent depths of the ocean—alone and unafraid.

This ceremony which marks the launching of the *Narwhal*, the SSN671, is a milestone in the annals of our submarine history. Just thirteen short years ago the world's first nuclear submarine, the *Nautilus*, designated SSN571, was launched from this same shipyard. Here we are a hundred submarines later, and of these, ninety-two have been nuclear powered. Only men of great foresight would have envisioned this tremendous accomplishment.

I can think of no other important technological advancement which has progressed as rapidly as has the use of nuclear propulsion for naval vessels.

It was not too long ago from this shipyard that the forty-first and last PO-LARIS missile firing submarine was launched, marking the completion of this program. There is little doubt that the POLARIS submarine represents our most formidable deterrent to an all-out war.

I must say that these achievements would not have taken place except for the persistent and aggressive support of the Joint Committee on Atomic Energy—with the help of Admiral Rickover and his associates—and I would want you all to know further that if world conditions persist in the way they are today, the Joint Committee expects to see many more nuclear submarines launched from these and other ways throughout this great Nation.

Now, however, we have come to the crossroads in the development of nuclear-powered submarines. With the present authorized POLARIS program completed, we must give serious consideration to a further expansion of this program and we must intensify our efforts to develop new and more advanced nuclear attack submarines to meet the expanding challenge of Soviet naval power and the new Chinese threat. I also believe that we should actively pursue the replacement of all our conventional submarines with nuclear submarines of advanced design.

We have developed an irreplaceable reservoir of highly skilled men, such as I see before me today, who have been largely responsible for the clear supremacy the United States holds over any nation in the world in the development of nuclear submarines. Many of you workers, I might add, are friends from Rhode Island who journey here each day to join in this great endeavor to strengthen our national security.

We should insure that the great skills and capabilities of the men who design and build our nuclear warships should not be dissipated.

But this is only one aspect of the continuing fight for American nuclear propulsion supremacy.

The nuclear-powered aircraft carrier ENTERPRISE has just returned from its second deployment in action off Vietnam. The ENTERPRISE has proven so effective in battle in Vietnam that the Secretary of Defense requested a new nuclear-powered carrier in last year's defense bill and has told Congress that he intends to ask for one more next year and another in a future year.

The nuclear-powered carrier approved by Congress last year has been named the NIMITZ after the late Fleet Admiral Chester W. Nimitz. You might be interested to know that about fifty-five years ago Lieutenant Nimitz was Commanding Officer of the first United States submarine NARWHAL, the predecessor of the nuclear submarine we are launching today.

The Joint Committee on Atomic Energy is proud of the active role it has taken and is taking to bring into being a Nuclear Navy.

Our reward has been to see the POLARIS nuclear submarine emerge as our first line of defense—and the *Enterprise* and its nuclear escort vessels perform admirably in support of our limited objectives in the Vietnam conflict.

The world into which the *Narwhal* will sail is a world of conflict and contradictions.

We are engaged in a military struggle *against* the forces of communism in Southeast Asia. At the same time we are working *with* communist nations at Geneva to produce a treaty banning the spread of nuclear weapons—a treaty which will lessen the possibility of a nuclear holocaust.

Our hopes and prayers are for a non-proliferation treaty and agreements—agreements to halt the arms race—and, indeed, agreements to eliminate all conflicts.

But we must understand military power and constantly be aware of the capabilities of our potential enemies. We must stay in tune with changing events.

A dramatic and upsetting event has recently taken place in the Far East. In less than three years Red China has become, not only a nuclear power—but a *thermonuclear power.*

I suggest that they have made amazing and astonishing progress in this brief span of time. Their accomplishments in the field of nuclear weaponry are all the more significant because the internal strife within China has apparently had little or no effect on their nuclear and missile programs. In light of these factors, it appears that Communist China presents a clear-cut threat to the free world.

At the beginning of the 90th Congress, as Chairman of the Joint Committee, I initiated hearings on Red China's nuclear capability. One of the most significant findings contained in the Joint Committee report that followed was the statement based on CIA and Defense Department testimony that:

".... The Chinese probably will achieve an operational ICBM capability before 1972. Conceivably, it could be ready as early as 1970-1971."

Add to this new threat the fact that the Soviet Union's offensive nuclear striking power is increasing in comparison to our own—while at the same time they are deploying one and probably two anti-ballistic missile systems to defend their country—which we are not doing—I repeat—which we are not doing.

While for the moment we can find comfort and a certain amount of security in the ideological schism that exists between Red China and the Soviet Union, we cannot discount the possibility that this breach could be healed and thereby greatly affect the balance of nuclear power in the world.

Which brings me to the important point that I want to make here today, and that is this—that the time has come for us to give serious and urgent thought to a reappraisal of our defense posture.

We cannot live in a world of atomic energy and discount completely the possibility of "surprise attack" on our Nation.

The Senate has just recently approved a budget of over seventy billion dollars for defense, the largest single appropriations bill in our history—and yet we have no effective anti-ballistic missile system.

I realize the cost to do this is high—indeed staggering—however, if we can afford to spend twenty-four billion dollars a year in defense of a neighbor, and I mean Vietnam, we can certainly spend as much to insure the life and security of our American society.

Our offensive weapons are second to none—but it has been our announced and continuing policy for generations never to strike first.

Today—in effect—we are asking the American people to be prepared to accept near nuclear annihilation because our strategy calls for absorbing the first nuclear strike.

We are not an aggressive people. We do not covet other nations' territory. We only ask that those who desire to be free—stay free. I merely point out that we must be as strong in defense to preserve our society as we must be strong in offense to discourage and deter an attack.

With *all* our offensive power, *our defense* posture could be our Achilles' heel.

We cannot sit back and let ourselves be lulled into a sense of false security, relying only on the hope that fear of retaliation will deter potential aggressors.

Development of an ABM system is, I repeat, extremely expensive but, indeed, necessary. In this kind of a world, the alternatives are few.

The security of our country—the ultimate in its defense—deserves the highest national priority.

An affluent America—with so much to lose—must not face this mortal challenge cheaply.

We should move full speed ahead on building an anti-ballistic missile system. In this connection, I am happy to say that Senator Henry M. Jackson of Washington, Chairman of the Subcommittee on Military Application of the Joint Committee on Atomic Energy, and one of the Senate's leading experts on military affairs, will soon hold hearings on the ABM question.

The Joint Committee on Atomic Energy will pursue the development of an ABM system with the same vigor that it pressed for the development of the H-Bomb and our first nuclear submarine, the *Nautilus.*

Both endeavors were successful and greatly increased the security of this great Nation.

This new submarine, the *Narwhal*, represents another link in the chain of undersea security so necessary in this turbulent world.

It is into this difficult and dangerous world that you—the officers and men of the *Narwhal*—will soon sail.

Your task is vital to our security.

Your mission will be difficult.

Your dedication is unsurpassed and our pride in you is unbounded.

APPENDIX 4.—REMARKS BY SECRETARY OF DEFENSE ROBERT S. McNAMARA BEFORE UNITED PRESS INTERNATIONAL EDITORS AND PUBLISHERS, SAN FRANCISCO, CALIF., SEPTEMBER 18, 1967

Ladies and Gentlemen, I want to discuss with you this afternoon the gravest problem that an American Secretary of Defense must face: the planning, preparation, and policy governing the possibility of thermonuclear war.

It is a prospect most of mankind would prefer not to contemplate.

That is understandable. For technology has now circumscribed us all with a conceivable horizon of horror that could dwarf any catastrophe that has befallen man in his more than a million years on earth.

Man has lived now for more than twenty years in what we have come to call the Atomic Age.

What we sometimes overlook is that every future age of man will be an atomic age.

If, then, man is to have a future at all, it will have to be a future overshadowed with the permanent possibility of thermonuclear holocaust.

About that fact, we are no longer free.

Our freedom in this question consists rather in facing the matter rationally and realistically and discussing actions to minimize the danger.

No sane citizen; no sane political leader; no sane nation wants thermonuclear war.

But merely not wanting it is not enough.

We must understand the difference between actions which increase its risk, those which reduce it, and those which, while costly, have little influence one way or another.

Now this whole subject matter tends to be psychologically unpleasant. But there is an even greater difficulty standing in the way of constructive and profitable debate over the issues.

And that is that nuclear strategy is exceptionally complex in its technical aspects. Unless these complexities are well understood, rational discussion and decision making are simply not possible.

What I want to do this afternoon is deal with these complexities and clarify them with as much precision and detail as time and security permit.

One must begin with precise definitions.

The cornerstone of our strategic policy continues to be to deter deliberate nuclear attack upon the United States, or its allies, by maintaining a highly reliable ability to inflict an unacceptable degree of damage upon any single aggressor, or combination of aggressors, at any time during the course of a strategic nuclear exchange—even after our absorbing a surprise first strike.

This can be defined as our "assured destruction capability."

Now it is imperative to understand that assured destruction is the very essence of the whole deterrence concept.

We must possess an actual assured destruction capability. And that actual assured destruction capability must also be credible. Conceivably, our assured destruction capability could be actual, without being credible—in which case, it might fail to deter an aggressor.

The point is that a potential aggresor must himself believe that our assured destruction capability is in fact actual, and that our will to use it in retaliation to an attack is in fact unwaivering.

The conclusion, then, is clear: if the United States is to deter a nuclear attack on itself or on our allies, it must possess an actual, and a credible assured destruction capability.

When calculating the force we require, we must be "conservative" in all our estimates of both a potential aggressor's capabilities, and his intentions. Security depends upon taking a "worst plausible case"—and having the ability to cope with that eventuality.

In that eventuality, we must be able to absorb the total weight of nuclear attack on our country—on our strike-back forces; on our command and control apparatus; on our industrial capacity; on our cities; and on our population—and still, be fully capable of destroying the aggressor to the point that his society is simply no longer viable in any meaningful twentieth-century sense.

That is what deterrence to nuclear aggression means. It means the certainty of suicide to the aggressor—not merely to his military forces, but to his society as a whole.

Now let us consider another term: "first-strike capability." This, in itself, is an ambiguous term, since it could mean simply the ability of one nation to attack another nation with nuclear forces first. But as it is normally used, it connotes much more: the substantial elimination of the attacked nation's retaliatory second-strike forces.

This is the sense in which "first-strike capability" should be understood.

Now, clearly, such a first-strike capability is an important strategic concept. The United States cannot—and will not—ever permit itself to get into the position in which another nation, or combination of nations, would possess such a first-strike capability, which could be effectively used against it.

To get into such a position vis-a-vis any other nation or nations would not only constitute an intolerable threat to our security, but it would obviously remove our ability to deter nuclear aggression—both against ourselves and against our allies.

Now, we are not in that position today—and there is no foreseeable danger of our ever getting into that position.

Our strategic offensive forces are immense: 1000 Minutemen missile launchers, carefully protected below ground; 41 Polaris submarines, carrying 656 missile launchers—with the majority of these hidden beneath the seas at all times; and about 600 long-range bombers, approximately forty percent of which are kept always in a high state of alert.

Our alert forces alone carry more than 2200 weapons, averaging more than one megaton each. A mere 400 one-megaton weapons, if delivered on the Soviet Union, would be sufficient to destroy over one-third of her population, and one-half of her industry.

And all of these flexible and highly reliable forces are equipped with devices that insure their penetration of Soviet defenses.

Now what about the Soviet Union?

Does it today possess a powerful nuclear arsenal?

The answer is that it does.

Does it possess a first-strike capability against the United States?

The answer is that it does not.

Can the Soviet Union, in the foreseeable future, acquire such a first-strike capability against the United States?

The answer is that it cannot.

It cannot because we are determined to remain fully alert, and we will never permit our own assured destruction capability to be at a point where a Soviet first-strike capability is even remotely feasible.

Is the Soviet Union seriously attempting to acquire a first-strike capability against the United States?

Although this is a question we cannot answer with absolute certainty, we believe the answer is no. In any event, the question itself is—in a sense—irrelevant. It is irrelevant since the United States will so continue to maintain—and where necessary strengthen—our retaliatory forces, that whatever the Soviet Union's intentions or actions, we will continue to have an assured destruction capability vis-a-vis their society in which we are completely confident.

But there is another question that is most relevant.

And that is, do we—the United States—possess a first-strike capability against the Soviet Union?

The answer is that we do not.

And we do not, not because we have neglected our nuclear strength. On the contrary, we have increased it to the point that we possess a clear superiority over the Soviet Union.

We do not possess first-strike capability against the Soviet Union for precisely the same reason that they do not possess it against us.

And that is that we have both built up our "second-strike capability" [1] to the point that a first-strike capability on either side has become unattainable.

---

[1] A "second-strike capability" is the capability to absorb a surprise nuclear attack, and survive with sufficient power to inflict unacceptable damage on the aggressor.

There is, of course, no way in which the United States could have prevented the Soviet Union from acquiring its present second-strike capability—short of a massive pre-emptive first strike on the Soviet Union in the 1950s.

The blunt fact is, then, that neither the Soviet Union nor the United States can attack the other without being destroyed in retaliation; nor can either of us attain a first-strike capability in the foreseeable future.

The further fact is that both the Soviet Union and the United States presently possess an actual and credible second-strike capability against one another—and it is precisely this mutual capability that provides us both with the strongest possible motive to avoid a nuclear war.

The more frequent question that arises in this connection is whether or not the United States possesses nuclear superiority over the Soviet Union.

The answer is that we do.

But the answer is—like everything else in this matter—technically complex.

The complexity arises in part out of what measurement of superiority is most meaningful and realistic.

Many commentators on the matter tend to define nuclear superiority in terms of gross megatonnage, or in terms of the number of missile launchers available.

Now, by both these two standards of measurement, the United States does have a substantial superiority over the Soviet Union in the weapons targeted against each other.

But it is precisely these two standards of measurement that are themselves misleading.

For the most meaningful and realistic measurement of nuclear capability is neither gross megatonnage, nor the number of available missile launchers; but rather the number of separate warheads that are capable of being *delivered* with accuracy on individual high-priority targets with sufficient power to destroy them.

Gross megatonnage in itself is an inadequate indicator of assured destruction capability, since it is unrelated to survivability, accuracy, or penetrability, and poorly related to effective elimination of multiple high-priority targets. There is manifestly no advantage in over-destroying one target, at the expense of leaving undamaged other targets of equal importance.

Further, the number of missile launchers available is also an inadequate indicator of assured destruction capability, since the fact is that many of our launchers will carry multiple warheads.

But by using the realistic measurement of the number of warheads available, capable of being reliably delivered with accuracy and effectiveness on the appropriate targets in the United States or Soviet Union, I can tell you that the United States currently possesses a superiority over the Soviet Union of at least three or four to one.

Furthermore, we will maintain a superiority—by these same realistic criteria—over the Soviet Union for as far ahead in the future as we can realistically plan.

I want, however, to make one point patently clear: our current numerical superiority over the Soviet Union in reliable, accurate, and effective warheads is both greater than we had originally planned, and is in fact more than we require.

Moreover, in the larger equation of security, our "superiority" is of limited significance—since even with our current superiority, or indeed with any numerical superiority realistically attainable, the blunt, inescapable fact remains that the Soviet Union could still—with its present forces—effectively destroy the United States, even after absorbing the full weight of an American first strike.

I have noted that our present superiority is greater than we had planned. Let me explain to you how this came about, for I think it is a significant illustration of the intrinsic dynamics of the nuclear arms race.

In 1961, when I became Secretary of Defense, the Soviet Union possessed a very small operational arsenal of intercontinental missiles. However, they did possess the technological and industrial capacity to enlarge that arsenal very substantially over the succeeding several years.

Now, we had no evidence that the Soviets did in fact plan to fully use that capability.

But as I have pointed out, a strategic planner must be "conservative" in his calculations; that is, he must prepare for the worst plausible case and not be content to hope and prepare merely for the most probable.

Since we could not be certain of Soviet intentions—since we could not be sure that they would not undertake a massive build-up—we had to insure against such an eventuality by undertaking ourselves a major build-up of the Minuteman and Polaris forces.

Thus, in the course of hedging against what was then only a theoretically possible Soviet build-up, we took decisions which have resulted in our current superiority in numbers of warheads and deliverable megatons.

But the blunt fact remains that if we had had more accurate information about planned Soviet strategic forces, we simply would not have needed to build as large a nuclear arsenal as we have today.

Now let me be absolutely clear. I am not saying that our decision in 1961 was unjustified. I am simply saying that it was necessitated by a lack of accurate information.

Furthermore, that decision in itself—as justified as it was—in the end, could not possibly have left unaffected the Soviet Union's future nuclear plans.

What is essential to understand here is that the Soviet Union and the United States mutually influence one another's strategic plans.

Whatever be their intentions, whatever be our intentions, actions—or even realistically potential actions—on either side relating to the build-up of nuclear forces, be they either offensive or defensive weapons, necessarily trigger reactions on the other side.

It is precisely this action-reaction phenomenon that fuels an arms race.

Now, in strategic nuclear weaponry, the arms race involves a particular irony. Unlike any other era in military history, today a substantial numerical superiority of weapons does not effectively translate into political control, or diplomatic leverage.

While thermonuclear power is almost inconceivably awesome, and represents virtually unlimited potential destructiveness, it has proven to be a limited diplomatic instrument. Its uniqueness lies in the fact that it is at one and the same time, an all powerful weapon—and a very inadequate weapon.

The fact that the Soviet Union and the United States can mutually destroy one another—regardless of who strikes first—narrows the range of Soviet aggression which our nuclear forces can effectively deter.

Even with our nuclear monopoly in the early postwar period, we were unable to deter the Soviet pressures against Berlin, or their support of aggression in Korea.

Today, our nuclear superiority does not deter all forms of Soviet support of communist insurgency in Southeast Asia.

What all of this has meant is that we, and our allies as well, require substantial non-nuclear forces in order to cope with levels of aggression that massive strategic forces do not in fact deter.

This has been a difficult lesson both for us and for our allies to accept, since there is a strong psychological tendency to regard superior nuclear forces as a simple and unfailing solution to security, and an assurance of victory under any set of circumstances.

What is important to understand is that our nuclear strategic forces play a vital and absolutely necessary role in our security and that of our allies, but it is an intrinsically limited role.

Thus, we and our allies must maintain substantial conventional forces, fully capable of dealing with a wide spectrum of lesser forms of political and military aggression—a level of aggression against which the use of strategic nuclear forces would not be to our advantage, and thus a level of aggression which these strategic nuclear forces by themselves cannot effectively deter. One cannot fashion a credible deterrent out of an incredible action. Therefore security for the United States and its allies can only arise from the possession of a whole range of graduated deterrents, each of them fully credible in its own context.

Now I have pointed out that in strategic nuclear matters, the Soviet Union and the United States mutually influence one another's plans.

In recent years the Soviets have substantially increased their offensive forces. We have, of course, been watching and evaluating this very carefully.

Clearly, the Soviet build-up is in part a reaction to our own build-up since the beginning of this decade.

Soviet strategic planners undoubtedly reasoned that if our build-up were to continue at its accelerated pace, we might conceivably reach, in time, a credible first-strike capability against the Soviet Union.

That was not in fact our intention. Our intention was to assure that they—with their theoretical capacity to reach such a first-strike capability—would not in fact outdistance us.

But they could not read our intentions with any greater accuracy than we could read theirs. And thus the result has been that we have both built up our forces to a point that far exceeds a credible second-strike capability against the forces we each started with.

In doing so, neither of us has reached a first-strike capability. And the realities of the situation being what they are—whatever we believe their intentions to be, and whatever they believe our intentions to be—each of us can deny the other a first-strike capability in the foreseeable future.

Now, how can we be so confident that this is the case?

How can we be so certain that the Soviets cannot gradually outdistance us—either by some dramatic technological break-through, or simply through our imperceptively lagging behind, for whatever reason: reluctance to spend the requisite funds; distraction with military problems elsewhere; faulty intelligence; or simple negligence and naivete?

All of these reasons—and others—have been suggested by some commentators in this country, who fear that we are in fact falling behind to a dangerous degree.

The answer to all of this is simple and straightforward.

We are not going to permit the Soviets to outdistance us, because to do so would be to jeopardize our very viability as a nation.

No President, no Secretary of Defense, no Congress of the United States—of whatever political party, and of whatever political persuasion—is going to permit this nation to take that risk.

We do not want a nuclear arms race with the Soviet Union—primarily because the action-reaction phenomenon makes it foolish and futile. But if the only way to prevent the Soviet Union from obtaining first-strike capability over us is to engage in such a race, the United States possesses in ample abundance the resources, the technology, and the will to run faster in that race for whatever distance is required.

But what we would much prefer to do is to come to a realistic and reasonably riskless agreement with the Soviet Union, which would effectively prevent such an arms race. We both have strategic nuclear arsenals greatly in excess of a credible assured destruction capability. These arsenals have reached that point of excess in each case for precisely the same reason: we each have reacted to the other's build-up with very conservative calculations. We have, that is, each built a greater arsenal than either of us needed for a second-strike capability, simply because we each wanted to be able to cope with the "worst plausible case."

But since we now each possess a deterrent in excess of our individual needs, both of our nations would benefit from a properly safe-guarded agreement first to limit, and later to reduce, both our offensive and defensive strategic nuclear forces.

We may, or we may not, be able to achieve such an agreement. We hope we can. And we believe such an agreement is fully feasible, since it is clearly in both our nations' interests.

But reach the formal agreement or not, we can be sure that neither the Soviets nor we are going to risk the other obtaining a first-strike capability.

On the contrary, we can be sure that we are both going to maintain a maximum effort to preserve an assured destruction capability.

It would not be sensible for either side to launch a maximum effort to achieve a first-strike capability. It would not be sensible because the intelligence-gathering capability of each side being what it is, and the realities of lead-time from technological break-through to operational readiness being what they are, neither of us would be able to acquire a first-strike capability in secret.

Now, let me take a specific case in point.

The Soviets are now deploying an anti-ballistic missile system. If we react to this deployment intelligently, we have no reason for alarm.

The system does not impose any threat to our ability to penetrate and inflict massive and unacceptable damage on the Soviet Union. In other words, it does not presently affect in any significant manner our assured destruction capability.

It does not impose such a threat because we have already taken the steps necessary to assure that our land-based Minuteman missiles, our nuclear submarine-launched new Poseidon missiles, and our strategic bomber forces have the requisite penetration aids—and in the sum, constitute a force of such magnitude, that they guarantee us a force strong enough to survive a Soviet attack and penetrate the Soviet ABM deployment.

Now let me come to the issue that has received so much attention recently: the question of whether or not we should deploy an ABM system against the Soviet nuclear threat.

To begin with, this is not in any sense a new issue. We have had both the technical possibility and the strategic desirability of an American ABM deployment under constant review since the late 1950s.

While we have substantially improved our technology in the field, it is important to understand that none of the systems at the present or foreseeable state of the art would provide an impenetrable shield over the United States. Were such a shield possible, we would certainly want it—and we would certainly build it.

And at this point, let me dispose of an objection that is totally irrelevant to this issue.

It has been alleged that we are opposed to deploying a large-scale ABM system because it would carry the heavy price tag of $40 billion.

Let me make it very clear that the $40 billion is not the issue.

If we could build and deploy a genuinely impenetrable shield over the United States, we would be willing to spend not $40 billion, but any reasonable multiple of that amount that was necessary.

The money in itself is not the problem: the penetrability of the proposed shield is the problem.

There is clearly no point, however, in spending $40 billion if it is not going to buy us a significant improvement in our security. If it is not, then we should use the substantial resources it represents on something that will.

Every ABM system that is now feasible involves firing defensive missiles at incoming offensive warheads in an effort to destroy them.

But what many commentators on this issue overlook is that any such system can rather obviously be defeated by an enemy simply sending more offensive warheads, or dummy warheads, than there are defensive missiles capable of disposing of them.

And this is the whole crux of the nuclear action-reaction phenomenon.

Were we to deploy a heavy ABM system throughout the United States, the Soviets would clearly be strongly motivated to so increase their offensive capability as to cancel out our defensive advantage.

It is futile for each of us to spend $4 billion, $40 billion, or $400 billion—and at the end of all the spending, and at the end of all the deployment, and at the end of all the effort, to be relatively at the same point of balance on the security scale that we are now.

In point of fact, we have already initiated offensive weapons programs costing several billions in order to offset the small present Soviet ABM deployment, and the possibly more extensive future Soviet ABM deployments.

That is money well spent; and it is necessary.

But we should bear in mind that it is money spent because of the action-reaction phenomenon.

If we in turn opt for heavy ABM deployment—at whatever price—we can be certain that the Soviets will react to offset the advantage we would hope to gain.

It is precisely because of this certainty of a corresponding Soviet reaction that the four prominent scientists—men who have served with distinction as the Science Advisors to Presidents Eisenhower, Kennedy, and Johnson, and the three outstanding men who have served as Directors of Research and Engineering to three Secretaries of Defense—have unanimously recommended against the deployment of an ABM system designed to protect our population against a Soviet attack.

These men are Doctors Killian, Kistiakowsky, Wiesner, Hornig, York, Brown, and Foster.

The plain fact of the matter is that we are now facing a situation analogous to the one we faced in 1961: we are uncertain of the Soviets' intentions.

At that time we were concerned about their potential offensive capabilities; now we are concerned about their potential defensive capabilities.

But the dynamics of the concern are the same.

We must continue to be cautious and conservative in our estimates—leaving no room in our calculations for unnecessary risk. And at the same time, we must measure our own response in such a manner that it does not trigger a senseless spiral upward of nuclear arms.

Now, as I have emphasized, we have already taken the necessary steps to guarantee that our offensive strategic weapons will be able to penetrate future, more advanced, Soviet defenses.

Keeping in mind the careful clockwork of lead-time, we will be forced to continue that effort over the next few years if the evidence is that the Soviets intend to turn what is now a light and modest ABM deployment into a massive one.

Should they elect to do so, we have both the lead-time and the technology available to so increase both the quality and quantity of our offensive strategic forces—with particular attention to highly reliable penetration aids—that their expensive defensive efforts will give them no edge in the nuclear balance whatever.

But we would prefer not to have to do that. For it is a profitless waste of resources, provided we and the Soviets can come to a realistic strategic arms-limitation agreement.

As you know, we have proposed U.S.-Soviet talks on this matter. Should these talks fail, we are fully prepared to take the appropriate measures that such a failure would make necessary.

The point for us to keep in mind is that should the talks fail—and the Soviets decide to expand their present modest ABM deployment into a massive one—our response must be realistic. There is no point whatever in our responding by going to a massive ABM deployment to protect our population, when such a system would be ineffective against a sophisticated Soviet offense.

Instead, realism dictates that if the Soviets elect to deploy a heavy ABM system, we must further expand our sophisticated offensive forces, and thus preserve our overwhelming assured destruction capability.

But the intractable fact is that should the talks fail, both the Soviets and ourselves would be forced to continue on a foolish and feckless course.

It would be foolish and feckless because—in the end—it would provide neither the Soviets, nor us, with any greater relative nuclear capability.

The time has come for us both to realize that, and to act reasonably. It is clearly in our own mutual interest to do so.

Having said that, it is important to distinguish between an ABM system designed to protect against a Soviet attack on our cities, and ABM systems which have other objectives.

One of the other uses of an ABM system which we should seriously consider is the greater protection of our strategic offensive forces.

Another is in relation to the emerging nuclear capability of Communist China.

There is evidence that the Chinese are devoting very substantial resources to the development of both nuclear warheads, and missile delivery systems. As I stated last January, indications are that they will have medium-range ballistic missiles within a year or so, an initial intercontinental ballistic missile capability in the early 1970s, and a modest force in the mid–70s.

Up to now, the lead-time factor has allowed us to postpone a decision on whether or not a light ABM deployment might be advantageous as a counter-measure to Communist China's nuclear development.

But the time will shortly be right for us to initiate production if we desire such a system.

China at the moment is caught up in internal strife, but it seems likely that her basic motivation in developing a strategic nuclear capability is an attempt to provide a basis for threatening her neighbors, and to clothe herself with the dubious prestige that the world pays to nuclear weaponry.

We deplore her development of these weapons, just as we deplore it in other countries. We oppose nuclear proliferation because we believe that in the end it only increases the risk of a common and cataclysmic holocaust.

President Johnson has made it clear that the United States will oppose any efforts of China to employ nuclear blackmail against her neighbors.

We possess now, and will continue to possess for as far ahead as we can foresee, an overwhelming first-strike capability with respect to China. And despite the shrill and raucous propaganda directed at her own people that "the atomic bomb is a paper tiger," there is ample evidence that China well appreciates the destructive power of nuclear weapons.

China has been cautious to avoid any action that might end in a nuclear clash with the United States—however wild her words—and understandably so. We have the power not only to destroy completely her entire nuclear offensive forces, but to devastate her society as well.

Is there any possibility, then, that by the mid-1970s China might become so incautious as to attempt a nuclear attack on the United States or our allies.

It would be insane and suicidal for her to do so, but one can conceive conditions under which China might miscalculate. We wish to reduce such possibilities to a minimum.

And since, as I have noted, our strategic planning must always be conservative, and take into consideration even the possible irrational behavior of potential adversaries, there are marginal grounds for concluding that a light deployment of U.S. ABMs against this possibility is prudent.

The system would be relatively inexpensive—preliminary estimates place the cost at about $5 billion—and would have a much higher degree of reliability against a Chinese attack, than the much more massive and complicated system that some have recommended against a possible Soviet attack.

Moreover, such an ABM deployment designed against a possible Chinese attack would have a number of other advantages. It would provide an additional indication to Asians that we intend to deter China from nuclear blackmail, and thus would contribute toward our goal of discouraging nuclear weapon proliferation among the present non-nuclear countries.

Further, the Chinese-oriented ABM deployment would enable us to add—as a concurrent benefit—a further defense of our Minuteman sites against Soviet attack, which means that at modest cost we would in fact be adding even greater effectiveness to our offensive missile force and avoiding a much more costly expansion of that force.

Finally, such a reasonably reliable ABM system would add protection of our population against the improbable but possible accidental launch of an intercontinental missile by any one of the nuclear powers.

After a detailed review of all these considerations, we have decided to go forward with this Chinese-oriented ABM deployment, and we will begin actual production of such a system at the end of this year.

In reaching this decision, I want to emphasize that it contains two possible dangers—and we should guard carefully against each.

The first danger is that we may psychologically lapse into the old over-simplification about the adequacy of nuclear power. The simple truth is that nuclear weapons can serve to deter only a narrow range of threats. This ABM deployment will strengthen our defensive posture—and will enhance the effectiveness of our land-based ICBM offensive forces. But the independent nations of Asia must realize that these benefits are no substitute for their maintaining, and where necessary strengthening, their own conventional forces in order to deal with the more likely threats to the security of the region.

The second danger is also psychological. There is a kind of mad momentum intrinsic to the development of all new nuclear weaponry. If a weapon system works—and works well—there is strong pressure from many directions to procure and deploy the weapon out of all proportion to the prudent level required.

The danger in deploying this relatively light and reliable Chinese-oriented ABM system is going to be that pressures will develop to expand it into a heavy Soviet-oriented ABM system.

We must resist that temptation firmly—not because we can for a moment afford to relax our vigilance against a possible Soviet first-strike—but precisely because our greatest deterrent against such a strike is not a massive, costly, but highly penetrable ABM shield, but rather a fully credible offensive assured destruction capability.

The so-called heavy ABM shield—at the present state of technology—would in effect be no adequate shield at all against a Soviet attack, but rather a strong inducement for the Soviets to vastly increase their own offensive forces. That, as I have pointed out, would make it necessary for us to respond in turn—and so the arms race would rush hopelessly on to no sensible purpose on either side.

Let me emphasize—and I cannot do so too strongly—that our decision to go ahead with a *limited* ABM deployment in no way indicates that we feel an agreement with the Soviet Union on the limitation of strategic nuclear offensive and defensive forces is any the less urgent or desirable.

The road leading from the stone axe to the ICBM—though it may have been more than a million years in the building—seems to have run in a single direction.

If one is inclined to be cynical, one might conclude that man's history seems to be characterized not so much by consistent periods of peace, occasionally punctuated by warfare; but rather by persistent outbreaks of warfare, wearily put aside from time to time by periods of exhaustion and recovery—that parade under the name of peace.

I do not view man's history with that degree of cynicism, but I do believe that man's wisdom in avoiding war is often surpassed by his folly in promoting it.

However foolish unlimited war may have been in the past, it is now no longer merely foolish, but suicidal as well.

It is said that nothing can prevent a man from suicide, if he is sufficiently determined to commit it.

The question is what is our determination in an era when unlimited war will mean the death of hundreds of millions—and the possible genetic impairment of a million generations to follow?

Man is clearly a compound of folly and wisdom—and history is clearly a consequence of the admixture of those two contradictory traits.

History has placed our particular lives in an era when the consequences of human folly are waxing more and more catastrophic in the matters of war and peace.

In the end, the root of man's security does not lie in his weaponry.
In the end, the root of man's security lies in his mind.
What the world requires in its 22nd Year of the Atomic Age is not a new race towards armament.
What the world requires in its 22nd Year of the Atomic Age is a new race towards reasonableness.
We had better all run that race.
Not merely we the administrators. But we the people.
Thank you, and good afternoon.

APPENDIX 5.—INTERVIEW WITH SECRETARY OF DEFENSE McNAMARA

[From Life Magazine of Sept. 29, 1967]

Q. Early this year, in testimony before a House committee, Mr. Secretary, you said, " . . . the Chinese threat, in itself, would not dictate the [U.S.] production of an ABM system at this time," Can you tell me why that statement is no longer valid?

A. The lead time then, as I pointed out, was longer for the Chinese than it was for us. It would take them longer to put in their offensive system—their ICBMs—than it would take us to put in our defensive system.

Since then nine months have passed and we are now at a point where, in a sense, our lead times are in conjunction, one with the other. It is appropriate, therefore, that if we are going to go ahead, we do so now.

Q. Is there any reason to believe that in the past nine months their pace in developing an ICBM system has been accelerated?

A. No, no. Their pace is almost exactly as we predicted at that time. They could have a first-test shot of an ICBM booster before the end of this year. If they do, they could have a small but militarily significant force of ICBMs in the mid-'70s. It is against that schedule that we have had to make our decision.

Q. When do you estimate China will have a "second strike capability" [the ability to absorb a nuclear attack and still have enough bombers and missiles to inflict unacceptable damage on the attacking country]?

A. It is very difficult to predict. I would say, not for 15 to 20 years.

Q. And hopefully, before that time, some kind of international agreement will be drafted?

A. Well, I don't want to anticipate what China might or might not agree to in 15 or 20 years.

Q. In your speech you also spoke of "conceivable conditions" under which China might "miscalculate" and attempt a nuclear attack on the U.S. Could you expand on that?

A. We can visualize a situation of tension between Red China and the U.S., brought about by some aggressive move by the Chinese. In that atmosphere, it is conceivable that someone in their government would predict that the U.S. was going to launch nuclear weapons to destroy their small and highly vulnerable missile force on the ground. Under those circumstances, some in China might be tempted to recommend that they pre-empt—that they launch ahead of time, because otherwise they would not be able to launch at all.

That kind of attack should be deterred by this system, and in any case we would be protected against it.

Our ABM has a second purpose, too, involving our friends in Asia. There has been lingering doubt in some Asian countries that if China in a few years were able to reach the U.S. with an ICBM, we would be deterred from taking actions that might risk a Chinese attack. Our decision to deploy a light ABM system ought to remove this doubt. Not only would it be utter suicide for Peking actually to attack the U.S. or our allies, but China would not be in a position to claim that we would back down because we feared civilian casualties at home.

Q. Now, if such an attack did occur in the late 1970s, what degree of success would it have?

A. Well, it would depend upon the number of weapons they have at the time. It is conceivable that, undefended, our fatalities would be between five and 10 million; and with the kind of defense that we will put in, the fatalities would range from almost zero to something less than a million.

Q. Is there any concern that Russia would provide China with penetration devices and other sophisticated equipment designed to get around our missile defenses?

A. Very unlikely. The Soviets are quite concerned with the Chinese, themselves.

Q. *China's missiles can be turned around?*

A. That's right. They can go in both directions.

Q. *The obvious question, Mr. Secretary, is: Why are we defending our cities against a possible Chinese attack and only our missiles against a possible Soviet attack?*

A. Our decision was based on their quite different technological and economic capabilities.

We can put up an anti-missile defense of our cities against China that will be effective and remain effective for many years to come. We can't against the Soviet Union, because they have already advanced so far in the development of the size and sophistication of their offensive force and are capable of still further advances.

Every ABM system that is now feasible involves firing defensive missiles at incoming warheads. It can be defeated by a sophisticated opponent with a large economy—like the Soviet Union—who can afford to launch more warheads and decoys than the defensive system can handle. The Soviets could equip themselves to overcome any system we could now deploy.

The Soviets not only have the capability, but strong motivation, too. Their leaders are determined to maintain their own ability to deter the launching of an American attack by having the capability to destroy our society in retaliation. If we deployed a defense that could, if the Soviets did not react, greatly reduce our expected casualties, the Soviets could and would respond by increasing the size of their offensive forces—just as we have done in response to their system. In the end we would be no more secure. That's why it doesn't make sense for us to waste resources in a futile effort to defend our cities against a Soviet attack.

Q. *Can you tell me a little about our projected "light" ABM system?*

A. The system has four major components—two types of radar and two types of missiles. It is designed to provide two kinds of defense: first, a so-called "area" defense of the entire U.S. population against the kind of small attack the Chinese might be capable of in the mid-1970s, and second, a "terminal" defense against Soviet attack on our underground Minuteman intercontinental ballistic missiles. In addition, our ABM also will protect us against a nuclear armed missile launched accidentally by any one of the nuclear powers.

Q. *How does the area defense work?*

A. A special, highly sophisticated kind of radar, called Perimeter Acquisition Radar [PAR], detects ballistic missiles at long ranges, tracks the incoming warheads and predicts their paths. Then a missile called the Spartan is fired to intercept and destroy the warhead well above the atmosphere, with no fallout hazard. That intercept point can be hundreds of miles from the Spartan battery location.

One installation will be able to protect a very large area of land around it. For that reason, only a few sites are necessary to cover the entire country. All the population within that area is protected.

Q. *What about the so-called terminal defense?*

A. It is very different; it is a defense of a point rather than an area. We now plan such a defense only for the ABM radar and the Minuteman missile silos, so that our second strike capability will survive. In case of an attack by the Soviets, we have to face the possibility that there will be enormous "clouds" coming at us—tens of miles across and perhaps as many as hundreds of miles long—composed of a variety of objects which will prevent our radar from seeing in detail which objects in there might be warheads.

Q. *When you say "clouds," do you mean some war-heads, some decoys—things of that nature to confuse the radar?*

A. Yes. Chaff, pieces of metal, boosters, everything. This stuff, however, gets separated out as it impinges on the atmosphere during descent. Atmosphere slows down particularly all the light objects. Heavy things bore through. So, when the actual enemy missiles are below a few hundred thousand feet, the terminal defense system can intercept them with individual missiles. If they are headed toward a Minuteman site or a radar installation, they can be taken under fire by Sprint, the short-range interceptor designed to destroy incoming missiles within the atmosphere. The danger to the population below is negligible.

We expect to have to attack each warhead separately. The enemy would not likely be so foolish as to place his re-entry objects so close together that we could annihilate them all with a single missile.

Q. *Can we adequately test an ABM system in view of the ban on atmospheric nuclear testing?*

A. Yes. The primary problems are not in the warheads, which can be satisfactorily tested underground, but in the coordination of all elements of the complex system. We are building sites in Kwajalein for that purpose.

Q. *Could the country which builds an ABM now conceivably come up with a technological breakthrough that would significantly improve its effectiveness?*

A. I think the reverse is more likely the case—that as you proceed in production, the project becomes so immense that there would be a great tendency and temptation to reduce your efforts to advance technology. I, myself, am certain that, had we gone ahead with Nike-Zeus in 1961 or 1962, it would have been an incorrect decision. We would now have a system that was obsolete before it was actually deployed. But also, in the interim, it would have taken away the emphasis we have put on research, development and advancing technology, which has led to the system we are deploying today.

So, it will be difficult to maintain the emphasis upon new developments while we are undertaking the ABM production program. We will plan to do so, however. We are spending about a half billion dollars a year in research on ABM systems today and plan to continue to spend that in the future.

Q. *In your speech, you warned that this Administration and the succeeding ones will have to resist pressure to expand the present system. From whom will pressure come?*

A. It will come from some private citizens who don't understand how futile an attempt to get an effective defense against the Soviets would be, from some members of Congress, from some of the military and from some in industry.

Q. *Does the U.S. possess nuclear superiority over the Soviet Union?*

A. Yes, we do, but I believe the notion of "nuclear superiority" has only limited relevance today. People become mesmerized by the word "superiority"; if you are superior, presumably you have some advantage you can translate to your own interest. But the advantage is certainly not what the words "superior military forces" connoted in the past.

A nation with an army of one million men used to have a significant military edge over a neighbor with an army of half a million. And under most circumstances, this military superiority could be translated into effective diplomatic leverage and political power. But today, in the nuclear age, nuclear superiority is of limited significance: despite our current superiority, or any realistically attainable superiority, the Soviet Union could still destroy the U.S. even after absorbing the full weight of an American first strike.

The U.S. and the Soviet Union can mutually destroy each other, regardless of who strikes first. And this fact narrows the range of Soviet aggression which can be effectively deterred by our nuclear forces. Even with our nuclear monopoly in the early postwar years, we could not deter the Soviet pressures against Berlin or their support of aggression in Korea. Today, they do not deter Soviet support of aggression in Southeast Asia.

What all of this has meant, of course, is that we—and our allies as well—have required substantial non-nuclear military forces to cope with the kinds of aggression upon which massive strategic forces have little effect.

Q. *While maintaining our nuclear superiority, right?*

A. Oh yes, and we will maintain it. Today our total forces can deliver 3 to 4 times as many warheads on the Soviet Union as they can deliver on us. We can also deliver more megatons, although the superiority there isn't nearly so great. We have about 4,000 separately targetable warheads—bombs and missile warheads—in our strategic offensive forces opposing the Soviet Union. They have roughly 1,000 which they could target against us.

We think that "separately targetable warheads" is the best single measure of the relative strength of the forces, rather than the number of launch vehicles or bombers, or megatons. We are in great danger of becoming obsessed with megatonnage as a measure of strategic force capability. It is the wrong measure. The number of targets each side can destroy is the important thing, not the total megatons each side can deliver.

Most targets can be destroyed by a megaton. That's equivalent to a million tons of TNT, 50 times as much as the weapon that destroyed Hiroshima. In fact, most targets can be destroyed by a much smaller weapon. Against such targets, a 20-megaton weapon is not more effective than a one-megaton weapon. If the target is destroyed, it's destroyed. Even for targets particularly suited to large weapons, such as very big cities, the destructive work of one 20-megaton weapon can be done by 4 or 5 one-megaton weapons. So, adding up megatons gives you the wrong answer.

Q. *Some people disagree. They speak of a "megatonnage gap." How do the Russians feel about megatonnage? A few years ago the Russians tested a 50-megaton weapon. . . .*

A. Yes, the Soviets have apparently gone for fewer and larger warheads. But we've bought more, smaller warheads—large and accurate enough to destroy their targets. And we're planning another big increase in the number our forces can deliver. We're doing it to be sure we can overcome the most powerful defenses the Soviets could build.

Q. *Does this mean that we will have to greatly increase the number of boosters in our strategic missile forces?*

A. No. We are replacing existing missiles with far more powerful ones—replacing Minuteman I and II with Minuteman III, and Polaris with Poseidon. More important, we're capitalizing on a major new technological advance. We can now equip our boosters with many warheads, each of which can be aimed at a separate target. We call this MIRV—Multiple Independent Re-entry Vehicles.

Q. *Does the public know about MIRV?*

A. There have been allusions to it in the press, but it has not been described publicly. We're buying MIRVs for both Minuteman and Poseidon. We believe that we have a substantial lead over the Soviets in this important technology. Through the use of MIRVs, we will redesign our strategic force to increase the total number of warheads. This will do two things: exhaust their defenses and at the same time better match the size of weapons to the targets to be destroyed. The net result will be an increase in military effectiveness with some reduction in the total megatons in our force.

Q. *A reduction in megatons?*

A. Yes. This reduction is like the one that President Eisenhower initiated in 1959 and 1960. Acting on the unanimous recommendations of the Joint Chiefs of Staff, he approved replacing the very large MK–36 nuclear bombs with larger numbers of the light, compact weapons that our bomber force now carries. Even though it reduced the megatonnage of the total stockpile by 40%, President Eisenhower was absolutely right to do so. President Kennedy carried out that decision.

Q. *To what degree does MIRV complicate the job of a missile defense system?*

A. Considerably. It's one of the things that makes us so confident that we can overcome the Soviet ABM. But in a few years the Soviets could have their own MIRVs and that is one of the reasons we are pessimistic about deploying an effective, more extensive ABM against them. Both our missile defense system and theirs were designed before MIRVs came along as a serious possibility. The optimistic statements made by ABM proponents on both sides haven't taken such things as MIRVs fully into account.

Q. *We have proposed talks with the Russians on the limitation of ABM defense systems. Are you at all hopeful that some agreement can be reached?*

A. We have tried on a number of occasions since last November to initiate discussions with the Russians. President Johnson spoke to Chairman Kosygin about it at Glassboro, as did I. The President is very anxious to engage in such discussions. We believe it is possible, either informally or formally, to agree with the Soviets on some form of limitations that would apply to both strategic offensive and strategic defensive weapons, to our mutual advantage. Early this month we tried again to initiate such discussions. We continue to hope that talks will be undertaken. In any event, the action we are taking now to deploy a system that has as its primary purpose the protection of our people against the Chinese threat would not be influenced by such discussions.

Q. *Are we making clear to the Russians, both privately and publicly, that this is a system not aimed at them?*

A. It is obvious from the technical design of the system. There will not be any misunderstanding by the Russians because they are sophisticated enough to see, in the deployment plans that will be made public, the distinction between Chinese-oriented and Soviet-oriented population protection systems. It is very important that our own people do not misunderstand that point.

Q. *Do we expect the Soviet ABM system to be expanded from the present modest system they are now deploying?*

A. Well, first there is some uncertainty as to the character of that system. We know that they are building one around Moscow which is not yet operational. They are deploying a second system elsewhere which may have an ABM capability. But the evidence is not conclusive. As Secretary of Defense I must assume that they will deploy a system across their entire nation, and that is the assumption on which we are developing and have developed our offensive weapons. Whether they will do that or not, I do not know.

Q. *Is our "light" ABM system more modest than theirs?*

A. Well, I think it is for a different purpose. Their Moscow system appears to be directed toward protecting Moscow against a potential U.S. attack. It is going to be ineffective for that. All of our senior commanders and all of our civilian officials in the Defense Department are very certain on that point. Ineffective because it is a very primitive system, which our existing weapons can overcome. Even if they later bought a better defense of Moscow, we would be able to overcome that too.

They undoubtedly made the decision to produce and deploy the Moscow system back in 1961 or 1962—when we, too, were considering deployment of a similar system; when many in our nation advocated deploying such a system. Had we followed that advice then, it would have been a serious error. Such a system would not be any more effective against the Soviets than their Moscow system will be effective against us.

Q. *Why, if the Russians know that any ABM system is ineffective—and I think their generals have admitted this—why does Russia persist in spending billions of dollars on it?*

A. You are quite correct. Some of their generals have admitted that their ABM system is ineffective. They have done that very recently, within the last six months. But they probably are not the same generals who made the decision several years ago to deploy it. The generals who made that decision are similar to some Americans, both civilian and military, who back in 1959, 1960, 1961, were strongly urging that we go ahead with what was then known as the Nike-Zeus, which would have been similar to the present Moscow system.

So, I think what the Soviets did then was to follow the same kind of advice we were getting, but which we decided against. And now some of their generals admit it was wrong.

But decisions like these have a way of acquiring a momentum of their own. And the Soviets have, for a decade and a half, spent far more on strategic air defense than we have, with little to show for it. There never has been any question that we could get through with bombers or missiles. So, the Soviets have wasted those expenditures on defense to a very substantial degree.

Q. *The momentum you speak of—I would think that might be more of a danger in an open society like ours, a demand that we expand our ABM. How are this and succeeding administrations going to control that?*

A. Well, we controlled it on the Nike-Zeus. We did not build it. We controlled it on the B-70. We didn't build it. The Hercules and the Hawk missile programs were controlled. I think we can control the ABM. We really control the momentum by informing our public of the pros and cons. And that was the reason for my 25-page speech in San Francisco. That is the reason I am sitting down here with you this morning.

Q. *You touched upon the theme of common interests with the Soviet Union. What are they?*

A. I do not want to exaggerate this theme because in many, many respects the Soviets are following an aggressive foreign policy that is contrary to the interests of the free nations of the world. I am not under any illusions as to that policy.

But the fact that we are in conflict in some spheres does not mean that there are not some areas in which our interests coincide. One of them is in avoiding a continuing escalation in strategic offensive and defensive weapons. We can each achieve the deterrent we need without that continuing escalation. It is unlikely that either one of us can achieve a meaningful advantage over the other.

The fact that there are within our society other desirable uses of the resources we devote to military hardware is so self-evident that it hardly needs elaboration. The same is true, to perhaps an even greater degree, in the Soviet Union. Just as important, both we and the Russians should be devoting much more of our national wealth toward improving conditions of life within the less-developed countries.

Q. *Besides a limit on arms expenditures, do you see other areas of mutual interest between the U.S. and the Communists?*

A. Avoiding nuclear war, of course. Trade is another, I think. Look at the failure of Congress to support the Administration's program of building bridges of trade with the Eastern European nations. Its actions included the denial of the Administration's request to participate in the $50 million loan to the Fiat Corporation to help the Soviets expand their automotive industry. This would be like putting them on dope. Once they get an automobile industry, they will never get off it. And that simply means they divert resources away from defense to consumer goods. How could that possibly be contrary to our interests? We are misguided if we fail to recognize these potential areas of common interest, as distinguished from their basic, aggressive foreign policy.

Q. *The U.S. and the Soviet Union are trying to agree on a draft for a nonprolifera-tion treaty which would commit us to seeking an end to the nuclear arms race. Isn't our ABM deployment a step in the opposite direction?*

A. One of the assumptions inherent in negotiation of the nonproliferation treaty is that the real deterrent to China's use of nuclear weapons is the overwhelming offensive nuclear capability of the U.S. We have emphasized this in our many conversations about the treaty with our friends in Asia.

China's leaders know that an attempt to attack the U.S. would invite the utter devastation of urban China. Our allies know that the same constraints that prevent China from attacking the U.S. prevent China from attacking them. At the time of the first Chinese nuclear test in October 1964, President Johnson said nations that do not seek national nuclear weapons can be sure that, if they need our strong support against some threat of nuclear blackmail, then they will have it. The capability to neutralize whatever nuclear threat China will be able to direct at the U.S. underscores our pledge of strong support against nuclear blackmail.

We firmly believe that it would serve no useful purpose for nations in Asia to acquire nuclear weapons of their own with all the financial burden, diversion of resources and needless competition that would entail.

Q. *In other words, those nations which depend on us for defense should be cheered by our announcement, because it assures that we will not be devastated by a Chinese attack?*

A. That is correct. Furthermore, it is extremely important that this ABM action of ours not be misunderstood in relation to our commitment to seek an end to the nuclear arms race.

I do not believe that a very limited ABM deployment is a step-up in the strategic arms race between the U.S. and the Soviet Union. Our deployment isn't designed to protect the cities of America against a Soviet strategic attack, and thus it in no way threatens the Soviet ability to deter an American attack.

The fact is, however, that they have been building up their strategic missile forces. We had no choice but to take some additional steps to maintain the adequacy of our own deterrent.

We considered a number of alternatives—adding more missiles, a new manned bomber, or even a new strategic missile system. We reached the conclusion that one of the most practical steps we could take, and the one least likely to force the Soviets into a counter-reaction, was the deployment of an ABM system which would protect our Minuteman sites, so that our own deterrent is not diminished.

Our ABM defense shouldn't have any adverse effect on negotiations of the nonproliferation treaty. Indeed, the arguments for signing such a treaty are more cogent than ever.

APPENDIX 6.—REMARKS OF PAUL C. WARNKE, ASSISTANT SECRETARY OF DEFENSE, INTERNATIONAL SECURITY AFFAIRS, BEFORE THE ADVOCATES CLUB, DETROIT, MICH., OCTOBER 6, 1967

At the start, I'd like to express appreciation and apology. Appreciation, of course, for the opportunity to be with you tonight and to share in your fellowship. Apology, for the fact that, inescapably, I'm cast as the skeleton at the feast.

But this is the risk that any group accepts when it invites a speaker from the Department of Defense. We deal necessarily with the implements of death. And to-day the implements of death are no longer reasonably selective but instead are the frighteningly impersonal instruments of mass destruction.

In recent talks in Washington a high official of an Asian country observed that: "The world is governed by the logic of deterrence." This got me to thinking. And I concluded that the statement, like so many oriental axioms, had a great deal of merit.

As has already been explained, my training and background is that of a lawyer. Accordingly, I have had day-to-day experience with the fact that adherence to the laws that are essential to the preservation of an ordered society turns largely on two kinds of motivation. One is the voluntary recognition by responsible members of society that its ability to function depends on conformity to the rules that protect both person and property. But responsible individuals never make up the totality of any population. Other elements can be compelled to comply with the basic laws only because they are deterred from anti-social conduct. Deterrence exists in the likelihood that deviation from society's rules will lead to punishment. And the surer that punishment, obviously, the stronger the deterrent becomes. As the likelihood of punishment diminishes, the likelihood that the laws will be flouted by irresponsible individuals obviously will increase. This inverse ratio is what has stimulated the lively debate as to whether our courts have gone too far in seeking to assure the Constitutional rights of those accused of crime. Concern about individual liberties admittedly detracts from the certainty that the guilty will be punished. But it also protects those mistakenly charged with crime and prevents the distortion of our free society into a police state.

Without getting further into a debate outside my present field, I would note that fear of punishment can never deter all criminal conduct. There is, in any population, a residuum of individuals who neither innate responsibility nor concern for the consequences can make adhere to the rules of organized society. There are individuals who, because of mental incapacity or a desperate conviction that they have nothing to lose, will stumble into criminal behavior or will seek determinedly to tear at the fabric of the society in which they find no place. This last phenomenon—of which you in this city have special knowledge—underlies the riots that have troubled our internal serenity during the past few years. Other crimes of course result when normally law-abiding persons are prey to panic or passion that overcomes both their normal responsibility and the fear of punishment.

Tonight I would like to discuss wlth you the implications of these universal principles to the field of international security. Because, as I see it, the logic of deterrence that permits any particular society to function applies as well in the sphere of international relations.

In the world community, the generality of nations conduct themselves responsibly because they recognize that their mutual interest is served by the responsible conduct of world affairs. A few, regrettably, may have to be deterred from aggressive efforts to better their own position at the expense of their neighbors. Today, we posses a deterrent force that permits certain response in sudden, sure and shattering strength. By all the logic of deterrence, therefore, fear of reprisal should be sufficient to make us safe from nuclear attack from any source.

Yet, as you know, Secretary of Defense Robert McNamara announced last month that the United States had decided to deploy a system of anti-ballistic missiles designed to protect against the possible Chinese threat.

This decision, of course, has very substantial implications for the area of my responsibility as Assistant Secretary of Defense for International Security Affairs. I would like therefore to consider with you this evening the likely impact of our deployment on international security.

In particular, I want to talk about the likely impact of this deployment upon our efforts to maintain the security of Asia. In addition, I will discuss its bearing on our efforts to negotiate a treaty to halt the spread of nuclear weapons and to secure an agreement on the limitation of offensive and defensive strategic systems with the Soviet Union.

Let me begin by trying to explain, in some more detail than was possible in Mr. McNamara's speech, what we hope and expect the bearing our deployment will have on Asian security.

I would like to stress that, contrary to the charges of some critics, this decision to deploy resulted solely from a careful consideration of the security interests of the United States and its allies. Outside and unrelated pressures were not a consideration. The positive advantages of the deployment, which I will discuss in a moment, seemed to us to make the decision to proceed a prudent, though close, choice.

Secretary McNamara has made clear his strong opposition to attempting to deploy an ABM system designed to protect our cities against a large Soviet attack. He is opposed, not because he does not want to protect our cities, but because of his belief, which I share completely, that this is not possible, that the Soviets would respond to our deployment in ways which would leave our cities still exposed. The deployment thus would not increase our security.

Secretary McNamara's consistent and determined public opposition to a Soviet-oriented ABM system has led to the misconception that he has been opposed to any ABM deployment. In fact, the Defense Department has been giving close consideration to the question of a Chinese-oriented ABM deployment for some time. Let me just remind you briefly about what we have said previously on this question. Secretary McNamara first noted the need to consider the possibility of a small nuclear attack on the United States by a nation other than the Soviet Union in February 1965. In his posture statement to the Congress for the coming fiscal year, he identified the risk of such attack as emanating from Communist China. However, he stated that the "lead time for that nation to develop and deploy an effective ballistic missile system capable of reaching the United States is greater than we require to deploy the defense."

The following year, Mr. McNamara's posture statement to Congress in February 1966 reflected his encouragement at the technical progress being made in the development of the ABM subsystem, particularly the long-range interceptor missiles. It also recorded his judgment that the system could be effective against the foreseeable Chinese threat. I quote him:

"Initially, the deployment concept for NIKE X contemplated the point defense of only a relatively small number of the larger cities against a heavy Soviet attack. Subsequently, as I described last year, it became feasible to consider extending protection to smaller cities by modifying certain NIKE X subsystems and using less extensive and sophisticated deployments. Even this concept, however, still left most of the country vulnerable to great damage even from a small attack deliberately designed to avoid our defended cities.

"This situation has now been changed significantly by the emergence of the possibility of developing an area missile defense based upon the use of long-range interceptor missiles which I mentioned previously. Against a relatively light attack, such as the Chinese Communists may be able to mount in the mid-to-late 1970's, an area defense might be very effective, offering the possibility of avoiding any substantial damage."

However, a production decision was not then deemed necessary. At background briefings and press conferences in November and December 1966, following the Chinese explosion of a nuclear weapon in a missile, Mr. McNamara maintained his position on the timing of a decision to deploy an ABM system to defend against the Communist Chinese threat.

We have delayed any decision until now, because one was not needed until now. During the interim, research and development on the Chinese-oriented system continued and the system has been greatly improved. However, the point in time has now been reached when we had to make the decision to deploy if we were to have a system in the field by the time the Chinese could begin to deploy ICBM's. The Chinese could test an ICBM as early as this year and they could have an ICBM capability of some significance by the mid-1970's. Since it will take us five years to deploy our defensive system, we need to begin now if we are to have our defense ready before the Chinese are capable of an attack against the United States.

I have frequently been asked, over the last several weeks, whether our deployment of an ABM system oriented against mainland China does not represent a step backward from our stated desire to try and build bridges to China. Some have suggested that the decision represents an exaggerated view of the actual threat which China poses to the United States and our friends and allies in Asia. I believe that close examination of our motivation in deploying a Chinese-oriented ABM system shows these views to be incorrect. A basic element in our approach to relations with the people of mainland China remains that stated in the President's State-of-the-Union Message. There he said:

"We shall continue to hope for a reconciliation between the people of mainland China and the world community—including cooperation in all the tasks of arms control, security, and progress on which the fate of the Chinese people, like the rest of us, depends. "We would be the first to welcome a China which had decided to respect her neighbors' rights. We would be the first to applaud were she to concentrate her great energies and intelligence on improving the welfare of her own people. And we have no intention of trying to deny her legitimate needs for security and friendly relations with neighboring countries."

Our ABM deployment will in no way interfere with these efforts. We continue to hope that China will evolve in a way which will make better relations with the leaders in Peking possible, not only on arms control matters but on a broad range of issues.

While hoping for changes in Chinese behavior, we have sought to analyze Peking's current views and attitudes which might affect their use of their developing nuclear capability. We see no reason to conclude that the Chinese are any less cautious than the rulers of other nations that have nuclear weapons. Nor do we believe that Peking is at all ignorant of the effects of nuclear weapons. On the contrary, we believe that the Chinese leaders understand the devastation which the use of nuclear weapons by China could bring to the mainland of China itself. Indeed the Chinese have shown a disposition to act cautiously, and to avoid any military clash with the United States that could lead to nuclear war.

In light of this view of China, then, why did we conclude that a Chinese-oriented ABM system makes sense?

I think one way to approach this question is to consider a hypothetical world without the Soviet Union. In that case, I believe that few would think our decision required much in the way of explanation. Hostile action by China is, unfortunately, not totally inconceivable; and nations have always deployed those defensive systems which could blunt an offensive attack from a possible enemy. If we can create, for a sum well within our means, a system which will greatly reduce if not eliminate the casualties we might receive from a Chinese attack, logic and prudence require that we do so.

Of course the Soviet nuclear force does exist; and, as Mr. McNamara pointed out in San Francisco, one of our major concerns in proceeding with this deployment was that it not trigger an acceleration of the strategic arms race with the Soviet Union. Because of this possible danger—which I wish to return to briefly at the end of my talk—we might well have concluded not to proceed with the deployment without some more specific reason to believe that it would enhance our own security and that of our friends and allies in Asia.

What then is the specific reason that led us to go ahead?

My answer to this question might begin by reemphasis that the cornerstone of our efforts to maintain the security of Asia is our ability to deter aggression. Our fundamental strategy remains deterrence and I want to make it clear that our decisions to deploy a China-oriented ABM system is wholly consonant with this strategy. The obligations of the United States in Asia stem most specifically and most importantly from our treaty commitments with a number of Asian nations. In addition, at the time of the first Chinese nuclear detonation in 1963, President Johnson declared that: "Nations that do not seek national nuclear weapons can be sure that, if they need our strong support against some threat of nuclear blackmail, then they will have it."

I have no doubt that the United States would honor these assurances, whether or not we deployed an ABM system. Our European allies have come to understand that the United States has both the will and the capability to deter Soviet aggression in Europe, even though the United States cannot achieve a credible first-strike capability that would prevent Soviet response, and even though American society—but not U.S. strategic forces—would be destroyed in a Soviet attack. Against the much reduced Chinese capability, there should be no doubt as to the credibility of our deterrent.

But despite this, some speculation had developed in Asia, and perhaps also in Peking, as to whether, when Chinese ICBM's were targeted on American cities, the United States would shirk its responsibilities in Asia. Some asked, for example, if the United States would really be willing to risk Detroit to save a small Asian nation. Similar questions had been asked by our European allies as the Soviet nuclear delivery capability grew. As we have learned in Europe, we must be prepared to run risks if our assurances are to have any credibility. But doubts did exist and we concluded that a Chinese-oriented ABM system could serve a valuable role in removing these doubts. In deploying this system, we seek to emphasize the present unique disparity in strategic nuclear capability and technology between the U.S. and China and to extend well into the future the credibility of our option for a nuclear response.

Our deployment will substantially reduce the Chinese Communist capability to threaten American cities and should leave, neither Asia in general nor the Chinese in particular, with any uncertainty as to whether or not the United States would act to prevent the Chinese from gaining any political or military advantage from their nuclear forces. We recognize that this deployment by itself would not be sufficient. The United States will continue to need to act in ways which make clear the credibility of our deterrent. And both we and Asian nations have to continue to maintain the necessary conventional forces to deal with lesser threats. But we believe our ABM deployment is an important, useful step. Hopefully the China-oriented ABM system will also help buy the time within which other political, economic, and social forces can be at work to bring China into responsible participation in an international community. We fully intend to help these forces do their work.

This, then, is how we believe the deployment of the Chinese-oriented ABM system will impact upon our efforts to maintain the security of Asia. What about the physical security of the United States itself?

Secretary McNamara referred, in his speech, to the possibility of Chinese miscalculation, and in a later interview with LIFE Magazine he made clear that his concern is with the situation in which there is the danger of a pre-emptive attack. Let me explain briefly what our concern is. In a crisis which they had brought on, if the Chinese came to believe that the United States might attack, they might be tempted to launch a pre-emptive strike, hoping to bring down at least a part of the American house in the face of the total destruction, or even only the destruction of their nuclear forces, which at the moment of crisis they feared we were about to wreak upon them. No matter how miscalculating or irrational such an act might seem—and I did say earlier we believe the Chinese leaders to be no less cautious than the rulers of other nations that possess nuclear weapons—under the current circumstances it is not impossible. This danger will pass when China develops, as the Soviets have done, a secure second strike capability. In the interim, we decided that as long as it was within our technical capability to provide an effective defense against this danger, prudence seemed to dictate that we deploy that defense which would further deter the Chinese from pre-empting, and eliminate or greatly reduce our casualties should they engage in such an act.

I am sometimes asked whether China could not nullify our defense by smuggling a bomb into the United States in a suitcase, or blowing up a junk off the California coast. Such activity is, unfortunately, technically feasible, although the magnitude of the potential destruction is not comparable to a missile attack. Moreover, we believe such action is extremely unlikely. As I have suggested, we do not view the Chinese as basically irrational. The suitcase bomb would require the Chinese, in the absence of an immediate crisis, to decide in advance that they wish to destroy an American city, knowing full well the retaliation which would follow. Such behavior seems to us totally unlikely. What our defense is directed toward, as I have said, is the possibility that at the height of a crisis the Chinese leadership might panic and press the button. Our ABM deployment will guard against that contingency, improbable though it too may be.

Of all the possible implications of our ABM deployment, none concerned me more than its impact on our efforts to negotiate a nonproliferation treaty—or NPT—designed to halt the spread of nuclear weapons. We analyzed very carefully the likely impact of a deployment on the on-going negotiations relating to the NPT. We came to the conclusion that our Chinese-oriented ABM deployment should make it easier, and not harder, for countries in Asia to sign the NPT. The increased credibility of the United States deterrent, which we expect to result from our deployment, should make even clearer the lack of any need for independent national nuclear forces in Asia. If any country in the area has been tempted to develop a nuclear capability because of a fear that we would cease to deter China, our actions should have removed these uncertainties.

One concern in regard to the NPT has related to the question of equality in obligation. The non-nuclear nations have been asserting, quite understandably, that the United States and the Soviet Union should demonstrate a willingness to move toward nuclear disarmament if they are asking the other nations of the world to forego the manufacture of nuclear weapons. Both we and the Soviets have accepted this obligation, and the language of the draft treaty reflects that commitment. However, that commitment does not mean, and I do not believe that other countries would want it to mean, that the United States would refrain from taking all steps that might improve our deterrent against China until China, herself, is prepared to enter into satisfactory arms limitation agreements. I believe our Chinese-oriented ABM deployment meets this criteria.

An additional cardinal point is that this ABM deployment does not signify in any way a change in our attitude toward the Soviet Union. Our view of that relation can be briefly summarized.

The relationship between any two great powers whose interests and activities are as far-reaching as those of the United States and the Soviet Union must necessarily be complex, a mixture of cooperation and conflict. During the first decade after World War II, the U.S.-Soviet relationship was primarily one of conflict. But in recent years, despite areas of deep disagreement—Vietnam and Germany are some examples—the necessity of co-existing in a highly armed world has led us to cooperate where we have interests in common.

Most important of these common interests is the need to prevent nuclear war. Each of us now has the ability to destroy the other's society. This is the most awesome power that men have ever possessed. We do not fear that the present leaders in the Kremlin, or any foreseeable successors, will employ recklessly or irresponsibly the vast resources of destructive capability which they possess.

Similarly, we think that we have given them ample evidence that they need fear no such behavior on our part. The costs of nuclear irresponsibility would be too great.

For this reason, another interest we share with them is to prevent the spread of nuclear weapons. This interest is not wholly altruistic: we are concerned not only that new possessors of nuclear weapons may employ them against each other, or against a non-nuclear state; we see an even greater danger in the possibility that the use of nuclear weapons by a third country could precipitate a war which would end in a nuclear exchange between the two so-called Superpowers. In our view, and I would think in that of the Soviet Union as well, each additional nuclear power increases the possibility of nuclear war, by design, by miscalculation, or even by accident.

The U.S. and the USSR have a third related interest: that of reducing the vast amounts of resources which each of us now devotes to military forces and to military hardware. That other and more rewarding uses can be made of these resources is so self-evident, despite the over-all prosperity of American society, that it demands no elaboration. The same is true, to an even greater degree, in the Soviet Union. Similarly, for the health of the world we inhabit, both we and the Russians should be devoting more of our national wealth to improving conditions of life within the less-developed countries.

Our decision to deploy a Chinese-oriented ABM system reflects no lack of concern about what Secretary McNamara called the "mad momentum" of the nuclear arms race. But because our proposed deployment poses no possible threat to the Soviet deterrent, it need lead to no acceleration of the Soviet-American strategic arms race.

We will continue to seek cooperation and agreement with the Soviets whenever our interests converge. In particular, we will continue to hope that by parallel actions, or by formal agreement, the two countries can undertake to limit their strategic offensive and defensive forces. There is no reason to believe that our deployment decision makes them any less willing to enter into talks, or to take parallel actions. In fact, although we cannot be sure, the contrary may well be the case. Moreover, should these talks occur, we hope to avoid bogging down in the perennially difficult issue of international inspection.

Since the end of the second world war, the United States has sought an international agreement to end, or at least slow down, the nuclear arms race. The United States has always insisted, and will continue to insist, on adequate verification of any arms control agreement with our potential adversaries. In deciding whether we need an agreed international inspection system, we assess very carefully the capability of our own unilateral verification systems. As you know, the United States agreed to the three environment test ban treaty, with the full concurrence of the Joint Chiefs of Staff and the consent of the United States Senate, despite the lack of provisions for international inspection. We did so because we were confident, and remain confident, that we can detect any violations of the treaty by the Soviet Union or any other signer. We have, in fact, accurately detected Chinese and French atmospheric nuclear tests.

In considering any possible agreement with the Soviet Union to level off or reduce strategic offensive and defensive systems, or even the possibility for parallel action on the part of the two countries, we may have to depend on our own unilateral capability for verification. We believe a number of possibilities for parallel action and even for formal agreement with the Soviets would permit our reliance on unilateral means of verification. Other more far-reaching agreements, particularly any involving substantial reductions, would require agreed international inspection. You may be sure that we would not accept any agreement unless we had high confidence in our ability to monitor Soviet compliance, either by unilateral means or by agreed inspection procedures. But you may be sure, also, that we will pursue, with diligence and determination, our efforts to bring the nuclear arms race under control.

For we do not believe that continuation of that nuclear competition is without risk, and that risk lies only in seeking agreement with our potential enemies. We now have lived with danger throughout most or all of our adult years. We recognize that all courses have risks and that it is folly, not prudence, to continue on the path that the world has been following without seeking a better way. The U.S. is fully prepared for an end to the nuclear arms race. For the sake of our own and future generations, we can only hope that neither the attitudes of our adversaries nor the gulf of suspicion which separates us will prevent attainment of the objective which is in our common interest.

It is my belief that the decision to go ahead with an ABM system directed against potential Chinese threat will not retard, but rather will advance our progress toward that objective.

APPENDIX 7.—NATIONAL SECURITY: BASIC TASKS, BY SENATOR HENRY M. JACKSON

ADDRESS TO THE HOOVER INSTITUTION ON WAR, REVOLUTION AND PEACE CONFERENCE ON 50 YEARS OF COMMUNISM IN RUSSIA

(Stanford University Memorial Auditorium, October 11, 1967)

I am delighted to be with you this evening. I am honored to share in this truly significant conference. It is also very good to be back at Stanford University.

I guess you would classify me as a Stanford drop-out. I attended school here during the summer of 1931 and took two courses under Dr. Graham Stuart, one on the League of Nations and the other on international relations. On his advice, due to the deepening depression and the manpower ceiling in the Department of State, I undertook the study of law rather than my previous plan to prepare for the Foreign Service. Your Dr. Stuart was and is a great inspiration to me.

I

Unlike the fabled Flu-flu bird—that didn't care where it was going, it only wanted to see where it had been—we are looking at the past in these meetings in order to find clues to the future. By gaining a better understanding of the last half-century we hope to be able to use our wits and wisdom to help shape events of the next half-century.

That comment reveals, I suppose, a political perspective. Some of you write history; the politician reads history to discover its operational significance to him in his work. What does it tell him that will help him to distinguish the wise from the less wise choices he faces from day to day.

II

In 1967, as throughout the postwar period, the conflict of purposes and policies between the United States and the Soviet Union is the conflict that must be successfully managed if our children are to inherit a nation and a world whose future possibilities have not been foreclosed.

There is a belief in some quarters that the cold war storms are abating and that the worst of our problems with the Soviet Union are behind us. The relative tempering of behavior since Stalin has encouraged many people to believe that the Kremlin, if not content with the *status quo*, is not acutely dissatisfied with it. Other people assure us that Moscow will not attempt to adjust by force existing spheres of influence. Some people even see Communist China as the one source of disturbance and danger in today's world—and tomorrow's—and the Sino-Soviet rift as the doorway through which the Soviet Union may step to rejoin Western society.

Experience *has* produced some leavening of world revolutionary dogmatism. The shaping forces of the modern world have not bypassed the Soviet Union. Moscow, like Washington, now is aware of the risks of nuclear war to Soviet society, and Soviet leaders seem to have some understanding of the need to prevent the accidents, miscalculations, or failures of communication that could lead to catastrophe. The vigorous development and application of science and technology have not only multiplied the capacity to wage war but also the capacity to produce consumer goods and services. The demand by Soviet citizens for improvements in living standards have thus been encouraged. These same advances in science and technology have brought about a somewhat wider diffusion of power internally. A restoration of Stalinism would today be difficult, if not impossible. The worldwide appeal of democratic ideas has touched Soviet society also—and where lip-service is paid to these ideas, in time mere lip-service may not be enough. The events of the century reveal no weakening of the political force of nationalism, as the Kremlin has learned in its relations with many communist regimes, and particularly with China.

Although everyone now says "polycentric" where some used to say "monolithic," it does not follow that Moscow is about to make common cause with the West. There is a hopeful side to the picture, but it is not the only side.

I do not know how to assess Soviet foreign policy in recent years except as an effort to extend the frontiers of Soviet influence whenever the risks seemed to be acceptable. How else should we read the several Berlin crises or the Cuban missile crisis? Khrushchev has not been criticized in Kremlin circles, by the way, for what he was trying to accomplish by installing missiles in Cuba, but for failing—by biting off more than he could chew.

Moscow's heavy responsibility for the situation in Vietnam also illustrates my point: it has given Hanoi steady and substantial military and diplomatic support. Moscow has helped to train and equip Hanoi's forces and is now the North's principal source of supply. Hanoi is one of the two or three best-defended cities in the world, thanks to Soviet anti-aircraft installations. Late-model Soviet rockets are being used against our bases and our forces on land and sea. In light of the evidence one must ask whether the Soviet Union desires a compromise settlement. Its behavior suggests that it would welcome our humiliation but that it will be careful to keep itself insulated against excessive risks.

On the other side of the world, Moscow is deeply involved in a political campaign, backed by all the elements of Soviet power, to reduce the influence of the United States in Western Europe to the point where NATO will disintegrate. Just this year, at the Karlovy Vary Conference of Communist and Workers Parties of Europe, Brezhnev took the lead in issuing a call to European communist parties and to West European socialist and social democratic parties to try to disrupt the NATO Alliance by 1969, in the expectation that Moscow could deal thereafter with a fragmented Europe of small and medium-sized states, with obvious implications for the ability of these states, including the German Federal Republic, to pursue policies not meeting with Soviet approval.

Moscow's large political, economic, and military investments in the Middle East underlie the events of last May and June, and dramatically support my point, even though, in the Kremlin's view, its efforts miscarried. It was not until events threatened to embroil the Soviet Union in an excessively hazardous enterprise that the Kremlin opted for a policy of caution.

My own reading of events, therefore, suggests that where we find the Kremlin acting with circumspection, it is because, to use their phrase, "objective conditions" impose this requirement. Where the "objective conditions" are propitious, however, the Kremlin is encouraged to act boldly to expand the frontiers of its influence. The circumstances are thus created for the most dangerous confrontation—a showdown between nuclear powers.

It is difficult, if not impossible, for anyone on the outside to know whether the Soviet leadership, at any given moment, is in a cautious or risk-taking mood. Nothing is more guarded than the discussions that take place within the Kremlin. Perhaps Kosygin, Brezhnev and company will avoid daring adventures—at least in Europe; I would be less sure about, say, the Middle East. For even a sense of caution about a direct US-USSR confrontation still leaves open a large arena for so-called "wars of national liberation" and political conflicts waged through proxies and mercenaries needled into action by Moscow. The constant danger is that any one such lesser war or conflict-by-proxy may lead to a nuclear showdown.

And how long will the present Soviet leaders lead? Few, if any, students of Soviet affairs anticipated Khrushchev's ouster, and few are likely to anticipate the next shift, or the policy changes it may precipitate.

In any event, as I look back upon our experience, I find a strong correlation between Soviet prudence and restraint and the firmness and capabilities of the West.

Also, as the record shows, Soviet leaders can be reasonable in one field and unreasonable in another—blunt and ready to do business on some issues, crafty and unpredictable on others. Indeed, on any given matter they can twist and turn, thaw and freeze, agree and disagree, and, with no embarrassment whatsoever, trot out on alternate days a black-hatted Fedorenko and a white-hatted Dobrynin.

We should have learned by now that the way to encourage a reasonable response from Moscow is not through weakness but through strength. The way to negotiate successfully with Soviet leaders is to maintain the strength to make negotiated agreements more attractive to them than continued disagreements—as in the case of the Austrian Peace Treaty and the limited nuclear test-ban treaty.

III

In relations with the Soviet Union the free world must pursue two consonant courses of action: to work with them where interests converge, and at the same time to maintain the strength and the resolve to discourage peace-upsetting moves by them.

It was with this point of view on East-West relations that I voted for the limited nuclear test-ban treaty—and also worked to obtain the Administration's pledges to continue actively with the nuclear testing permitted under the treaty and to maintain in a state of readiness a program for atmospheric tests in the event of abrogation of the treaty or other circumstances placing the supreme interests of the nation in jeopardy.

It is with this point of view that I have favored efforts to limit the spread of nuclear weapons—and at the same time have opposed major concessions in the treaty negotiations without any compensating changes of policy on the Soviet side.

For similar reasons I have favored discussions with Moscow about freezing the development of strategic defensive weapons—and at the same time voted to appropriate funds to begin the production and deployment of a "thin" ABM system, and argued against indefinitely delaying such a deployment. I have sought a high priority for a research and development program to develop, if we can, the tools for an effective defense against the kind of missile attack that, as of today, only the Soviet Union could launch.

For similar reasons I have supported West German efforts to move toward normal relations with Eastern Europe and the Soviet Union, including expanded cultural, scientific, trade, and diplomatic contact. At the same time, I have opposed substantial unilateral reductions of American forces in Western Europe and I have argued the still fresh and compelling need for the Atlantic Alliance and its international commands.

It is with this point of view that I have urged the importance of frequent and frank discussions between the United States and the Soviet Union, in order that each side might gain a clearer understanding of the range and limits of the other's intentions and actions and that we and they might work toward an identification of areas of common or parallel interest, in Vietnam and elsewhere. At the same time, I have tried to counteract the siren song that goes: "if we trust the communists, they will trust us." A favorite quotation of mine is one from Reinhold Niebuhr:

> "If the democratic nations fail, their failure must be partly attributed to the faulty strategy of idealists who have too many illusions when they face realists who have too little conscience."

IV

Frankly, I am deeply concerned at a tendency I discern in some current thinking about American military policy. Some scientists and civilian officials have a mirror image interpretation of Moscow's decisions relating to its military establishment, seeing them as reflex actions—a tit-for-tat, action-reaction view of the Soviet arms buildup. Implicit (and sometimes explicit) in this view is the belief that if the U.S. did not act the Soviet Union would not act. Sometimes the argument is taken even farther: if the U.S. acted to reduce its military programs, the Soviet Union would reciprocate, in what could be called *a policy of minus-tit for minus-tat.*

That is one possible model of Soviet behavior, but the policy-maker cannot rely on it until and unless it is supported by convincing evidence that the model describes not how the Soviet Union *might* act, but how it *does* act. There is, of course, a relationship between the U.S. strategic posture and that of the Soviet Union. I am sure the Russians have a real fear of our awesome military might. Yet as I read the evidence, the Russian aspiration to possess a first-rate military establishment stems from other factors as well, from a perspective that goes beyond the theories of deterrence that have gained popularity over the last twenty years.

One factor is the long-implanted belief that Russia is threatened at various points along its tremendously long land borders. The Soviets have lost tens of millions in the wars of this century and it is not surprising that they display a passionate, at times paranoid, concern for the security of their frontiers. Another factor is the propensity of Soviet leaders, given their interpretation of history, to impute to the "capitalist-imperialist" West, the worst of intentions. Over and beyond this, of course, the thinking of Soviet leaders is conditioned by their own conception of the Soviet Union's historic role, which is still defined in the familiar vocabulary of world revolution.

We cannot ignore the fact that it was the Soviet Union which acted first to develop long-range intercontinental surface to surface missiles, and the U.S. which followed. It is the Soviet Union which has acted first to deploy an ABM set-up, and the U.S. is following.

Some American scientists and civilian officials have done the nation a poor service by propagandizing a notion contrary to all the evidence, namely, the idea that military technology has arrived at a "plateau," that the "scientific military revolution" has been "stabilized," and that no new technological upsets which could affect military relationships are likely. Ordinary economic technology is always finding better ways to do things and there is no reason to suppose that military technology will cease in this effort. Missile technology, for example, is advancing in almost all fields of offense and defense—payload, accuracy, guidance, maneuverability, and multiple warheads.

What is the evidence that if we unilaterally reduce our own military programs, the Soviet Union will reciprocate? We do have some experience to go on. It may not be conclusive, but we should face up to it.

Sometime ago our government announced a top limit on the number of our strategic missiles for deployment—both land and sea-based. But Moscow, according to its own statements, has been working hard to narrow the missile gap that limited its range of options in the Cuban crisis of 1962. Moscow has just increased by 50 percent in one year the number of its operational intercontinental ballistic missiles. A year ago the ratio of American to Russian ICBMs and submarine-launched ballistic missiles was 3 to 1; the present ratio is less than that.

The argument is made that this declining ratio in offensive strategic capability can be offset by the U.S. move to multiple warheads. If past experience in the development of critical weapons is any guide, however, we must assume that the Soviets are also on the multiple warhead course. We need to remember that the larger missile payload the Soviets can mount on their bigger missiles gives them the capability to deploy more nuclear warheads per missile than we can.

Sometime ago our government phased out our land-based intermediate-range ballistic missiles and we have reason to believe the Soviet Union understood that we were trying to eliminate a possible source of misunderstanding about our intentions. Yet the Russians have maintained 700 to 800 medium-range and intermediate-range ballistic missile launchers, most of which are targeted on Western Europe.

Consider also our experience with the anti-ballistic missile. Our government put off a decision to start deploying a "thin" ABM system in the hope that the Soviet Union would see the mutual advantages in mutually foregoing further developments in defenses against missiles, thus releasing Soviet and American resources for urgent and constructive purposes in the world.

Moscow, however, is going about *its* business, not *ours*. An ABM system in Soviet hands lends itself superbly to the bluffing and blackmail that have all too often been hallmarks of Soviet policy. Would a U.S. without ABMs maintain its firm resolve if a USSR with ABMs began a series of step-by-step moves against Berlin? As Soviet planners "cold-war game" with the forces of the 1970s, they are surely asking themselves questions of this kind. So should we.

Obviously the Soviet rulers do not accept the notion that military technology stands on a "plateau." Perhaps no single breakthrough would be as significant as the developments leading to the H-bomb or the ICBM, although I would not want to bet on that. In any case an accumulation of less dramatic inventions could have major significance, and could critically affect the present balance of forces.

v

I must also say, I am profoundly concerned at another tendency I note in the current discussion of American military policy. Top Defense officials are telling us that "nuclear superiority has only limited relevance today" and that "today, in the nuclear age, nuclear superiority is of limited significance." What do statements like that mean? While continuing to describe our policy as one of maintaining nuclear superiority over the Soviet Union, are we in fact embarked on a different course? Have top Defense officials accepted the hypothesis that nuclear superiority constitutes a provocation to the other side to build up its strength? Is nuclear parity now our goal? Have top Defense officials come to think that missile defense against the Soviets is a destabilizing influence in world affairs, and that an effective missile defense should not be one of our objectives?

These are not rhetorical questions. I do not know the answers. I do suggest that if such assumptions are entering into the making of American military policy, they should be ventilated and debated thoroughly—and not quietly substituted for the assumptions on which we have been acting. The questions involve what would be a radical change in American policy. I believe it could be the road to catastrophe.

If, for example, the Soviet Union comes out ahead in the search for an effective anti-missile system, the relationship on which our defense planners have counted to maintain political stability by discouraging a diplomacy of blackmail will be reversed. The consequences for the West could be calamitous.

As I see things, international peace and security depend not on a par ty of power but on a preponderance of power in the peace-keepers over the pieace-upsetters.

Our aim is not, of course, an unlimited accumulation of weapons. Our policy has been—and I believe it should continue to be—to create and maintain, in cooperation with our allies, a relationship of forces favorable to the deterrence of adventurism and aggression. The road to disaster would be to permit an unfavorable relationship of forces to arise.

VI

In all this the productive power of the American economy is a factor of great importance. Last year our gross national product exceeded $740 billion. By the end of this year it will approach an $800 billion rate. Total current output of our NATO allies is more than $500 billion, so that together the fifteen allies have a productive capacity well over $1 trillion. Although GNP comparisons must be used with care and do not necessarily indicate what societies can or will allocate to military purposes, it is worth noting that Soviet productive capacity is estimated at less than $350 billion, and that the figure for all communist countries combined is estimated at less than $600 billion.

The USSR with a large command economy can afford to build a fairly complete arsenal of sophisticated weapons. But in terms of outlays of money, materials and manpower for military and foreign programs, there is no doubt that the Soviet Union is operating under more severe economic constraints than the West. We have the economic power to help build a healthier world economy and to give prudent support to the efforts of developing countries to raise their productivity. The superior industrial and agricultural power of the West might yet be a trump card in the long effort to arrive at mutually advantageous arrangements and agreements on the control and limitations of arms and in other fields. If this card is to remain in our hand, however, the Executive Branch and Congress must be ready to make the hard decisions needed to assure continued, steady, non-inflationary growth.

We want to walk the road of cooperation with any who will accompany us. We want a world in which reconciliation and peace prevail. It is a noble cause. But a cause must have its champions, and we may take pride in being counted among them.

APPENDIX 8.—NEWS CONFERENCE OF SECRETARY OF DEFENSE ROBERT S. MCNAMARA AT PENTAGON, NOVEMBER 3, 1967

Mr. GOULDING. Gentlemen, this is our normal Thursday backgrounder with a couple of exceptions: first, that we are holding it on Friday instead of Thursday, and second, we have a couple of announcements so the entire thing will be on the record.

Secretary MCNAMARA. We do have two announcements that I want to make. Afterwards I'll be happy to take your questions. The first relates to what we call a Fractional Orbital Bombardment System, and in connection with this I want to discuss with you certain intelligence information we have collected on a series of space system flight tests being conducted by the Soviet Union. These relate to the possible development by the Soviets of something which, as I say, we call a Fractional Orbital Bombardment System, that I'll hereafter refer to as FOBS—a rather inelegant term.

Let me distinguish the FOBS from the traditional intercontinental ballistic missile. An ICBM, as you know, normally does not go into orbit, but rather follows a ballistic trajectory from launch point to impact point. On this trajectory it reaches a peak altitude of about 800 miles.

Now, unlike the ICBM and this ballistic trajectory, the vehicle launched in a FOBS mode is fired into a very low orbit about 100 miles above the earth. At a given point—generally before the first orbit is complete—a rocket engine is fired which slows down the payload and causes it to drop out of orbit. The payload then follows a re-entry path similar to the re-entry of a ballistic missile.

Even now it is impossible to be certain of what these Soviet tests represent. It is conceivable that the Soviet Union has been testing space vehicles for some re-entry program. But we suspect the Russians are pursuing the research and development of a FOBS. If this turns out to be true, it's conceivable that they could achieve an initial operational capability during the next year, 1968.

Some years ago we ourselves examined the desirability of the FOBS and there was agreement among civilian and military leaders that there was no need for our country to develop a FOBS. While development of it could be initiated at any time for relatively rapid deployment, our analyses conclude that it would not improve our strategic offensive posture and consequently we have no intention of revising the decision made some years ago.

Like other possible variations, the FOBS offers some characteristics which differ from traditional ICBMs. In our opinion, the disadvantages of the FOBS are overriding.

Because of the low altitude of the FOBS' orbits, some of their trajectories would avoid detection by some early warning radars, including our BMEWS. Also, the impact point cannot be determined until ignition of the rocket engine that deboosts the payload out of orbit—and that occurs roughly three minutes and some 500 miles from the target. And the flight path can be as much as 10 minutes shorter than that of an ICBM.

For these characteristics, severe penalties are paid in two critical areas—accuracy and payload. The accuracy of the Soviet ICBM modified to a FOBS weapon would be significantly less, and the payload of the FOBS vehicle would be a fraction of the ICBM.

The FOBS weapon would not be accurate enough for a satisfactory attack upon United States Minutemen missiles, protected in their silos. Perhaps the Soviets might feel it could provide a surprise nuclear strike against U.S. soft land targets such as bomber bases.

However, several years ago, anticipating such Soviet capability, we initiated the deployment of equipment to deny that capability. For example, already we are beginning to use operationally over-the-horizon radars which possess a greater capability of detecting FOBS than do the BMEWS. These will give us more warning time against a full-scale attack using FOBS missiles than BMEWS does against a heavy ICBM launch.

As you know, our deterrent rests upon our ability to absorb any surprise attack and to retaliate with sufficient strength to destroy the attacking nation as a viable society. With three-minute warning, a 15-minute warning or no warning at all, we could still absorb a surprise attack and strike back with sufficient power to destroy the attacker. We have that capability today; and we'll continue to have it in the future.

Now in the second announcement, I want to tell you that we have approved the name SENTINEL for the Chinese-oriented anti-ballistic missile system. Moreover, Lieutenant General Alfred D. Starbird, USA, has been named as the Army's System Manager for the Sentinel System. General Starbird is currently serving as Director of the Defense Communications Agency as you know. He'll assume his new position on November 15.

The System when deployed will provide a defense against the Chinese ICBM force (assuming they go ahead to deploy such a force), of the mid-1970's. As System-Manager, General Starbird will be responsible for the Sentinel's development and deployment.

His organization will have three main elements. The first will be the System Office in this area. It will be an element of the Office, Chief of Staff of the Army. The second will be the Systems Command at Huntsville, Alabama. They will develop, procure, and install the Sentinel System and the third element will be an Evaluation Agency with headquarters at the White Sands Missile Range, responsible for the evaluation, review and testing of the system.

The Sentinel organization will be supported by existing Army agencies such as the Corps of Engineers, the Materiel Command, the Army Communications Command, the Continental Army Command, and the Air Defense Command.

The NIKE-X organization will continue separately from the Sentinel organization. NIKE-X will carry on research and development on systems, the objective of which would be to protect population centers against large-scale attacks. The

NIKE-X program will also design equipment to be used for tests of the penetration capabilities of our offensive missiles. Lieutenant General Austin W. Betts, who as you know is Chief of Research and Development for the Army, will continue to be responsible for the NIKE-X program.

Now I will be happy to try to take your questions.

Question. Of the two possibilities you mentioned in the FOBS announcement, either the development of FOBS or a new re-entry program for space, to which do you give the greater weight at this stage?

Secretary McNAMARA. I think it more likely they are working on the Fractional Orbital Bombardment System than they are on new re-entry vehicles for space systems. It's too early to be absolutely sure, but the weight of evidence is in favor of the former.

Question. Would this stimulate our effort in Bambi type of concepts as interception by satellite?

Secretary McNAMARA. No, I think not.

Question. Why is that?

Secretary McNAMARA. We have other ways of obtaining warning and the problem of protecting the population by destruction of the warhead as we have said before cannot be met by technology available to us today, taking account of the almost certain reaction of the Soviets to any ballistic missile defense that we would put up.

Question. Mr. Secretary, is this the orbital bomb that the Russians themselves have referred to and if it is as bad as you say it is, sir, why on earth are they considering the thing? I don't mean to be facetious . . .

Secretary McNAMARA. Let me first say I don't know what they were referring to when Khrushchev made the statement. I believe it was Khrushchev who made the statement about an orbital bomb. I don't know whether this was what he had in mind or not. He didn't tell us, but secondly, why are they doing it? I think the most logical explanation is that we have maintained a very large bomber force in contrast to their bomber force, intercontinental bomber force, and as you know, we have plans to continue to maintain such a force in the future. They have perhaps thought that this force was a problem to them and that they could reduce the effectiveness of the force by designing a weapon that would eliminate the warning that the force needs to survive. As you know, our bomber force is highly vulnerable to missible attack, and we have protected a percentage of the bomber force against missible attack by putting it on an alert status such that it could take off and advance into the atmosphere during the period of warning of the missile attack. That is the primary advantage of BMEWS.

What the FOBS does is circumvent BMEWS. So if you were a Soviet planner, possibly concerned about the bomber element of our force, this might be one action you would take to meet that threat.

We countered their action with a reaction which is our over-the-horizon radar to recapture the warning time necessary to preserve a portion of our bomber force.

Question. Mr. Secretary, some of us met this morning with Senator Jackson and he brought up this Fractional Orbital device problem, and he is not at all as sanguine as you are about our ability to detect. In fact, he made the statement it would completely confound our defense and would come in by the back door. Do you have any comment on that?

Secretary McNAMARA. He hasn't said that to me so I don't want to try to read what was in his mind, but we do have as I say an over-the-horizon radar system which we have been working on for some time, which we are beginning to use operationally at the present time and which will be fully operational early next year. And which does provide warning of potential attacks of this kind. Whether he is aware of that or remembered it when he made the statement he did, I can't say. Perhaps he can raise the question again. Mr. Nitze is appearing in public session before his Committee on the subject of ABMs on Monday.

Question. What you have on your hands here—I know what the headlines are going to be—that they have a three-minute bomb. It's not going to make any difference about whether it's aimed at a soft target like our bombers, as far as the American public is going to be concerned, is possibly a terror weapon. Is this the kind of irresponsible act that perhaps the German scientists did on the V-2 when they were sending these things over London?

Secretary McNAMARA. I think any such headline, of course, would be a false statement of the characteristics of the weapon and a misleading indication to the American people of the character of that weapon. This is a less accurate, less efficient weapon than the intercontinental ballistic missile. It does have the characteristics of flying, if you call it that, at an altitude and in certain areas of space such that it perhaps would not be detected by our Ballistic Missile Early Warning System. In anticipating that possibility several years ago, we developed a supplementary warning system—the over-the-horizon radar. I recall speaking of it publicly, I believe in 1964, so we've had it under development for a long period of time for exactly this purpose. It's becoming operational at the present time, it will be fully operational before their FOB system is in effect, and therefore the FOB system is just what we indicated—a system in which the disadvantages far outweigh the advantages as far as the attacker is concerned.

Question. There are four parts to this. (a). does this make an attack from over the South Pole far more likely? (b). how long have we known about their development of the FOBS? (c) where are they testing it? (d) what do we think of it as our main defensive weapon against it—the Thor-based system you referred to in '64, anti-satellite, or the NIKE-X?

Secretary McNamara. Taking the last one first, as we have said before, we don't believe that there is a defense today in their hands or ours against a large-scale intercontinental ballistic attack on population centers. That, of course, is why we decided against deployment of an anti-ballistic missile system designed to protect population centers against heavy missile attacks.

Secondly, it's only been in the past month or two that we've seen enough evidence of testing to lead us to believe that it's more likely than not that these space shots are associated with a FOB system in contrast to a possible re-entry development of the space system.

Thirdly, where are they testing from? I'd rather not discuss that. It exposes some of our intelligence gathering information.

Fourthly, does this make an attack from the south more likely than not? I think not because there are severe penalties, as I have indicated, they pay for a FOBS orbit. A FOBS orbit need not come from the south. It could come from the north. But in any case, where it's to come from the south, it would be a far less efficient way of delivering their warhead than an intercontinental missile trajectory, and I think that if they were to use it, it would be a specialized form of attack against such soft targets as, such time-urgent soft targets, as bomber bases.

Question. Will you go into why you are announcing it at this point? Is it in some way an effort to convey something to the Russians?

Secretary McNamara. No. It's only been in the last month or two that we've seen enough tests, enough evidence of tests, to lead us to this conclusion, and it has only been in the matter of the past few days that we've finished classified briefings on the subject of Congressional Committees. It was quite appropriate, therefore, I think, that we announce it publicly at this time.

Question. Could you describe how far along they are, Mr. Secretary, in an advanced stage of experimentation?

Secretary McNamara. As I indicated to you, we think it could become operational, if they choose to deploy it, sometime in 1968.

Question. Is this tied in with the 7 Cosmos shots in the past week? Are they related?

Secretary McNamara. I don't think they are related.

Question. Are these connected with the mystery shots?

Secretary McNamara. Let me just take this. I'll come to you next.

Question. I was going to ask that, too. Also, what do you estimate the payload is of these things? In terms of megatons?

Secretary McNamara. I don't know whether to give that out or not. I'd say one to three megatons.

Question. Are they multi-warheads, sir?

Secretary McNamara. No.

Question. Is our third stage, the new stage for the _____ sufficient to counteract this?

Secretary McNamara. The Chinese-oriented ABM system is designed to protect against a Chinese attack in the mid-70s and not a Soviet attack.

Question. We are developing a new third stage against the FOBS system?

Secretary McNamara. The Chinese-oriented ABM system is designed to effect against the Chinese and not against the Soviets. Yes?

Question. I asked earlier whether these recent space shots were described as so-called mystery shots that we were not discussing, were those so-called FOBS tests, there were about eight or nine?

Secretary McNamara. Let me ask Phil to check this. I'm not entirely sure that I know which shots you're talking about—the mystery shots. Well let me ask Phil to ask the question. I don't think of these shots as mystery shots. I hope there aren't any mysteries.

Question. Talking about over-the-horizon radar and warning. What kind of warning will you be able to get if this takes only about a few minutes for the warhead to come down?

Secretary McNamara. We will have warning of the movement to us, toward us of . . . . objects.

Question. How will we know if it is one of the FOBS?

Secretary McNamara. When we see the kind of the FOBS attack that would be designed against our bomber bases, we'll know it's that, it's a FOBS, by over-the-horizon radar.

Question. . . . . Do you have this over-the-horizon radar deployed all around the city too?

Secretary McNamara. The over-the-horizon radar warns of the incoming objects whether they be targets against cities or bombers. There's no particular reason for them to use a FOBS as opposed to an ICBM against the city. The only purpose of using FOBS instead of ICBM's would be to avoid the warning, reduce the warning time and this becomes important only in relation to time-urgent targets. Cities aren't going to move in the next ten minutes, we can't do anything to move them. The bombers can move and we can act to move them and its this characteristic of the target that leads to this choice of weapon to be used against it and we counter that threat as I say by a new type of warning that recaptures the warning time.

Question. But my question sir is do you have enough of this over-the-horizon radar to protect the countries residents—

Secretary McNamara. To warn of attacks on any part of the country and the answer is yes.

Question. Mr. McNamara, is it possible, though . . . . I want to get one thing straight on this thing, when you speak of an orbit. Is it possible for them to put this thing up in orbit and go around and around the earth several times before they fire this rocket off?

Secretary McNamara. The answer is it is possible, but there is no advantage to it. As a matter of fact, there is a penalty to them for doing that. It exposes the weapon to destruction, it's a violation of an agreement they've entered into, it gives additional warning and for all of these reasons it's a very unlikely tactic.

Question. But if this thing is capable of orbit, how are you going to know when they put this thing up and its starts orbiting that they are not simply orbiting some sort of satellite and that they are actually orbiting a FOBS. Couldn't they orbit this thing, let it go around once, and then fire the damn thing off. And you only have 3 minutes warning.

Secretary McNamara. And of course it isn't one you are thinking about. One is of no value to them. We have roughly 40 SAC bomber bases. It would take a very substantial number of warheads targeted on those bases to destroy them and quite clearly they are not going to put that substantial number X into orbit.

Question. Mr. Secretary, you said they were destroyable? What would you destroy them with?

Secretary McNamara. We have systems that are capable of destroying them—Satellites. We can put objects in orbit if that becomes desirable or necessary.

Question. Sir . . .

Secretary McNamara. Let me take someone else, yes.

Question. On the over-the-horizon radar, I understand this is one of the first developments in which we were actually using it as we were developing it. What I want to get clear is whether this is what you mean by saying it has become operational and also is it still confined to the test area—whether it be Florida or wherever?

Secretary McNamara. No. The over-the-horizon radar has been in development for several years. In a test made, we have been actually using it to—

Question. Where is that?

Secretary McNamara. We don't disclose the sites of it.

Question. Is this airborne radar?

Secretary McNamara. No. Ground-based radar. A ground-based system. I'm not going to discuss it any more than I have. It has been in development for a number of years. It has been in use as a test system for a number of years, measuring and obtaining flight information on Soviet launches for that period of time; and within the last 60 days—am I right on that—within the last 60 days we've put it in the operational status. It's not yet fully operational. It won't be fully operational until February of next year.

Question. Can I ask you a question of——

Secretary McNamara. I'll take this one.

Question. What kind of warning time does it give us on the FOBS?

Secretary McNamara. Roughly the same as the BMEWS. Slightly more, but roughly the same.

Question. Fifteen minutes?

Secretary McNamara. Roughly fifteen minutes.

Question. On the warhead itself, just to get it into perspective, you say that the payload of the FOBS would be a fraction of the ICBM and you put the actual as between one and three megaton. Isn't that about equivalent to Polaris or Minuteman?

Secretary McNamara. They have to use a very large launch vehicle, and the large launch vehicle would carry a larger warhead on an intercontinental ballistic missile flight. But you degrade the capability in order to use it for this purpose, and you degrade it in two respects. One, is in reducing the payload, and the other, and far more important, degradation, is in reducing the accuracy.

Question. Well, actually the warheads would be equal to our own warheads?

Secretary McNamara. Yes, roughly so. The accuracy, of course, is far, far less than our warheads and therefore the destruction capability which is a function of accuracy and payload is far, far less.

Question. As a follow-up on that, would they be capable of using MIRV in these bombs to get really messed up, multiple warheads in the bombs? And why couldn't they increase the accuracy?

Secretary McNamara. They have a number of inaccurate objects, possibly.

Question. Can't they increase—just like everything else is perfected, just increases accuracy where it would be?

Secretary McNamara. The length of the flight and the characteristic of the orbit—they will never be able to get the accuracy in this kind of a system that they could get, applying the same technology to an intercontinental ballistic missile system. The object, therefore, is to reduce warning time. That's why you sacrifice payload, why you sacrifice accuracy, and our counter to that, as I say, is to develop a new warning system. I am correct in saying, Phil, Dan, and I announced this in 1964, am I not?

Mr. Goulding. It was before I was on board, sir.

Question. How do they get them in orbit? Doesn't that imply improved accuracy?

Secretary McNamara. No. Low orbit is one of the things that takes additional power.

Question. Isn't that a new re-entry vehicle?

Question. There are so many important questions asked about this today, won't you please give us a little more time and a few more questions?

Secretary McNamara. No. I have a terribly busy day. Let me just take this question here. I can't answer the question of yours about the new re-entry vehicle, but Phil, will you get the answer to that?

*Question. Will your satellite observation station network at Hawaii and * * *, will they be able to identify those objects?*

Secretary McNamara. These objects are identified by the over-the-horizon radar system, the sites of which are classified, and I just don't want to get into a discussion that throws any light at all on where these sites are, or the character of the over-the-horizon system.

Question. Your whole presentation here seems to be based on the assumption that the Russians don't think much of our over-the-horizon radar. If this thing works, then it knocks the hell out of their reason for using it.

Secretary McNamara. It negates the advantage that they may have hoped to get from it. It's exactly the reason why we decided not to go ahead with it. On the other hand, they are faced with the bomber threat that is very substantial and they are quite clearly taking action to counter that bomber threat. There's no question but what if you are sitting in the Soviet shoes and you look at our bomber force as it has been, and as it is, and as it will be, it's a much larger bomber force than they have.

Question. We're not developing a new bomber?

Secretary McNamara. We have today how many bombers?

Voice: 600.

Secretary McNamara. 500 to 600? How many are we going to have tomorrow?

Question. We're phasing out the B-52s.

Secretary McNamara. Oh, no, we're going to have hundreds of bombers as far in the future as any of you can look. . . . If you are looking at this problem from a Soviet point of view, you are going to be concerned about it. Particularly you would have been concerned about it 4 or 5 years ago. I don't think there is any doubt but that is what is behind the Tallinn system. For our planning, we must assume the Tallinn system has an ABM capability. There's an uncertainty whether it does or doesn't. But it's very clear indeed that it is an advanced air defense system. It was designed to take account of the stated plans of the United States to maintain a large bomber force for a number of years. So it's very clear that our decision to maintain a bomber force has led to their reaction.

There's no argument about that. This is simply another illustration of the theme I tried to advance in San Francisco, that in strategic force planning, action leads to reaction. It's absolutely fundamental to each party that they maintain a deterrent, so long as technology and financial capability permits, and technology and financial capability both the Soviets and the U.S. make possible the reaction of one to the action of the other. So this is—you are seeing it every day. You see it in our action. Our Posiedon is in part a reaction to their potential ABM force, we said so at the time we introduced the Posiedon into the research and development program two or three years ago; we said it again when we introduced it into the deployment schedule this past year.

You can continue to expect that, and this is the reason why this government so strongly believes that it is in our national interest to engage in discussions of this subject with the Soviets.

Question. Did we have an agreement with them—I've forgotten the status of the agreements—did we have an agreement with the Soviets that we wouldn't get into using weapons in space?

Secretary McNAMARA. No. They have agreed not to place warheads in full orbit. That is why this is a fractional orbit, not a full orbit, and therefore not a violation of that agreement.

Question. You said a moment ago, it could go around the earth.

Secretary McNAMARA. I said they could, but they haven't.

Question. Well now, maybe they will.

Secretary McNAMARA. Maybe they will violate and if they will we will observe it, but the point is that this Fractional Orbit Bombardment System is not a violation of that agreement.

Question. You are going to say this is not a violation of that agreement?

Secretary McNAMARA. Read the agreement and you will see why it isn't. I will be happy to give you a copy of the text.

Question. You say we have systems which are capable of destroying satellites of this nature. I take that to mean, the very limited installations we have out in the Pacific.

Secretary McNAMARA. Yes, that is right.

Question. This doesn't provide very much coverage, does it?

Secretary McNAMARA. I don't want to imply that we can defend population centers of this country against heavy Soviet attacks. We can't.

Question. Is your position now that we are still relying on deterrence as your basic defense against it?

Secretary McNAMARA. Yes, very, very, definitely so. We are still relying on the deterrent and that is what they are relying on. There is no other basis on which to rely at the present time and no technology, either ours nor theirs, would permit any other basis. One more question.

Question. We would like to have you characterize your concern, whether this means a new round in the arms race. . . .

Secretary McNAMARA. I'm not concerned for the reasons I have outlined to you.

Question. Should our European allies be concerned, Mr. Secretary, who don't have over-the-horizon radar?

Secretary McNAMARA. The European allies face different problems. They face the medium-range ballistic missiles and the intermediate-range ballistic missiles and they did not have and cannot obtain the period of warning that we have. Theirs is quite a different problem.

Thank you very much.

APPENDIX 9.—DEPARTMENT OF THE ARMY, OFFICE OF THE SECRETARY OF THE ARMY, NOVEMBER 15, 1967

SENTINEL SYSTEM POTENTIAL SITES TO BE SURVEYED

The Department of Defense today identified the first ten geographical areas to be surveyed as possible site locations for the SENTINEL System, the Communist Chinese oriented anti-ballistic missile system recently approved for deployment.

The Sentinel system is an area defense system. Because of the long range of the Spartan missile, a relatively few batteries can protect the entire country against the kind of light and relatively unsophisticated attack that the Communist Chinese may be capable of by the mid-70s. The system will give protection to all U.S. cities, not only those near missile site locations. The potential areas which will be studied now are among those which will probably provide optimum locations for the area-defense weapons and their radars. It should be emphasized that those areas are not final choices and that this list is not complete. In some cases, even the preliminary potential areas have not yet been determined.

Initial areas to be surveyed are in the vicinity of:

Albany, Georgia.
Chicago, Illinois.
Dallas, Texas.
Grand Forks Air Force Base, North Dakota.
New York, New York.
Oahu, Hawaii.
Salt Lake City, Utah.
Seattle, Washington.
Boston, Massachusetts.
Detroit, Michigan.

Rights of entries to affected properties will be obtained for site selection surveys of possible feasible sites. Surveys will include topographic surveys, foundation explorations and radio frequency interference measurement tests. These surveys and tests will be conducted over a period of several months depending upon results obtained and other factors such as weather and ground conditions.

In most cases, sites being considered are located on government-owned lands.

Announcements regarding the identification of other areas to be selected for a detailed survey will be made at a later date.

INFORMATION SHEET

COMMUNIST CHINESE ORIENTED ANTIBALLISTIC MISSILE SYSTEM

On September 18, 1967, the Secretary of Defense announced a decision to produce and deploy an antiballistic missile system oriented toward a possible future Communist Chinese threat.

The Sentinel System plan provides for the deployment throughout the United States of from 15 to 20 SPARTAN batteries. The SPARTANS will provide area coverage for the continental United States, Alaska, and Hawaii against a Communist Chinese attack for many years to come. The current plan also provides for the use of SPRINT missiles to further defend radar sites and certain MINUTEMAN missile sites, but it is not necessary to make the decision on whether to implement this section of the plan at this time.

Cost of the program is estimated at $5 billion. Break-out of funds for specific components has not yet been determined. Cost of the missiles is classified, in order to prevent premature release of exact numbers of missiles in the system. However, on the average, missiles will cost roughly $1 million each. SPARTAN and SPRINT will not cost the same.

Each of the radars will cost in the neighborhood of $100 million.

Year-by-year funding has not been determined. It will be over a 5 to 6 year period. The $5 billion production and deployment figure does not include operating costs, which will be about $500 million a year. Contracting for the system will begin in about four months.

It is expected that the system will have the first battery operational in the early 1970's. The entire system will be operational in five or six years.

The R&D program on ABM components of the Nike-X system, as contrasted to this ABM deployment program, will continue, with tests being conducted at Kwajalein. Exact nature of the tests and the time schedule for them is classified.

Generally, the system will work as follows: if missiles are launched against the U.S., the radars will locate, track, and provide discrimination data for the system. As this information is fed into the computers, intercept times will be determined and defensive missiles will be fired at the appropriate time. The SPARTAN will engage targets generally outside the earth's atmosphere at several hundred miles range; the SPRINT will engage generally within the earth's atmosphere at a range of about 15–25 miles. Both missiles will be armed with nuclear warheads. When intercepts are made, the ground effects of these detonations will be negligible for blast and radiation. Lethal fallout will not be produced by these air bursts.

Volume of fallout will be less than that produced by previous U.S. and Soviet nuclear testing in the atmosphere.

Throughout the operation, the radars provide information on targets and command guidance for defensive missiles; computers operate the radars, compute trajectories of incoming missiles, sort out the threat, and provide guidance for defensive missiles; the missiles intercept the in-coming offensive missiles at long ranges for the area defense and at both long and short ranges for the areas defended by SPRINT and SPARTAN.

New Antiballistic Missile System Named and System Manager Designated

Secretary of Defense Robert S. McNamara announced today that the Communist Chinese oriented antiballistic missile system recently approved for deployment will be named the SENTINEL SYSTEM.

Lieutenant General Alfred D. Starbird, USA, has been named as the U.S. Army's System Manager for the Sentinel System. General Starbird is currently serving as Director, Defense Communications Agency, Washington, D.C. He will assume his new position on November 15, 1967.

The System when deployed will provide a defense against the Communist Chinese ICBM force of the mid-1970's. As System Manager, General Starbird will be responsibile for Sentinel's development and timely deployment.

General Starbird's organization will have three main elements. The first will be the Sentinel System Office in the Washington, D.C., area, an element of the Office, Chief of Staff, U.S. Army. The second will be the Sentinel System Command, at Huntsville, Alabama, which will develop, procure, and install the Sentinel System. Third element, the Sentinel System Evaluation Agency with headquarters at the White Sands Missile Range, will provide General Starbird with independent evaluation, review and testing.

The Sentinel System organization will be supported by existing Army agencies such as the Corps of Engineers, the Army Materiel Command, the Strategic Army Communications Command, the Continental Army Command, and the Army Air Defense Command.

The existing NIKE-X organization will continue separately from the Sentinel System. It will carry on research and development on systems, the objective of which would be to protect against large-scale attacks. The NIKE-X program will also design equipment to be used for tests of the penetration capabilities of our offensive missiles. Lieutenant General Austin W. Betts, Army Chief of Research and Development, will continue to be responsible for the NIKE-X program.

Appendix 10.—Remarks on Nuclear Test-Ban Treaty Safeguards by Senator Henry M. Jackson, on the Floor of the Senate, November 30, 1967

Introduction

Mr. President, four years have passed since the Nuclear Test-Ban Treaty was favorably considered here in the Senate following extensive hearings by the responsible committees. That Treaty, welcomed by so many, was counted on by some as a first step in a continuing march of arms limitation and control agreements to be negotiated between the nuclear powers and also among the nonnuclear countries. Unfortunately, the yearned for series of agreements on the control of arms has not progressed far beyond the first limited step. It is noteworthy that while meaningful arms limitation agreements have eluded our efforts the danger to our national security and that of other countries as well has been increased by determined moves by Soviet Russia and Red China in the vital field of nuclear arms.

With respect to offensive weapons, Moscow has been working hard to narrow the missile gap that limited its range of options in the Cuban missile crisis of 1962. It has recently doubled the number of its operational ICBMs, and the larger missile payload it can mount on its bigger missiles gives it the capability to deploy higher yield nuclear warheads per missile than we can. Moscow is also developing the capability to launch orbiting nuclear bombs ready for sudden attack from relatively low altitudes. With respect to defensive weapons, the Soviet leaders have deployed an ABM system around Moscow, and our best intelligence is that they will expand and improve that system over the years. Meanwhile, through her six nuclear and thermonuclear tests to date, Communist China is emerging as a thermonuclear power with all the potentialities for trouble that foreshadows. Communist China, of course, was not a signatory to the Nuclear Test-Ban Treaty, and has stated she will not agree to the nuclear non-proliferation agreement now being considered in Geneva.

These recent developments constitute a serious challenge to the strategic superiority of U.S. power on which our defense planners have counted to maintain political stability and to keep the peace. As I read events, where Moscow acts with circumspection, it is because, to use the Kremlin's phrase, "objective conditions" impose this policy. Where the "objective conditions" are favorable, however, Moscow is encouraged to act boldly to expand the frontiers of its influence and to enter into distant conflict situations around the globe. The circumstances are thus created for the most dangerous confrontation—a showdown between nuclear powers.

Even when the Soviets have been in a condition of admitted strategic inferiority to U.S. power, Moscow has periodically pursued adventurous policies— in Berlin and the Cuban missile probe—and to take advantage of opportunities for mischief in the less developed areas of the world. This is exemplified by the Kremlin's recent strong encouragement to the radical Arab forces in May and June 1967.

As Professor Philip Mosely of Columbia University testified in the recent hearings of our Military Applications Subcommittee, in each of these past probings, "the strategic inferiority of Soviet power has set definite limits to the extent of the risks that the Soviet policy-makers were willing to run. It is painful and disturbing to contemplate the far wider range of risks which the Kremlin might have accepted if it had been confident of possessing an equality or a superiority of over-all deterrent strength." Professor Mosely correctly warned that "in any future period in which Moscow might attain either nuclear equality or nuclear superiority however that may be measured in terms of the ratio between offensive and defensive systems, we would be prudent to assume that Soviet policy would be tempted to undertake a more extensive, more acute, and more dangerous range of risks in order to pursue its declared long-range ambition to reshape the world according to its own dogma."

Also, we must take into consideration the possibility of facing not only the continuing strategic threat of the Soviet Union but that threat *combined with* the new threat of China. Distinguished American experts on Sino-Soviet affairs predict that Communist China and the Soviet Union will be cooperating again two or three or five years after Mao's death or incapacitation. Obviously, if Moscow and Peking begin to coordinate their strategies in Asia and the Middle East, the United States will be in for a very dangerous time. For example, if the Soviet Union and Communist China agreed on a plan of action, and Moscow by then considered that it had nuclear equality or even superiority over the United States, the Chinese nuclear power could be used to blackmail China's neighbors while the Soviets neutralized the major United States nuclear capability. This may be what some Chinese leaders are looking forward to.

Looking ahead, if we are to maintain the necessary posture of strategic superiority, there are *two prime requirements:*

The *first* requirement is a strategic offensive capability which will be able to penetrate Soviet ABM defenses whatever their nature several years from now. This means we will need another generation of land-based ICBMs with larger payload capacity and reliance on Multiple Independently-targetable Re-entry Vehicles (MIRVs). This also means we will need another generation of nuclear submarines with more and larger missiles, and reliance on MIRVs.

A *second* requirement is the best ABM defense in the West that science and technology can provide us, to protect our retaliatory second-strike force and to safeguard our people and our society, and to take into account the needs of our allies. For if the Soviet Union comes out ahead in the search for an effective anti-missile system, the relationship of forces on which the U.S. has depended to discourage adventurism and a diplomacy of blackmail will be reversed. The consequences for the West could be disastrous. We can now begin to deploy a "light" ABM system which will be useful at least in the near future against any Chinese threat and to provide some protection for our nuclear retaliatory force. But we do not yet have the tools for an effective missile defense against the kind of missile attack that today only the Soviet Union could launch. The development of such a defense is in the hands of the scientists and engineers. At this stage the need is for a high priority R & D program to develop, if we can, an effective defense against a full-scale Soviet type missile attack.

I would like now to report on the implementation of the Nuclear Test-Ban Treaty safeguards because they are of central importance in giving us the flexibility and the opportunity to take actions to meet these prime requirements for U.S. strategic superiority.

BACKGROUND OF THE TEST-BAN TREATY SAFEGUARDS

By way of a quick review, it will be recalled that in 1963, when the Senate committees were reviewing the then proposed Limited Nuclear Test-Ban Treaty, the Preparedness Investigating Subcommittee shared with the Joint Chiefs of Staff a serious concern about the treaty and whether it would serve the best interests of the United States. The Joint Chiefs informed the Senate that in their opinion certain "safeguards" would be necessary if the treaty was not to operate against our national security interests. At the request of the Preparedness Subcommittee and the Committee on Armed Services, the Joint Chiefs developed a statement of the specific requirements to implement the necessary safeguards they had defined.

The safeguards, in brief, are: (1) the conduct of comprehensive, aggressive, and continuing underground nuclear test programs; (2) the maintenance of modern nuclear laboratory facilities and programs; (3) the maintenance of the facilities and resources to resume promptly atmospheric testing should it be deemed essential to our national security or should the treaty be abrogated by others; and (4) the improvement of our capability to monitor and detect violations of the treaty, and to maintain our knowledge of foreign nuclear activity.

It is significant that the assurances to the Senate given by President Kennedy in August of 1963 that he would fully and effectively implement the safeguards were reaffirmed in their entirety by President Johnson in April 1964.

The Preparedness Subcommittee, because of its role in the formulation of the safeguards, has assumed the role of monitoring the implementation and of making an annual report to the Senate on the implementation. The Joint Committee on Atomic Energy likewise has a deep interest in the safeguards implementation and for the past three years the safeguards monitoring and reviewing has been a joint undertaking. The staff members of both committees follow the safeguards throughout the year and the committee members then conduct a periodic review of progress, the latest of which has just been completed, and this fourth annual report to the Senate on the implementation of the safeguards is a result of that review.

The implementation of the Nuclear Treaty safeguards is the joint responsibility of the Secretary of Defense and the Chairman of the Atomic Energy Commission. To facilitate coordination of the activities of the two agencies in support of the safeguards, the Secretary and the Chairman, in June 1964, formally established joint procedures for the development and periodic review of a National Nuclear Test Program. That program has been developed and submitted to the President, and as directed by the President, plans for implementation are being maintained. The latest White House approval of the current nuclear test program was made in early July 1967.

SAFEGUARD NO. 1: UNDERGROUND TESTING

Turning now to the first safeguard, Underground Testing. During the past year the Department of Defense, charged with the responsibility of determining the effects of nuclear weapons, has continued to develop methods of conducting underground tests in which results are being obtained that were previously thought impossible under the treaty restrictions. The accelerated underground test program of the DoD for the next 18 to 24 months consists of a relatively large number of tests on new reentry vehicles, guidance systems, and our anti-ballistic missile systems now under development. As a result, the actual detailed test program has developed into a fast moving and changing program because of numerous scientific discoveries and proposals for new testing techniques that are being developed.

The Atomic Energy Commission has been somewhat handicapped this past year in nuclear testing, first by continuing labor difficulties at the National Nuclear Test Site in Nevada from early July through early November, and, second, by the lack of a suitable test site for the detonation of high yield weapons underground safely and in compliance with the treaty. However, in spite of these problems, a large number of underground tests were conducted and very significant advances made in the area of weapons technology development, new and radically different weapon design concepts, and in the science of peaceful uses for nuclear explosives.

The basic aims of upcoming underground tests are for the furthering of our knowledge of weapon effects, for improving weapon reliability, increasing penetration capability, and advancing technology.

The AEC and the DoD determined in mid-1966 that it was essential to establish a capability for conducting higher yield tests underground than was determined to be possible at the National Nuclear Test Site in Nevada. Originally, the Pahute Mesa, at the north end of the regular test site, was thought to be suitable for higher yield tests, but experience disproved this hope and other sites have been selected. The first, still in Nevada, is about 70 miles northeast of Tonopah, Nevada, in an area named Hot Creek Valley. This area is thought suitable for going beyond the yields possible at the Pahute Mesa site. Next, an uninhabited island near the western end of the Aleutian Chain, Amchitka Island, is being developed for possible higher yield explosions.

In the high yield area the USSR has conducted nuclear tests of higher yields both in the atmosphere and underground than has the United States. In the high yield test area it is interesting to note that the USSR has, on at least three occasions, violated the Nuclear Test-Ban Treaty, in that nuclear debris from their tests was detected outside the continental boundaries of the Soviet Union. Upon being challenged by the United States the USSR has either denied the charge or said it was a negligible accident and unworthy of further concern.

I mentioned in my report on the safeguards implementation to the Senate last year that we thought the money being provided for underground nuclear testing was insufficient and that the Joint Atomic Energy Committee added $10 million to the FY 1967 funds for this. Later the Atomic Energy Commission determined that even this additional $10 million was not enough and a supplemental budget request for $20 million more was required. This year, for FY 1968, the same situation has developed and again the Joint Committee added $15 million to the funds for weapon development and testing. We did this because of the importance and vitality of the underground testing program and because we thought the 20% cut by the Bureau of the Budget in the amount requested by the Atomic Energy Commission was too heavy handed. For FY 1968, the Department of Defense increased their planned expenditures in this underground testing area by some 50% over the amount requested in FY 1967, and this increase is stated by the responsible officials to be sufficient. However, we have been told recently that there are some planned reductions in the DoD funds from the amounts requested in their budget for safeguards support. I would hope that these cuts, if made, will not be applied in this most important area of underground testing.

SAFEGUARD NO. 2: THE MAINTENANCE OF MODERN LABORATORIES

As to the second safeguard, our nuclear laboratories and their support and work, we very recently had an opportunity for lengthy and detailed discussions with the Directors of our National Nuclear and Weapon Laboratories and they assured us that their laboratories were well supported, excellently staffed and completely loaded with work. A possible concern we might have for this safeguard is not on present status, but a caution that in the near future more money will need to be provided for the construction of some new facilities and the purchase of some new expensive equipment, such as additional computers.

The problems and work of the laboratories are exceedingly complex and require a systematic analysis of many related phenomena, many of which require new theoretical and experimental techniques. This program has some advantages over full-scale nuclear tests. Laboratory experiments are generally less expensive, they can be performed many times, and the important parameters can be more easily controlled. To provide positive correlation between laboratory research and the actual effects of nuclear explosions, laboratory results are tested in the underground nuclear test program to the maximum extent possible.

Increased emphasis is being placed on high altitude phenomenology because of the degrading effects of nuclear weapons upon military radar and communications systems. This is a particularly urgent requirement in light of the anti-ballistic missile system deployment decision. These effects are of prime significance in the employment of offensive and defensive tactics and operational techniques for our missiles, aircraft, and command and control systems.

SAFEGUARD NO. 3: READINESS TO RESUME ATMOSPHERIC TESTING

The third safeguard, readiness to quickly resume nuclear testing in the now prohibited environments in the event the treaty is abrogated, is in a condition of effective support but also one of change and study.

During the year since my last report here, the overseas testing facilities at Johnston Atoll and the Hawaiian Island complex and the equipment there have been maintained in a high readiness status and thoroughly exercised and tested. During FY 1968 it is expected that maintenance and reliability improvement efforts will continue compatible with the laboratory-generated advances in technology and with certain specific replacements of test equipment. Airdrop readiness exercises, both on the continent and overseas-based, have been conducted to maintain and increase technical proficiency and to exercise the airborne diagnostic capability.

Recent evaluation of the AEC–DoD nuclear test readiness program indicate that it should be updated. The majority of tests in the present readiness program were derived from the most pressing questions in weapons development and effects that existed in 1963 when the treaty was ratified. Since 1963, however, the testing capabilities and problems have changed considerably. In particular, the ability to acquire data in the underground test program has been better than had been expected. The AEC and the DoD are now studying revisions in the readiness plans, including the scope and frequency of exercises, for the purpose of updating the program should testing restrictions be removed. It is our intention that the Committee staffs will be kept informed on a day to day basis of changes as they are planned in the program and that periodic updating briefings will be presented to the Committee members who follow the safeguards implementation.

SAFEGUARD NO. 4: TEST DETECTION AND FOREIGN NUCLEAR PROGRAMS

The fourth safeguard is the maintenance and improvement of our capability to monitor and detect nuclear explosions by other countries and to maintain and improve our knowledge of foreign nuclear programs. In the past four years, in addition to the United States, the United Kindgom, the USSR, France and Communist China have all conducted nuclear tests. A great deal of effort is required to keep informed of these tests as they might bear on the national security of our country. Our present Atomic Energy Detection System (AEDS), designed to detect and identify nuclear detonations, now represents a facilities investment of some $85 million. Commencing in FY 1964, a $100 million program was initiated to increase the number of stations and modernize the equipment. About $58 million has been provided in the past four years for this effort and it is planned that about $16 million more will be spent for this purpose in FY 1968.

The national research program for the development and systems design effort aimed at improving our ability to detect, identify, locate, and verify the occurrence of a nuclear explosion in all environments is called Project VELA. This project includes developments applicable to the Nuclear Test-Ban Treaty and also additional results to increase the capability for detection, identification, location, and verification of underground nuclear explosions now legal under the treaty, but which would be barred if ever a total test ban is agreed to between all nations. The VELA program to detect nuclear tests in the atmosphere and in space is directed toward development of satellite-based instruments and systems. A broad variety of radiation detectors and associated electronics and logic circuitry has been developed and fabricated for incorporation into satellite payloads and placement into earth orbit. There have been four successful launches on four attempts, October 1963, July 1964, July 1965 using Atlas-Agena boosters, and the last in April 1967 using a TITAN IIIC booster, each resulting in the placement of two satellites in near circular earth orbits on opposite sides of the earth. This program with its four successful launches in four attempts and long lived payloads, is recognized in the field of space technology as a highly successful endeavor. All satellites, including those from the first launch, continue to operate and provide mission data. A fifth launch is planned for 1968 using a TITAN IIIC booster to place two earth-oriented spacecraft into near circular orbits. The detectors to be used will be similar to those for Launch IV with a general upgrading together with additional capabilities for optical and electro-magnetic-pulse systems and with an added diagnostic capability.

CONCLUSION

In summary, it is our belief that all of the four Nuclear Test-Ban Treaty safeguards are being supported and implemented in a satisfactory manner. The programs have permitted us to detect and improve what might have been fatal shortcomings in our strategic missile systems, to develop the warheads for our forthcoming ABM systems, and to be kept aware of the developments in other countries.

The costs involved in the four safeguards are significant and are indicative of the sincerity of purpose of the United States in maintaining and protecting our national security. In FY 1964 the costs were $706 million; in FY 1965, $724 million; FY 1966, $697 million; FY 1967, $702 million; and in FY 1968 are budgeted for $ 753 million.

The members and staffs of the Joint Committee on Atomic Energy and the Preparedness Investigating Subcommittee of the Committee on Armed Services will continue to follow the safeguards implementation, will make inquiry and conduct hearings on these matters, and will periodically, as I have done again today, make the appropriate reports to the Senate.

APPENDIX 11.—ADDRESS BY DR. JOHN S. FOSTER, JR., DIRECTOR OF DEFENSE RESEARCH AND ENGINEERING, AT DALLAS CHAPTER OF THE ASSOCIATION OF THE U.S. ARMY AND DALLAS COUNCIL ON WORLD AFFAIRS, DALLAS, TEX., DECEMBER 13, 1967

Mr. President and Distinguished Guests, it is a pleasure to be with you this evening. I plan to talk to you tonight about research and development in the interests of our national defense. The fact that research and development is making many contributions to our society must be apparent to every citizen. We have television programs coming to us live from Europe via satellite. We have astronauts circling the earth. We send instruments to other planets to measure their atmospheres and report back. We have transplanted tissues from the dead to aid the living. We find computers teaching classes in our schools. That the pace of introduction of new technical results into our society is accelerating is attested by the fact that over 80% of all the scientists and engineers who have ever lived are alive today, and most of them are practicing their profession. In the last 35 years, our scientific and technical manpower has increased 400% while the labor force increased 50%. The research and development community is capable of accomplishing great things for our society, but it is not capable of accomplishing all things, and it can suggest many more possibilities than it can realize.

So let me invite your attention to an important question. By what mechanisms does our society select the goals and opportunities which our research and development community will pursue? How is it decided what priorities and what efforts will be given to putting a man on the moon, transplanting tissues from the dead to the living, giving us safer automobiles, better housing technology, more powerful computers or military research and development? Some of these are national goals established and supported by the Federal Government by the processes of our democratic society. Some are set by the actions of competitive free enterprise in seeking potential profit. Some are set by the tastes and convictions of individuals and institutions within our society. Many are pursued because they are possible or because they are exciting.

In Defense research and development, too, there is a great ferment of scientific and technical activity. One-third of all the research and development activities in the United States is sponsored by the Department of Defense for purposes of national security. This activity has enabled us to restore to health 98% of U.S. Servicemen wounded in battle in Southeast Asia, to deploy a system which will protect the United States against Chinese nuclear missile attack, to equip aircraft with sensor systems and weapons which make them one hundred fold more effective against vehicles, gun emplacements and personnel in the jungles. In some fields of technology, Defense is pioneering for the country. In others, we are following the lead of other government agencies or of private enterprise. Each year we are presented with a tremendous range of opportunities to improve every weapon system in our possession and to introduce wholly new and revolutionary weapon systems into our arsenal. Now, if we were to push all of the opportunities which we generate it would require much more than the gross national product of the United States to procure and operate the products which resulted. And we would tie up the entire research and development resources of the United States for five to ten years in getting the systems to work. Thus, the crucial problem for us is the selection of opportunities which we shall pursue and exploit.

Naturally, I'm constantly approached by enthusiasts for some particular improvement or innovation or system with an exciting story. They say that their innovation had been proven feasible by research and will be much faster and more powerful and cheaper and lighter weight than any system which we have in operation today. And usually they are absolutely right! Yet we don't always pursue their system and it's necessary to know why. Frequently, the answer is— We have systems already developed, already paid for, already proven feasible which are adequate to do the job. Therefore, we can wait a few years before we must introduce a new system. That means that we will have the opportunity to take advantage of further progress in research and development. Thus, when we do commit our resources to a new system it will give us still greater performance and advantages. The fact is that we must defer nearly all of the opportunities each time they are presented to us, until technical progress or change in our needs requires the new system.

There is another less obvious purpose in our research and development besides technical progress for our own use. Bear in mind that the Soviet Union and the Chinese Peoples Republic pursue an aggressive foreign policy. They have shown themselves willing to sacrifice many domestic goals in order to exploit research and development for military advances. They perform much of their research, their development and even their deployment in secrecy. From time to time, they have surprised us in the past with innovations of military technology but by scrambling, we have responded to the challenge. To avoid such surprises, it is important that we know what it is possible for them to create. To be ready for such surprises, we must be prepared to respond fast to new threats as they emerge. We must always have in readiness feasible advances which we could deploy in one year, in two years, or in five years from now, adequate to counter the worst challenges which may be brought against us.

In summary then, there are two simple reasons why we emphasize research and development. First, to find out what is possible, so that we will find the technological surprises and be ready to exploit them before our adversaries do. Second, through research and development to provide the opportunity to achieve new objectives or to maintain the capability for present ones at less cost.

To give you some feeling for the amounts of money involved, I should point out that for this fiscal year the Defense Research and Development funding is 8.0 billion dollars.

Of this, about 400 million is to be spent on basic research in fields important to defense. It is the work that uncovers what nature has to offer. This effort is limited primarily by the supply of first rate talent and good ideas rather than by a conviction it should not be bigger.

However, the discovery of a scientific principle or phenomenon does not automatically or easily suggest its most important uses, and so we will spend almost a billion dollars in an effort to extract from basic research the results of potential significance to Defense and to explore them.

To transform the opportunities from nature into potential options for weapons systems, we will spend more than a billion dollars. This transformation is exceedingly important because an option for defense is much more than the further development of a given technology. A weapons system is a complex integration of hundreds of technologies. It is defined by objectives and by threats and there are many changes and substitutions to the technologies and to the threats during the development and during the operation of a weapons system.

Over a billion dollars will go into the specific engineering development of those options which are feasible, to show how they can be made, at what cost, schedule and performance. One of the most agonizing parts of the R&D management process is the motivation of the people who are carrying out these programs. We must encourage in them the drive and determination to make their own options available and economical and viable. Yet, we must also hold back on the decision to deploy, waiting to see how the threat emerges, hoping to see a still superior system emerge from R&D in time before a deployment decision must be reached. Holding in immediate readiness, but on tenterhooks in this way, is a cause of more controversy and difficulty than any other single aspect of our R&D management.

In addition, almost two billion dollars are spent on management and support of facilities, ranges, ships and aircraft used to test and evaluate weapons systems, equipments and devices.

All of the above is invested to provide tested feasible viable options for possible deployment. Finally 2½ billion dollars are spent on research and development in support of items which have been selected for deployment or actually deployed.

And what are some of the new systems we are producing to maintain our national security?

To counter the Soviet deployment of additional ballistic missiles and defenses against our ballistic missiles, we are pursuing two major developments.

Both involve a major breakthough in missile technology called MIRV. That stands for Multiple Independently Targeted Reentry Vehicle, for those of you who love acronyms. For the others and for tonight lets just call it the Space Bus. This bus carries many individual reentry vehicles with thermonuclear warheads. After the main booster has cut off, the bus keeps making minute adjustments to its speed and direction and after each adjustment it ejects another warhead. Thus each warhead is delivered on a trajectory to a different city, or if desired, all can be delivered within one city.

One development is a new missile called POSEIDON, planned for deployment on our POLARIS nuclear submarines. It will carry a larger payload to greater range. But more importantly, it will carry the space bus.

The other development is a new missile for the Minuteman land-based missile system called Minuteman III. It too will carry a larger payload to a greater range, and it too will carry the space bus.

These two, together, will multiply the capability of our missile systems manyfold; they will assure penetration of any Soviet anti-missile defenses, and deliver unacceptable damage to them even after we have been subjected to an all-out nuclear surprise attack.

To counter possible improvements in the Soviet strategic air defenses, we are introducing the FB-111 bomber which can fly long distances at high speeds and at very low levels to avoid radar detection, and in addition a new Short Range Attack Missile (the SRAM) which will allow the bombers to attack targets from a distance and thus avoid the intense fire from surrounding defenses.

In the area of tactical weapons, we have introduced several major new systems which are being used very effectively in Viet Nam.

For the ground forces, we have introduced the ability to move an entire Army division—troops, headquarters, equipment, supplies, kitchens, hospital—all by helicopter and set it up anywhere on short notice. This gives our Army a whole new concept in mobility. And, as you know, we have recently upgraded our helicopter capability with the introduction of the Huey Cobra gunship. This gives our Army a whole new concept in mobility. Our troops now have the ability to see clearly at night using only natural starlight for illumination. They also have new miniature radars which can detect individual Viet Cong in the jungle.

At sea the Enterprise, our new aircraft carrier, is a complete self-contained warfare unit with the ability to attack land, air, sea and submarine targets. It is nuclear powered, carries an integrated computer system for command and control of the aircraft fleet, carries new radars for early warning and new attack, reconnaissance and defensive aircraft.

We have deployed a worldwide military satellite communication system with transportable terminals which can be moved to any spot in the world with the first wave of our forces so that the Pentagon or the White House can be in continuous and private communication with the local commander. In addition, these satellites are now used to transmit high quality reconnaissance photographs from Saigon to Washington in a matter of minutes.

The fruits of research and development in Defense present us with a tremendous range of opportunities to improve our weapon systems and introduce new ones.

At the same time, the uncertainty as to what the Communist societies may be preparing to confront us with next, and the uncertainty as to where they may next incite conflict—these uncertainties generate a very great drive to improve our entire arsenal.

But if we were to develop, produce, deploy and operate every major advance which technology offers to us, we would quickly paralyze ourselves, because the cost would soon exceed the gross national product. In addition, we would tie up all of the scientists and engineers of the United States in trying to make the systems work.

On the other hand, if we were never to buy any advances, the United States would soon lose its position of pre-eminent military power. Therefore, we must select, and the process of selection is the most excruciating task in the management of research and development for Defense.

There is a great deal of anguish involved in making these selections because the security of our country is involved. Because the economic well being of a community is often affected. Because the convictions of dedicated proponents are involved. Because threats and capabilities and requirements are very complex and hard to project, and men of ability and integrity will judge them differently even after great effort.

Now, looking back over the last decade we can see a number of cases where we made a bad decision and where precious resources were wasted. You will recall that in response to the unexpected Soviet leap forward in missiles, we started development of the SKYBOLT missile and of the B–70 bomber. Both were designed to deliver nuclear warheads from aircraft, and each had its own way of circumventing the massive air defenses that the Soviets were then deploying. The SKYBOLT was a ballistic missile which could be launched from an aircraft to travel hundreds of miles to a target. The aircraft could remain outside of the Soviet air defenses and launch the missile from the borders. In the case of the B–70, the aircraft was to penetrate the defenses by flying very high and very fast. Within five years, both of these systems were canceled, but only after two billion dollars had been spent. So, what went wrong? In the first place, we selected options whose feasibility had not been established so they were not realistically available options. They, therefore, suffered schedule delays and major overruns in cost and compromises of performance. In the second place, both were attempting tasks that could, in fact, be done as effectively with much less cost by other systems such as B–52 and B–58 bombers and the POLARIS and the MINUTEMAN missiles. A more careful analysis of suitability for the mission revealed that the SKYBOLT, in fact, offered the disadvantages of aircraft which are vulnerable to surprise attack while on the ground and require long delivery times to get in position. Better threat analysis showed that the B–70 was vulnerable, in spite of its extremely high altitude and supersonic speed, to surface-to-air missiles which the Soviets could have had by the time the B–70 could be introduced. Our current understanding is that the best way for aircraft to penetrate a sophisticated defense system is to fly at very low altitudes and the B–70 was much less capable at low altitudes than the B–52 and B–58 bombers which it was designed to replace.

In retrospect, the failure to think through the missions and the anticipated threats contributed as much to the failure of the systems as the inadequate technological basis. If our goal had been to get the fastest, highest, newest bomber, the B–70 was certainly the answer. If our goal was to get weapons delivered to targets which were defended by sophisticated defenses at reasonable cost, the B–70 was a poor choice of a delivery means. Have there been cases where we have had the technology but we have delayed overlong in developing a system to utilize it? One case is the C5–A. That is a subsonic transport jet that we are now producing for operation in 1969. This airplane plays a crucial role in providing the very fast mobility required for limited warfare. It will be able to move one hundred tons of cargo more than 3000 miles in seven hours. Now the key technological requirement to produce such an aircraft was the development of a powerful, reliable, inexpensive jet engine. By 1960, it has been shown that such an engine was definitely feasible. When we analyzed the role of very large transport aircraft in limited war, we found that it offered a substantial advance in effectiveness. The delay in initiating a valuable and important program was partly our failure to think through carefully the requirements of limited warfare and partly the fact that the technological advance called for was not so challenging as to have its enthusiastic technical proponents.

From such histories as these, we have repeatedly learned that money is not enough. That enthusiasm is not enough. That technical innovation is not enough. We need critical analysis of purposes, missions, threats and requirements. We also need realistic tested advanced alternatives produced by our investment in research. And to gain wise management decisions, we must join these together in constructive confrontation.

One of the great contributions Mr. McNamara has made to the Department of Defense is his insistence upon a documentation of the essential ingredients necessary to guarantee the security of the United States. And furthermore that this documentation be arrived at by full participation of all responsible authorities in the Department.

Thus whenever possible, we have today an explicit careful formulation of the objectives of Defense. It has been hammered out by agonizing study and sharp debate. The result is presented annually to Congress by Mr. McNamara.

We have an explicit careful formulation of the *threats* posed by potential enemies, giving both the most probable threats to the United States now and over the next several years, and giving a greater than expected threat based on potential capabilities.

We have a Five-Year Defense Plan giving the inventory of all weapon systems, personnel and equipment planned and committed for incorporation in our force structure.

The five year defense plan is backed up by documents giving the analysis of the effectiveness with which the components of the force structure can achieve their assigned objectives against the specified threats.

These careful formulations provide a structure and discipline for our decision making which removes much of the heat and emotion by creating a foundation of agreements already reached, and by sharpening the issues on which decisions will be made. Thus, it permits us to concentrate our attention on those areas where judgment must be made.

Whereas our major strategic objectives can be formulated with some clarity and precision, the range of possible threats identified, and the role and effectiveness of weapons systems considered relatively quantitatively, the treatment of limited warfare is much more difficult and uncertain because the subject is so varied in its possible locales, participants and developments. However, even in these areas, the same disciplines force the debate to center on the definitive issues of objective, threat and weapon effectiveness.

Now, I'd like to tell you what happens when a major new development is proposed.

Usually we have several alternatives. Each serious alternative will have its dedicated proponents deeply persuaded by the possibilities for improvement it offers and seeing the emerging threat against which it is needed in a stark light. Or they may be preposing a new objective for the United States that would be made accessible by their system.

And each option will have its opponents who are as deeply persuaded of the adequancy of the systems already in our forces or of the superiority of some other planned systems, or who question the feasibility of the proposed new one. They usually see the threat and the capability of their favored system differently.

In the past, each protagonist would have written a separate and probably impassioned dissertation to the Secretary setting forth his arguments. The differences amongst the several views would appear wide and diffuse because each would be using assumptions and critieria appealing to his own judgment and supporting his own case.

We have now introduced a new tool and procedure called the Development Concept Paper. It is a short single document, prepared when there is an important decision to be made by the Secretary on a major development program. It forces the essential confrontation between proponents and opponents to take place in preparation for the Secretarial decision. It requires that the issue be addressed in terms of objective, threat assessment, the adequacy and effectiveness of present and planned systems and the estimate of performance, technical risk, cost and schedules for the proposed development. It requires that both parties agree to a common document that states the issues, the assumptions, the alternative courses of action available, the pros and cons for each. Often this exercise itself brings agreement on most issues. If not, the single document states the position of each. When this document has been well prepared the decision making is greatly simplified because the options, arguments and consequences are clear and complete.

Once the decision has been made and the paper approved by the Secretary, its contents can be transmitted to the implementors in the Services and in industry who can then understand the reasons, assumptions and considerations which weighed most heavily at the highest levels of Defense and guide his own actions accordingly.

Let me summarize: One-third of all our nation's research and development supports National Defense. We faced a closed Communist society which does its development in secrecy and which has the initiative to choose the time, the place and the type of aggression with which they will confront us. We, on the other hand, maintain the aggressive initiative in research and development so that we can find the surprises first and anticipate the worst that our potential adversaries can bring against us and we exploit these surprises to our own advantage. We do this in order that we can quickly contain any threat as it emerges. Because we maintain an aggressive R&D, and because we buy enough capabilities to cover our uncertainties regarding the threats, we guarantee the security of the United States. Forceful, deliberate tools and procedures for the management of research and development have been introduced so that we may provide for our national security without placing an inordinate burden on the national economy.

Ladies and Gentlemen—National Defense is so important that it is the proper concern of every citizen. Recent history shows that we have made costly mistakes in Defense R&D and, despite the greatest care, we will make more. I have stressed the challenge to us of Soviet and Chinese secrecy, but our society has a very great advantage over these closed societies. Our decisions and directions are taken in full public view and they are subject to thorough search and critical debate, and it is only through this process that the soundness of our plans and efforts can be adequately tested and assessed in advance. Therefore, we welcome your serious continuous interest, your discussion and challenge. With that help, the chance for error on the part of those of us charged with decision making for National security will be greatly reduced.

My deep thanks for your attention.

Appendix 12—Correspondence Concerning an Article in Look Magazine of November 28, 1967, on "The Case Against an Antiballistic Missile System"

Congress of the United States,
Joint Committee on Atomic Energy,
Washington, D.C., December 12, 1967.

Gen. A. W. Betts,
Office, Chief of Research and Development,
Chief of Research and Development and Nike-X Systems Manager,
Department of the Army,
Washington, D.C.

Dear General Betts: I have reviewed an article on ballistic missile defense by Dr. Jerome Wiesner in the November 28, 1967, issue of Look magazine. Dr. Wiesner brings up some very serious questions concerning missile defense which I believe should be answered.

Would you please review the points brought up in the article and provide me with the results of your evaluation. I believe that the public record, within the bounds of security classification, should contain an evaluation of the points brought up by Dr. Wiesner. Therefore, it would be appreciated if you would attempt to prepare an unclassified evaluation of the article for inclusion in the published hearings of the Subcommittee on Military Applications.

Thank you for your cooperation in this matter.

Sincerely yours,

Henry M. Jackson,
Chairman, Subcommittee on Military Applications.

[From Look Magazine, Nov. 28, 1967]

The Case Against an Antiballistic Missile System

By Dr. Jerome B. Wiesner, Provost, Massachusetts Institute of Technology; Special Assistant to the President for Science and Technology, 1961–64; longtime member, President's Science Advisory Committee and consultant to the Department of Defense on military technology

When China exploded a hydrogen bomb, waves of concern spread around the world. Renewed calls were raised in the United States for a defense that would protect us from Chinese nuclear ballistic missiles. These calls have now been heeded by President Johnson. Scientists agree that neither the United States nor the Soviet Union can protect itself completely from a nuclear attack by the other. But as long as Communist China's primitive missile force is very small, some protection *can* be achieved—and this is what the President has decided to buy. Because he couldn't persuade the Russians to consider limitations on missile defenses, the President has now ordered the building of a "thin" defensive system to protect us from the Chinese. The logic of the President's decision seems mighty tortured.

The word in Washington is that President Johnson was forced to bend under the pressure of the military, congressional and industrial sponsors of the antiballistic-missile system. Enormous pressure certainly existed, but such pressure on a President to build a missile-defense system is not new. Both President Eisenhower and President Kennedy were exposed to it. One of the most difficult decisions President Kennedy had to make concerned the Nike-Zeus missile-defense system. The pressures on him were tremendous, but after long, careful study, he decided, on technical grounds, not to build the Nike-Zeus. Today, we know that to have built that system would have wasted between $20 and $30 billion. It would have been already obsolete. I am certain that the system we are now planning will be regarded as ineffective before it is installed.

Secretary of Defense McNamara estimates that the United States could build an ABM system (for between $3 and $6 billion) that would provide a reasonably effective defense against Chinese ballistic missiles—for 10 to 15 years. But he concedes that such a system would do us little good against an attack by the Russians. Even if the thin ABM system is as effective as the Secretary of Defense says—and I strongly question this—should we take the portentous step of deploying an ABM system for protection against Red China? I think we should not.

In his long statement announcing the President's decision to build an anti-Chinese ABM system. Secretary McNamara concludes that the arguments marginally support its construction. This is obviously a matter of judgment. I think the arguments are overwhelmingly against building it. In fact, I believe that this decision could be as wrong and have as serious domestic and international consequences as the disastrous conclusion six years ago that a few military advisers and some weapons would lead to an early victory for South Vietnam's forces.

In the late 1950's, the United States first began to examine the problem of defense against ballistic missiles. At that time, the only useful concept involved low-altitude interceptor missiles armed with nuclear weapons. The idea was that radars would track an incoming enemy missile and guide our "anti-missile missile" near enough so that the nuclear warhead, exploded at the right time, would destroy the enemy missile. One defensive rocket would be fired against each incoming object. But an enemy could easily confuse the radars—by including along with the real nuclear warheads high-altitude "decoys," such as lightweight metallic balloons. Since decoys break up or slow down when they hit the earth's atmosphere, we hoped that by waiting, we could pick out the real warheads and launch a defensive attack. The antimissile missiles would have to be placed near each city to be defended, and the tremendous heat and blast caused by the explosion of the defensive warheads, low over the cities, could inflict terrible civilian casualties. It was possible that such a defensive system would do as much damage as enemy warheads. The Nike-Zeus plans, therefore, included a major fallout-shelter program.

During the past two years, it has appeared feasible to build high-altitude defensive missiles for use against small-scale attacks. The nuclear warheads on the high-altitude missiles would be exploded far out in space—in an attempt to destroy both the decoys and the real enemy warheads. In this way, some defense of a much wider region, farther from each antimissile site, would be possible. The proposal is that, with enough sites, the entire United States can be protected. But this will not work if an attacker staggers his decoys and warheads in time and spreads them over a large area, or precedes them by a nuclear explosion of his own to "black out" our defending radars. High-altitude defense represents an improved approach to the problem of defense against ballistic missiles, but it is by no means a solution.

The basic technical fact about an ABM defense is that a sophisticated opponent can overcome any defense currently possible. Offense has all of the advantages; any defense system can be overpowered.

Today, the nuclear powers rely on the deterrent effect of their offensive missiles to keep the peace. A powerful incentive, therefore, exists for either side to increase its offensive-missile forces the moment the other starts to build an ABM system.

The Russians appear to be building a simple ABM defense around Moscow, and possibly other areas, though it is yet unclear that they have decided on a full-scale, antimissile defense system. In response, the United States has taken steps to add decoys and multiple warheads to its own offensive-missile force. These actions on our part are still quite limited, but the steps we have already taken, especially the introduction of multiple warheads on each missile to overwhelm possible Soviet defenses, will greatly increase the number of missile warheads in our inventory. The Russians appear to have been taking similar steps in anticipation of a U.S. decision to build an ABM system. An ABM system in the U.S. will stimulate the Soviets to increase the number of their offensive warheads.

The United States is earnestly seeking some agreement with the Soviet Union to limit the deployment of ABM systems and missiles, in order to forestall a new spiral in the arms race. Unofficial conversations have been held with individual Russians, but we have not succeeded in getting discussions started at an official government level. In Glassboro, President Johnson repeated to Mr. Kosygin our willingness to explore the problem. The Soviet Union does not seem ready to discuss such questions—yet. But there is no need for us to rush into an ABM deployment.

There is little relation between a Russian decision to deploy an ABM system (if, indeed, they have made a decision for more than an experimental system) and such a decision here. Our security would be seriously endangered if the Russians installed an effective ABM defense that could prevent our missile force from reaching their territory and if they simultaneously developed an effective defense against our Strategic Air Force bombers—something they have not been able to do so far. Since it is obvious folly for us to build a defense against missiles while we also are so vulnerable to a bomber attack, the Pentagon has quietly decided to spend four billion more dollars improving our air-defense system.

I do not believe that a really effective antimissile system is remotely possible for either the U.S. or the Russians. And even if the Russians could develop one, and a truly effective defense against our SAC bombers as well, our installing an ABM system would not restore our powers of deterrence. Only improvements in our own offensive-missile force, including "penetration aids" such as decoys and electronic jammers to ensure that our missiles could get through the Russian defense, could achieve this. This is our Defense Department's basic strategy.

The United States has embarked on a large, expensive program of outfitting ballistic missiles with multiple warheads and other devices to penetrate Russian defenses. We have also started a $2 billion program to replace our submarine-based Polaris missiles with the larger Poseidon missiles, which can carry more and better penetration aids. As long as we continue to improve our missile forces and maintain our B-52 bomber force, our deterrent power will remain effective. An ABM system is not required to preserve the power and the effectiveness of our deterrents.

We should build an ABM system only if it gives us greater security. And in deciding this, we must assume that the Russians will respond to our ABM system by upgrading and enlarging their missile force—just as we are doing in response to their ABM activities. If the Russians were to do this, an American ABM system would leave us with less security and more vulnerable to destruction.

Secretary McNamara and many proponents of an ABM system concede that an anti-Soviet ABM defense would not be worth the huge expense, because the Russians could nullify its effectiveness at considerably lower cost to themselves. So the proponents now argue: We can at least provide ourselves with protection against Red China at a more modest cost and without starting a new Russian-American arms spiral. Is this so? Again, I think not.

An ABM system would grant us some protection against China's missiles during the early years of its missile buildup; but this protection would not be complete, and it would be short-lived, certainly, much shorter than 15 years. Once the Chinese can build intercontinental missiles, the cost to them of producing additional missiles would be relatively small (perhaps $5 to $10 million per missile). Within a short time, they would have enough missiles (say, 50 to 100) to penetrate our "anti-Chinese" ABM system.

The Chinese would certainly build penetration aids into their missile force. The techniques of designing such aids are neither highly complex nor exceedingly costly (one can learn all about them in American aerospace journals). I do not believe, therefore, that an ABM system will give us either complete or lasting protection against Chinese missiles. I am convinced we must rely instead on the offensive deterrent, as we must with the Russians; that is, we must rely on our known ability to retaliate devastatingly in case of a nuclear attack. Ten percent of our SAC bomber force could kill 200 million Chinese.

I am very skeptical that any ABM system based on the present approach will ever work at its calculated effectiveness. No one has even succeeded in developing an antiaircraft defense that is as much as ten percent effective (three percent is a more common actual effectiveness). An ABM system that was only this effective would be almost worthless. Even if an ABM system were as much as 90 percent effective, it could still not prevent an opponent from inflicting millions of fatalities on us.

Besides, whenever an ABM system might be installed, how could a realistic test be made? We could not fire missiles at it (it would be located within the continental United States), and from hard experience during World War II, we know that far simpler devices (such as submarine torpedoes) fail to work the first time. I realize that a model system is being tested on Kwajalein, but these tests are under laboratory conditions and cannot simulate a nationwide installation manned by GI's and technicians. Even if we were willing to fire missiles at the system, the test would not be completely realistic, for we would be testing against our missiles, not enemy warheads. Few competent people expect the extremely complex ABM system to work the first time; yet it must to have any effect!

There will always remain a big chance that even if the system is working as designed, it will not intercept all of the enemy missiles. They will obviously know how our ABM system works; we will know little about their offensive weapons. Imagine the advantage a football team would have if it knew precisely its opponents' defense on every play. Remember that if a single enemy nuclear weapon leaks through the defense to a city, the city will be destroyed.

Besides, the Chinese could bypass our ABM system completely—either with low-altitude missiles launched from submarines or with aircraft, which, surprisingly enough, are more difficult to intercept than intercontinental ballistic missiles because they come in at relatively low altitude and do not follow predictable projectories the way a missile does. We simply cannot rely upon an ABM system to give us a sure defense against a Chinese attack.

Many people also fear that the deterrent power on which we rely against the Soviet Union will not be effective against China. The exceptional anxiety expressed each time the Chinese carry out a nuclear test seems related not to their military potential but to our view of them as irrational or unstable. This anxiety rises more from Chinese rhetoric than Chinese actions. Although the words of China's leaders have been inflammatory in the extreme, in action, they have been exceedingly cautious.

China's actual military capacity is, most likely for decades to come, hardly comparable to that of either the United States or the Soviet Union. The Chinese have an extremely limited industrial capacity (until now, they have produced no aircraft of their own!). They also lack the broad base of technically trained manpower that is absolutely necessary for a modern military establishment. Nonetheless, they have made remarkable progress in developing nuclear weaponry. They took less time than any of the other nuclear powers to carry out a thermonuclear explosion. In this, they received considerable help from the Soviet Union, in the late 1950's, as well as a good deal of technological information from open sources and their own intelligence network. And they do appear to be making progress on missiles capable of carrying nuclear weapons. Apparently, they launched one of their nuclear weapons on a short-range missile. Though we have no evidence of a Chinese long-range ballistic missile, we know that their resources are adequate to develop one and, I believe, produce it in moderate numbers (100–200) in less than a decade.

During the late 1950's, many statements by Chinese leaders minimized the importance of nuclear weapons, arguing that they did not really change the relative power balance. We heard boasts that China alone among the great powers would be able to survive a nuclear war. All this has changed. The Chinese now renounce any intention of being the first to use their nuclear weapons, and they show every sign of a growing sophistication in nuclear matters, which is to be expected as they acquire knowledge of the terrible effects of nuclear explosions.

It is China's neighbors, not we, who would be most directly threatened by any Chinese missile force, and an ABM system in the U.S. would be of little help to them. We could not deploy an ABM system in India and Japan; they are too close to China to permit the system to work effectively. What, then, must the leaders and people of Japan and India think as we make plans to hide under an ABM umbrella while they have no way to defend themselves? If the United States is so fearful of China that it must create an ABM defense, should not Japan and India conclude that it is time for them to make their peace with the Chinese? There is no easier way for us to build up China in Asian eyes. No Asian can afford to believe that we are prepared to lose New York to counter a Chinese nuclear attack against them. Some Indian officials are already asking for a missile-defense system.

Can we build a limited ABM system to protect us against China without stimulating the Soviet Union to respond with an offensive-force buildup of its own? I think not. Just as we are enlarging our missile forces because we cannot wait to see whether the Soviet Union is building a limited or an extensive ABM system, so the Russians could not wait to see whether our system would be a limited one before embarking on an offensive-missile buildup. Even if, as the President proposes, we build a thin ABM system, it would be unlikely to remain small; pressures from the military and industrial establishment to improve—and expand—it would be irresistible. Most military planners expect the system to expand rapidly, and in fact do not consider the initial system to be of much use.

This is the reality of the President's decision. I am convinced that once we decide to take the ABM route, we cannot avoid an enlarged arms race.

Three other consequences of the President's decision are not generally appreciated. First, an expanded ABM system will be needed eventually to cope with decoys and multiple warheads. It will almost certainly raise the issue of fallout shelters to protect the population both from Russian nuclear weapons and our own protective system.

Secondly, no one has bothered to mention the several hundred million dollars a year that it will cost to maintain and operate even this thin system or the billions of dollars it would take to run the final one.

Finally, our only substantial arms limitation accomplishment, the limited test ban treaty, is likely to be a victim of this step-up in the arms race. The developers of the ABM system will soon be telling us that they cannot assure its effectiveness without nuclear tests in the atmosphere. The pressure on the President to renounce the treaty in the interest of national security and protecting our multi-billion-dollar investment will be overwhelming.

The United States and Russia are learning to work together to create a more rational world order. Gone are those deep fears of a surprise attack that dominated the 1950's. The best hope for the future lies in joint efforts by the Soviet Union and the United States to eliminate the arms race. Such efforts will be impossible if each side is forced to offset the defensive and offensive buildup of the other.

Under the present circumstances, we are going to have to accept and live with a "deterrent balance." We have done it with the Russians. We will have to with the Chinese. There just is no way to avoid this; there is no magical or technical escape from the dilemmas of the nuclear age through defense. A sensible course would be to reduce greatly the offensive-missile forces on both sides, achieving the deterrence with much less danger to all of us.

Like most other scientists who have studied its problems, I am convinced that much mutually coordinated disarmament is technically achievable with considerably less risk, effort and cost than is involved in our current deterrent position. The blocks to disarmament are political and psychological, not technical. Unfortunately, disarmament has no effective political support, no vested interests backing it, and no power base in the Government bureaucracy or in the Congress. Some of the same senators who have been pressing the President to spend tens of billions of dollars on defense against a missile attack have consistently tried to cut the tiny budget of the Arms Control and Disarmament Agency. Substantial balanced disarmament is sensible, safe and technically achievable, and even partial disarmament would release many tens of billions of dollars for constructive uses. But it is not coming very fast. Until statesmen take disarmament efforts seriously and fashion international security arrangements more appropriate to the nuclear age we all live in, the best we can hope for is an increasingly nightmarish peace insured by only a balance of terror.

A real defense against nuclear-armed missiles is a mirage. Our only real security lies in peace itself. Nuclear weapons are just too potent for effective defense. The best defense is to prevent a nuclear war.

DEPARTMENT OF THE ARMY,
OFFICE OF THE CHIEF OF RESEARCH AND DEVELOPMENT,
Washington, D.C. January 4, 1968.

Hon. HENRY M. JACKSON,
Chairman, Subcommittee on Military Applications,
Joint Committee on Atomic Energy,
Congress of the United States, Washington, D.C.

DEAR SENATOR JACKSON: Furnished herewith in response to your letter of December 12, 1967 is an evaluation of the article in the November 28, 1967 issue of LOOK magazine by Dr. Jerome Wiesner.

Sincerely,

A. W. BETTS,
Lieutenant General, GS,
Chief of Research and Development.

Comments of Lt. Gen. A. W. Betts on "The Case Against an Antiballistic Missile System," Look Magazine, November 28, 1967, Issue, by Dr. Jerome Wiesner

1. *Quotation.*—"The word in Washington is that President Johnson was forced to bend under the pressure of the military, congressional and industrial sponsors of the antiballistic-missile system."

Comment.—I know of no evidence to support the claim by Dr. Wiesner that the President was forced by internal pressures to make the decision to deploy a ballistic missile defense. It has been reported that in an investigation conducted by Senator Javits, which included looking for evidence of this sort, no evidence of pressure was found.

2. *Quotation.*—"The antimissile missiles would have to be placed near each city to be defended, and the tremendous heat and blast caused by the explosion of the defensive warheads, low over the cities, could inflict terrible civilian casualties. It was possible that such a defensive system would do as much damage as enemy warheads. The NIKE-ZEUS plans, therefore, included a major fallout-shelter program."

Comment.—The inference that a major fallout-shelter program was, and is, required because of the detonation of defensive nuclear warheads over our cities is without basis. In fact, the intercept altitudes and defensive yields of the NIKE-ZEUS and SENTINEL ballistic missile defense systems would not cause a significant direct threat to our population by either fallout, thermal or blast overpressure effects. A civil defense shelter program has been, and continues to be, a complement to active defense which would further reduce casualties due to enemy nuclear weapons.

3. *Quotation.*—"The basic technical fact about an ABM defense is that a sophisticated opponent can overcome any defense currently possible. Offense has all of the advantages; any defense system can be overpowered"

Comment.—First, the approved deployment of a U.S. ballistic missile defense is intended to counter the Chinese Communist ICBM threat of the 1970's. The Chinese Communist threat in this time period can not be sophisticated enough to penetrate our planned defensive system.

Second, we have not decided to deploy our defense against the Soviet ICBM offense. We are continuing a vigorous R&D program which will enhance our defense capability. Until these concepts are developed, it would seem premature to conjecture on the relative advantages of defensive and offensive systems.

4. *Quotation.*—"Secretary McNamara and many proponents of an ABM system concede that an Anti-Soviet ABM defense would not be worth the huge expense, because the Russians could nullify its effectiveness at considerably lower cost to themselves."

Comment.—I know of no statements made by the Secretary of Defense to the effect that the Russians could nullify at considerably lower cost to themselves the effectiveness of a U.S. ballistic missile defense. I believe that the deployment of a ballistic missile defense can be cost effective if our research objectives are realized. As stated in my answer to quotation 3, we cannot accurately predict the cost trade-offs of future systems at this time.

5. *Quotation.*—"An ABM system would grant us some protection against China's missiles during the early years of its missile buildup; but this protection would not be complete and it would be shortlived, certainly, much shorter than 15 years. Once the Chinese can build intercontinental missiles, the cost to them of producing additional missiles would be relatively small (perhaps $5 to $10 million per missile). Within a short time they would have enough missiles (say 50 to 100) to penetrate our 'anti-Chinese' ABM System."

Comment.—Full cognizance of the Chinese Communist capabilities was taken into account in the decision to deploy the SENTINEL ballistic missile defense system. If the size of the Chinese Communist ICBM force proves to be somewhat larger than originally expected, these quantitative increases can be offset by the defense by changes in the SENTINEL system.

6. *Quotation.*—"The Chinese would certainly build penetration aids into their missile force. The techniques of designing such aids are neither highly complex nor exceedingly costly (one can learn all about them in American aerospace journals.)"

Comment.—In making the decision to deploy the Chinese Communist-oriented Sentinel system defense, the range of possible and probable penetration aids development by the Chinese Communists was considered. The availability of data on penetration aids techniques in US unclassified literature does not serve as a reasonable yardstick for measuring the degree of difficulty the Chinese Communists would have in developing operational systems employing penetration aids. We fully intend to continue our research and development program on ballistic missile defense to provide for new and improved ways of maintaining a viable defense.

7. *Quotation.*—"Even if an ABM defense were as much as 90% effective, it could still not prevent an opponent from inflicting millions of fatalities on us."

Comment.—Against the relatively low number of ICBM's which the Chinese Communists may possess in the 1970's, we fully expect the SENTINEL defense to provide an effective defense of the US population. It must be remembered that the defense problem and its effectiveness are greatly different against tens of ICBM's compared to a massive attack consisting of many hundreds of ICBM's. A near perfect defense against a small threat is technically possible whereas against a massive threat the defense must be thought of in a damage limiting role.

The value of the SENTINEL defense can be illustrated to be large even using the suggested 90% effectiveness. Thirty Chinese Communist warheads arriving over the US could inflict severe damage on the 30 largest US cities without defense. If the defense were only 90% against this same threat, the number of cities which would suffer damage would be drastically reduced.

8. *Quotation.*—"I realize that a model system is being tested on Kwajalein, but these tests are under laboratory conditions and cannot simulate a nationwide installation manned by GI's and technicians." . . . "Few competent people expect the extremely complex ABM system to work the first time; yet it must to have any effect."

Comment.—The first time a prototype SENTINEL System will be put to the test will be at Kwajalein, during an intensive test program. The Army has had, however, many years of valuable experience in ballistic missile defense through testing the NIKE–ZEUS and NIKE–X equipments. The results of the prior test combined with the upcoming program will provide a confident basis for insuring the SENTINEL defense system will be effective if called upon to counter an attack.

9. *Quotation.*—"Many people also fear that the deterrent power on which we rely against the Soviet Union will not be effective against China. The exceptional anxiety expressed each time the Chinese carry out a nuclear test seems related not to their military potential but to our view of them as irrational or unstable."

Comment.—As Secretary McNamara explained on September 18, 1967, the danger of the Chinese Communists equipped with ICBM's is not that they are considered irrational in their use of force. In times of major confrontation with the US, they could become convinced that the US was about to attack their ICBM force. They might feel compelled to preempt by releasing their forces against US cities. With the 50–100 Chinese Communist ICBM's suggested in the article by Dr. Wiesner and their preemption, they could literally wipe out the top 20 to 50 cities, if we have no defense. The SENTINEL system defense would save most, if not all, of these cities and reduce US civilian casualties by many millions.

10. *Quotation.*—"It is China's neighbors, not we, who would be most directly threatened by any Chinese missile force, and an ABM system in the US would be of little help to them."

Comment.—A defended versus undefended US population can have a significant effect with regard to our Asian allies. With a capability to defend our cities against the threat of Chinese Communist ICBM's, our Asian allies are more apt to believe that we would come to their aid when and if they are threatened by the nuclear forces of the Chinese Communists.

APPENDIX 13—JOINT COMMITTEE ON ATOMIC ENERGY PRESS RELEASE, SEPTEMBER 18, 1967

STATEMENT BY SENATOR CLINTON P. ANDERSON, CHAIRMAN, SUBCOMMITTEE ON SECURITY, JOINT COMMITTEE ON ATOMIC ENERGY, ON DECISION TO PROCEED WITH ANTIBALLISTIC MISSILE SYSTEM

Let me say at the outset that I agree with Secretary of Defense McNamara's statement today in which he announced our decision to proceed with a thin Anti-Ballistic Missile (ABM) system. I support this decision. I am sure it is a decision that has been reached after much deliberation and is a decision that has taken into consideration the President's strong and continuing desire to work out an agreement with the Soviet Union and other nations, whereby we could mutually reduce the threat of nuclear war. Regrettably attempts to negotiate with the Soviet Union to reach agreement in the field of anti-ballistic missiles have not been fruitful. The decision to proceed with the production and eventual deployment of an ABM system was required to insure our national security particularly in light of the Communist China nuclear threat.

It is my hope that the Soviet Union and other nations will see that the United States is serious in its decisions both for peace and for insuring that our country is safe from nuclear attack.

APPENDIX 14—JOINT COMMITTEE ON ATOMIC ENERGY PRESS RELEASE, NOVEMBER 1, 1967

JOINT COMMITTEE ON ATOMIC ENERGY ANTIBALLISTIC MISSILE HEARING ANNOUNCED

The Joint Committee on Atomic Energy will begin its Anti-Ballistic Missile hearings in public session starting at 2:00 p.m. Monday, Nov. 6, 1967 in Room 1202, New Senate Office Building, it was announced today by Senator Henry M. Jackson, Chairman of the Subcommittee on Military Applications of the Joint Committee.

The first witnesses will be Mr. Paul H. Nitze, Deputy Secretary of Defense, and Dr. John S. Foster, Director of Defense Research and Engineering.

On Tuesday, November 7, 1967 experts on the Soviet Union and Communist China are scheduled beginning at 10:00 a.m. with Professor Philip E. Mosely, Columbia University, as the first witness.

An executive session will be held by the Subcommittee on Military Applications in the Joint Committee's classified hearing room in the U.S. Capitol on Wednesday, November 8, 1967. General Earle G. Wheeler, Chairman, Joint Chiefs of Staff, is scheduled to appear at 10:00 a.m. He will be followed at 2:00 p.m. by Mr. Richard Helms, Director, Central Intelligence Agency.

Additional witnesses to testify before the Subcommittee on Military Applications will be announced at a later date.

In announcing the hearings, Senator Jackson said:

"The Joint Committee has had a long and continuing interest in developments in the field of ballistic missile defense. The purpose of these hearings is to bring the Joint Committee up to date on plans and programs relating to our ABM program, with particular emphasis on the scope, magnitude, and implications of the U.S. program as announced by Secretary of Defense McNamara on September 18, 1967.

"We expect that the Executive Department will describe in detail this complex and vitally important subject.

"Mr. Helms will, of course, report on foreign activities relating to the U.S. defense posture vis-a-vis potential aggressors."

Senator Jackson also said:

"I believe that a thorough review in both public and executive session will be of value to the Congress and to the public. I want to stress that I believe it is important that as much information as possible, within the bounds of national security, should be made available to the American people."

Senator Jackson added:

"We also will review the implementation of the nuclear test ban treaty safeguards, jointly with members of the Nuclear Safeguards Subcommittee of the Senate Committee on Armed Services. This is an annual review in connection with the annual report to the Senate on the implementation of the safeguards program.

JOINT COMMITTEE ON ATOMIC ENERGY, LIST OF WITNESSES, ANTIBALLISTIC MISSILE HEARINGS

MONDAY, NOVEMBER 6, 1967—2 P.M.—PUBLIC—ROOM 1202, NSOB

Paul H. Nitze, Deputy Secretary of Defense.
John S. Foster, Director of Defense Research and Engineering.

TUESDAY, NOVEMBER 7, 1967—10 A.M. AND 2 P.M.—PUBLIC—ROOM 1202, NSOB

Philip E. Moselv, Director European Institute, Columbia University; former Director Russian Institute, Columbia University.

Thomas W. Wolfe, Senior Staff Member, the Rand Corporation; member faculty Sino-Soviet Institute, George Washington University.

Alice Langley Hsieh, Senior Staff Member, the Rand Corporation (analyst Communist China's external political and military policies).

WEDNESDAY, NOVEMBER 8, 1967—10 A.M. AND 2 P.M.—EXECUTIVE—ROOM AE–1, U.S. CAPITOL BUILDING

General Earle G. Wheeler, Chairman, Joint Chiefs of Staff.

Richard Helms, Director, Central Intelligence Agency.

O

www.ingramcontent.com/pod-product-compliance
Lightning Source LLC
Chambersburg PA
CBHW021333090426
42742CB00008B/593